W9-BBX-430

SERVING POWER

Recent Titles in
Contributions to the Study of Education

Brainpower for the Cold War: The Sputnik Crisis
and National Defense Education Act of 1958
Barbara Barksdale Clowse

In Opposition to Core Curriculum:
Alternative Models for Undergraduate Education
Edited by James W. Hall with Barbara L. Kevles

Peer Teaching: Historical Perspectives
Lilya Wagner

School Law for the Practitioner
Robert C. O'Reilly and Edward T. Green

The Search for Quality Integrated Education:
Policy and Research on Minority Students in School and College
Meyer Weinberg

From Little Rock to Boston: The History of School Desegregation
George R. Metcalf

American Higher Education: Servant of the People
or Protector of Special Interests?
E. C. Wallenfeldt

School Desegregation Plans That Work
Charles Vert Willie

Education and Poverty: Effective Schooling in the
United States and Cuba
Maurice R. Berube

Learning from Our Mistakes: A Reinterpretation of
Twentieth-Century Educational Theory
Henry J. Perkinson

Getting What We Ask For: The Ambiguity of Success
and Failure in Urban Education
Charles M. Payne

SERVING POWER

The Making of the Academic Social Science Expert

EDWARD T. SILVA

SHEILA A. SLAUGHTER

Contributions to the Study of Education, Number 11

Greenwood Press
Westport, Connecticut • London, England

Library of Congress Cataloging in Publication Data

Silva, Edward T.
  Serving power.

  (Contributions to the study of education, ISSN 0196-707X ; no. 11)
  Bibliography: p.
  Includes index.
  1. Social sciences—United States. 2. Social
scientists—United States. 3. Policy sciences.
I. Slaughter, Sheila,   II. Title.   III. Series.
H53.U5S54 1984   300'.973   83-18518
ISBN 0-313-24058-2 (lib. bdg.)

Library of Congress Catalog Card Number: 83-18518
ISBN: 0-313-24058-2
ISSN: 0196-707X

First published in 1984

Greenwood Press
A division of Congressional Information Service, Inc.
88 Post Road West
Westport, Connecticut 06881

Printed in the United States of America

10 9 8 7 6 5 4 3 2 1

To our fathers, Obdulio Silva
and Wayne Benjamin Slaughter

Contents

Chart and Tables

Acknowledgments

In this work, we have gained greatly from colleagues everywhere. We are particularly grateful to the people we worked with at the University of Wisconsin, the University of Toronto, Virginia Polytechnic Institute, and the State University of New York at Buffalo for their constructive criticism and scholarly solidarity during five years of writing. And we are most thankful to those who helped us present and improve preliminary versions of our analysis at conferences and in articles. Finally, we are extremely indebted to our parents, siblings, peers, and children who have instructed us in the character of emotional, material and intellectual dependency, the key concept used in this analysis.

SERVING POWER

AALL	American Association for Labor Legislation
AAUP	American Association of University Professors
ACE	American Council of Education
ACLS	American Council of Learned Societies
ACLU	American Civil Liberties Union
AEA	American Economic Association
AFT	American Federation of Teachers
AHA	American Historical Association
AJS	American Journal of Sociology
APSA	American Political Science Association
APSR	American Political Science Review
ASS	American Sociology Society
ASSA	American Social Science Association
BAAUP	American Association of University Professors Bulletin
CEIP	Carnegie Endowment for International Peace
CIWY	Carnegie Institute of Washington Yearbook
DAB	Dictionary of American Biography
DIE	Department of Industrial Relations
ES	Economic Studies
HUAC	House Un-American Activities Committee
ICC	Interstate Commerce Commission
IRC	Industrial Relations Committee
JSS	Journal of Social Sciences
MLA	Modern Language Association
NC	National Cyclopedia of American Biography
NCCC	National Conference of Charities and Corrections
NCF	National Civic Federation
NML	National Municipal League
NMR	National Municipal Review
OAS	Organization of American States
PAEA	Publications of the American Economic Association
PASS	Publications of the American Sociology Society
PAPSA	Proceedings of the American Political Science Association
PAU	Pan American Union
PSQ	Political Science Quarterly
RF	Rockefeller Foundation
SSRC	Social Science Research Council

1
Why Read This Book? Experts, Power and the Higher Learning

Ours is a world of experts. Our cars, our bodies, our minds are serviced and cured by occupational specialists controlling monopolies of automotive, medical and psychiatric knowledge. When we face critical collective issues, we routinely turn to experts in the social sciences. We who work in higher education not only rely on others' expertise while claiming to be experts in our own subject matters, but we also create new generations of socially certified experts.

Since expertise is so much a part of our everyday work and leisure experiences, we have become insensitive to the social forces shaping its creation and practice in democratic societies. Worlds of experts depend on the establishment of knowledge monopolies. A specialized division of expert labor implies that each occupational niche creates and maintains its own knowledge boundaries, defining currently correct ideas and their practical application. But creating and maintaining such boundaries requires a continuing capacity to mobilize material and social resources from the community-at-large. It requires social power.

Normally, we in higher education assume that our knowledge monopolies are legitimate; that we receive our resources from an approving community in tacit exchange for the good we do. We transmit to our students the finest thoughts, the highest ideals, the most advanced techniques known in our cultures. This enables our societies to meet their humanistic needs and solve their social problems. In return, we receive our careers: college and university positions, our pay, our prerogatives, our pensions.

This book challenges these assumptions of tacit exchange between higher educationists and the community-at-large. In so doing, its intellectual aim is to shift the thrust of both the sociology of knowledge and the study of higher education in three ways. First, it broadens the sociology of sociology into a much wider concern for all the social sciences by detailing their common origins in the transformation of political economy into economics, political science and sociology in an America undergoing rapid industrialization. Second, it insists on the importance of applied knowledge--on the social uses of social science--in the shaping of these academic disciplines. It holds that extra-university service by leading practitioners decisively shaped the intellectual limits of these disciplines and those of the professorate-at-large. Third, it moves analytical emphasis from individuals to organizations, painting a collective portrait of the leaders of the major social science associations during the transformation of American higher education. Here its theory and method are sensitive to the weight of social structure yet open to the necessity of choice by those organizing academic knowledge production in support of the new industrial order. Thus, the book urges a substantively broader, and more organizationally sophisticated, sociology of applied knowledge upon all who would understand both the origins of the specialized social sciences and the more general present-day crisis of America's higher learning.

Our work traces the development of the role of social scientist as expert. Our primary concern is to show the shaping of an ideology and practice of expertise within the leadership of the American Economic Association, the American Political Science Association, and the American Sociological Association. Leading academics forged links with political economic elites able to deliver resources for the institutionalization of social science within the higher education system. We see academics as able to procure resources by using their expertise outside the university and demonstrating to possible clienteles the uses of social knowledge. The ways social scientists served the powers-that-be included their work on the trust and labor problem, their work on municipal reform and imperialism, and their work with foundations. We argue that academics as experts linked the economy and the state, and in return for this mediation received resources, on the one hand, and responsible positions with some power, on the other hand. The price they willingly paid was binding knowledge to power within the limits of the existing political economic system.

Further, our work places social science role development in its broader educational context. We connect the making of the university-based social science expert to the rise of the graduate school. And we examine the major unappreciated part played by social science association leaders in forming the American Association of University Professors. Here we see the special problems encountered by social scientists in bringing their knowledge to bear on sensitive social problems translated into system-wide guidelines for academic freedom. Thus, we argue that social scientists had an unacknowledged and substantial hand in shaping the role for the twentieth-century American academic.

In essence, our study explores the organizational and institutional roots of academic expertise. We use a systematic sample of leaders representing all the major social science associations of the period and a blend of exchange and professionalization theory to offer a broad and well-grounded interpretation of the relation of role to resources. Of course, our work is indebted to historians who are immersed in turn-of-the-century historiography. But it seeks a much wider audience: social scientists interested in their origins and the institutional articulation of their fields with both the political economy and the growth of higher education. Indeed, we hope that the broad dimension of our book will interest everyone concerned with the relation between power and knowledge, and with the wider problems of culture creation and transmission in Western democracies. It should also interest North American academics concerned with their professional past, present and future in a time of retrenchment, when their roles are once again changing under the press of resource reorganization.

At nub, then, this work holds that contemporary American university-based social science tends to support vested political economic interests. Its fundamental problematic is to explain how this came about. Its theory blends professionalization and resource exchange notions to account for the institutional biasing of the expert social scientist's role in the direction of these vested interests.

Accordingly, in this book we explore the social creation of our own occupational niche in the academic division of labor. We trace the formation of American social expertise from the Civil War until the

1920s. Using the major social science associations--American Social Science Association (ASSA), American Economic Association (AEA), American Political Science Association (APSA), American Sociological Society (ASS)--as a research base, we explore the relationship between experts and the wider society at that point where knowledge is put to social use. We are particularly concerned with the strategies that a sample of social science association leaders developed to procure the resources necessary to create and maintain their emerging occupational monopoly of knowledge. Here, we find these leaders serving power as they worked at defining the role of the modern social science expert.

Chapter 2 sets forth theory and method. Our sample of association leaders includes 43 officers from the ASSA, 81 from the AEA, 43 from the APSA and 17 from the ASS. We argue the importance of these organizations in defining the expert role, and we demonstrate that these officers dominated association knowledge production. Thus, they can be considered intellectual as well as organizational leaders and their lives can be used to clarify the relation between knowledge and power in the making of the social science expert.

In Chapter 3, we view the ASSA as the organization from which the modern social science role emerged. Here we present (1) the social origins and careers of 43 ASSA leaders, (2) their ideas on social science expertise as found in the ASSA's Journal of Social Science, and (3) their practical experience as social science experts in government and the private sector between 1865 and 1886. Examination of the ASSA allows us to establish the role of the expert prior to the university-based institutionalization of the social science disciplines.

In Chapter 4, we document the inter-relationships among (1) political economic resource holders, (2) university managers, and (3) leaders in the emerging social science associations. We are concerned with role limitations established as social science made its way into the graduate university. We look at AEA leaders creating their professional association and the rewards available for such activity. We also look at the leaders who were sanctioned by university managers for their deviant use of knowledge. Thus, we examine the part the AEA's early leaders played in adapting to the resource dependence inherent in housing their intellectual speciality in the university.

Chapters 5 and 6 focus on the AEA's collective understanding of the expert role by examining presidential addresses from its founding in 1885 until 1904, the point at which political scientists and sociologists formed separate specialist associations. We analyze the association debates precipitated by these addresses and look at the leaders' careers in the service of power. We also present contemporary critiques of the association's emerging consensus on the expert role and suggest the alternatives available. We conclude that the AEA leaders successfully (1) identified the executive branch of government as a primary arena of occupational opportunity, (2) secured resource support for expert service, and (3) constructed a professional ideology that both justified their service as advocates for the existing order and offered a rationale for building the discipline firmly into the graduate university.

Chapter 7 explores the way in which the APSA and ASS differentiated from the AEA. It presents a collective biography of the leaders of these three disciplines. An analysis of their social origins, education and careers reveals their continued recruitment from the middle and higher reaches of society, locations predisposed to serving established power. The chapter concludes with the leaders' conception of their fields as presented at the International Congress of the Arts and Sciences sponsored by the 1904 St. Louis World's Fair, a festival of the mind announcing the coming-of-age of American social science expertise.

In Chapter 8, we examine in more detail social scientists' work with resource elites. Here we look at leaders' participation in the National Civic Federation, an organization dominated by owners and managers of increasingly concentrated industrial capital (1900-1914). In Chapter 9, we focus on the leaders' continuing concern with "imperialism" and "urbanism," two problems they saw as critical both to their own occupational opportunities and to the wider society's problems of industrialization (1900-1916). In Chapter 10, we treat leaders' participation in projects funded by American philanthropic foundations, particularly the Carnegie, Sage and Rockefeller foundations (1900-1916). These three chapters document the modern social science expert's role in action, offering technical and ideological skills in exchange for material and social support to consolidate their disciplines' place inside the university. This consolidation's costs are inventoried by noting the criticisms of oppositional social scientists working outside the university.

In Chapter 11, we detail the way social science leaders rejected oppositional alternatives and protected their expert role in a period of social turbulence. We examine their efforts to shape the AAUP's Declaration of Principles to accommodate academic experts' continued service to power. We also analyze the leaders' participation in the First World War as another opportunity to serve power--for the new experts somewhat unscientifically enlisted for the duration.

In the final chapter, we argue that the expert role was sufficiently delineated by 1920 to supply the foundation for subsequent professional development. Our position is that modern social science expertise was and continues to be defined as much by its organizational leaders' ability to form alliances with political economic power as by its own special knowledge. While such ties create the resource base sustaining a widely proclaimed "professionalization," they also shape the social knowledge produced. Thus we hold that social science's earliest leaders willingly accepted the limits of political economic power as they helped make the social sciences' expert role. It remains to be debated if such limits are appropriate to our times and problems.

2
Theory and Method

The rise of the graduate school was predicated on academic specialization, and modern professors are experts. Through its power to grant higher degrees, the university confirms our monopolies of specialized knowledge. Theoretically, all professors are certified as experts. The Ph.D.--our highest degree--attests to its holder's original work on a specialized question that is part of the problematic of a larger field. As experts in academe our role is tripartite: we use our specialized knowledge for teaching, research and service to society.

In this volume, we argue that the service component of the expert role was of critical importance during the institutionalization of social science in the graduate school. Leaders of newly formed specialist associations used their service to demonstrate the utility of their disciplines to university managers and resource holders. Expert service showed what social science could do for society in an era struggling with the problems of industrialization. Thus, we focus on expertise at the point where it is put to social use: in government, private policy-making forums and foundations.

However, academically trained specialists were not the only claimants of expert knowledge in the last quarter of the nineteenth century. Uncertified specialists organized and successfully presented themselves as experts, as did representatives of popular social movements and proponents of reformist schemes. To link certification with specialization as the only legitimate way of defining expertise, leaders of social science associations had to strengthen their claims at the expense of these others. This meant using the associations to formulate an understanding of their role as experts, incorporating the associations into the university via the department system, winning approval from university managers to field their expertise, and finding acceptable outlets for their service. Securing support for their routine service as experts was crucial: it was a means of legitimating university-certified expertise. The specialist associations, then, were the arenas where social scientists worked out the shape of their exchanges with university managers and groups in the wider society able to provide resources for expert service.

In this chapter, we consider current explanations of the way social scientists shaped their roles and present an alternative theory, one blending professionalization and resource exchange notions to account for the rise of centralist social science. Then we explain our methodology and identify our sample of specialist association leaders. Finally, we demonstrate that these officers dominated knowledge production in their associations; thus, they can be considered intellectual as well as organizational leaders and their lives used to approach the relation between knowledge and power in the context of professionalization.

Until quite recently, we knew very little about the social forces shaping the occupational role of social science experts. Fortunately, students of intellectual roles, particularly historians, have been quite active of late, and we have begun to accumulate some considerable appreciation of how American society at the turn of the century shaped this role.[1] However, this welcome emerging literature tends toward a premature closure, opting, as it does, for a "professionalization" interpretation. We believe that this interpretation is theoretically incomplete. Accordingly, we will first present a critique of the professionalization view and then outline our alternative--a notion of "role complementarity" rooted in exchange theory.

In the emerging literature, the new social scientists are viewed as one of several occupations organizing themselves into professions during the Progressive period. The Progressive period itself is the culmination of a much longer crisis of ideology[2] --a period of intense normative uncertainty and questioning generated by the experiences attending the accelerating pace of American industrialization after the U.S. Civil War. Indeed, as many have noted, Northern victory in[3] that war unleashed long pent-up forces of industrial production and quickened the normative rethinking and social reorganization usual to industrialization.[4]

The long search for order between the Civil War and the First World War found a wide variety of popular expressions, each marking the extent to which established ideological formulas were called into question. Capital and labor conflicts often flared into lengthy and widespread violence. Such disorders were almost invariably contained and extinguished by the state's superiority in force of arms.[5] But this political-economic fire fighting inevitably added fuel to the normative crisis, weakening a popular certitude in an equality under the law which was already undermined by reports of extensive political corruption.

Furthermore, imperfect coordination of the newly nationalizing economy created frequent economic breakdowns with virtually half the years between the Civil War and the First World War being years of economic depression.[6] These tumultuous years of boom-and-bust and unplanned development shook the confidence of the respectable strata in the promise of American progress through rapid industrialization, fostering the rise of middle-level reform efforts such as the charity organization and social gospel movements.[7] The boom-and-bust cycles also increased the material deprivation of the rapidly growing, landless, polyglot, urban work force dependent on industrial employment,[8] creating the possibility of a class-oriented labor movement.

Finally, treating the farming West and South mainly as a market for northeastern manufactured goods and a supplier of cheap food and fiber for the increasingly urbanized labor force resulted in years of virulent and determined regional opposition to the centralizing thrust of eastern-based finance capital.[9] In sum, the dynamics of American industrialization after the Civil War resulted in extensive capital-labor disorders, frequent boom-and-bust, and enduring regional disparities that severally and together contributed to a continuing and nation-wide questioning of established ideological formulas. This questioning amounted to a society-wide search for order culminating in the Progressive period's reassertion of ideological stability.[10]

During ideological crises like the one attending American industrialization between 1865 and 1921, social science expertise was important, for it claimed to supply the community-at-large with objective solutions to the widely appreciated problems of the day. And in these times of ideological crisis, social science was sought out and asked its views more frequently and fervently than in periods of relative stability or "normalcy." As they practiced their occupation, social scientists necessarily offered normative and practical paths through the disorders of the times and inevitably offered themselves as guides in the broadly based search for a new social order, one more appropriate for the rapidly emerging industrial commonwealth.

In the American case, at least three groupings claimed social science expertise. One set of social science experts offering advice during the search for order was centered in the American Social Science Association (ASSA). It was modeled on British examples and founded in Boston at the time of Northern victory (1865). In the emerging literature, its members are commonly referred to as the traditional or "old" social scientists. A second group offering the nation social science expertise reflected the German rather than the British industrial experience. They were the "new social scientists," largely recruited from the ranks of students who studied in Germany after the Civil War and who formed the disciplinary associations upon their return to the U.S.: the American Economic Association (AEA, 1885), the American Political Science Association (APSA, 1903), and the American Sociological Society (ASS, 1905).

With the forming of these associations, the literature argues the new social scientists came into direct ideological competition with the traditional social scientists centered in the ASSA. They also came into an as yet under-analyzed ideological conflict with a third set of social scientists claiming expertise on the issues of the day. United mainly by their whole-hearted opposition to both the new and traditional social science, a loosely affiliated network of indigenous American social thinkers—single taxers, Bellemyites, socialists, populists, anarchists and other radicals—offered their challenge on the lecture circuit, the debating platform and in the press.[11]

The conflict among the old, new and radical ended with the triumph of the new in the Progressive period. How is this victory accounted for? The bulk of the literature stresses professionalization as a key element in deciding the struggle's outcome. There are several interconnected points to the explanation. First, professionalization fostered the growth of an occupational subculture and an ideology guiding the new social scientists' conduct and thought along common lines. Second, this occupational subculture included the elaboration of new methods as a basis for expertise, thereby providing technical rationale for reform that the traditionals and radicals lacked. Third, professionalization gained the new social science experts the exclusive right to create and exercise a monopoly of knowledge. This monopoly was granted in tacit exchange with the community-at-large for the new social scientists' disinterested solution of problems. In short, the victory of new social scientists was yet another instance of occupational specialists organizing themselves during the Progressive period.

There are a number of extremely difficult problems raised by the use of professionalization theory to explain the triumph of the new over the traditional and radical social scientists. First, the rise of the new social science was not simply a triumph over an older version. Rather it was an adaptation of an established social science requiring new forms of knowledge, broader geographical representation, and a more detailed defence against both left and right critics of American industrialization. Thus, the "losers" in the period's ideological contest were the radicals, and not the traditional social scientists. In addition, one might note that the traditionals were about as professionalized as their period allowed. Indeed, they exhibited most of the characteristics of professional organization save that of formalized schooling, a characteristic unavailable, since graduate social science education had not yet emerged.[12] And a number of the radicals, who organized somewhat later, held doctorates from the emerging American graduate school and elaborated new methods of social analysis. Further, the explanation reflects the views of the triumphant social scientists, views endlessly reproduced and expanded by those trained by the victors. Professionalization theory is then a congratulatory occupational self-justification becoming, in time, an ideology for all mental workers.[13] Finally, the analysis omits the oppositional voices of radical social thinkers whose analyses were as methodologically subtle and theoretically sophisticated as those offered by old or new social scientists.

However, the most important problem, and the one that argues decisively against the present professionalization analysis, involves the theory's incomplete attention to power and resource exchange. On the one hand, the theory of professions is centered on power. The thrust of the theory explains why the professional's knowledge monopoly is not used in the expert's own interest, as one might suppose in a profit-maximizing market society such as the United States. Here, a notion of tacit exchange is invoked. The community-at-large allows professionals to create a knowledge monopoly only if that monopoly is used disinterestedly in the community's best collective interests. On the other hand, the literature's theory of professions, reflecting its origins in structural functionalism, ignores the exact nature of exchange between community and organized professionals. In particular, it is blind to the reality that all professions must relate themselves to ongoing structures of power, since the creation and continuation of a profession requires considerable resource expenditures. Such expenditures, and thus professionalization itself, are inconceivable without at least the tacit approval of those interest groups which control the ebb and flow of societal resources.[14]

In the case of the new social scientists, the provision of resources was the critical issue, for their method of discourse requires nothing less than the industrialization of social science expertise. They wanted to move from the traditional's style of scholarship that was hand- and mind-crafted, one that involved knowing a relatively few books and arguments very well, and elaborating those arguments to handle a large number of emergent social issues. Instead of a few books and arguments, the new social science required the creation of new means of knowledge production. The industrialization of social science required the procurement of massive amounts of material resources--for research libraries, graduate schools, journals of record, data creation, processing and storing operations--in short, for the establishment of the entire material infrastructure underlying modern social science.

However, as Max Weber noted in 1918, industrialization of universities created its own structural problem: dependence. This dependence, "found wherever capitalist enterprise comes into operation," was manifested on two levels in the industrialization of social scientific expertise. First, the bureaucratic organization of knowledge production made intellectual workers as dependent on university managers "as the employee in a factory on management." Second, in the transformation of the mode of cultural production itself, the academic "craftsman," like the "artisan of the past," no longer "personally owns the tools, essentially the library," but instead has to depend on "enterprises, which cannot be managed without very considerable funds."[15]

Such reorganization of knowledge production created multiple points of organizational mediation. As intellectual workers in organizations fueled by the spirit and resources of American capitalism, social scientists in the industrializing university had to filter their expertise through their university's managers (deans, presidents, trustees). They also had to pass muster with its particular budget-allocating apparatus, especially political leaders and private donors. Furthermore, they had little opportunity to pursue their work independently, since their mode of knowledge production required an infrastructure the individual academic craftsman could no longer sustain. In sum, their massive resource requirements made the new social scientists quite vulnerable to the role definitions held for them by those in the community with readily available resources: economic elites, educational managers, political bureaucrats and leaders.

Since professionalization theory as used in the literature on academic roles does not focus on such vulnerabilities and exchanges, it is ill equipped to account for the rise of the new social science (or indeed any other academic speciality, or even occupation).[16] If professionalization alization theory and its recent academic applications are flawed, what alternatives are possible?

Neo-Marxist theory, which sees the educational system integrated into the occupational system by class power and not meritocratic authority, offers some possibilities. However, these theorists have not turned to the problem of the professionalization of social science, and their current hegemonic interpretations of the relation between knowledge and power are not sufficient to explain their professions' limited--but real--tolerance for their own work. While the resource requirements of professions obviously render them vulnerable to the pressures of class power, the disciplines' ability to provide a measure of protection for ideological deviants also indicates a degree of autonomy.

We offer an alternative rooted in the details of the period that emphasizes role, resource exchange and social science leaders' construction of an ideological center to match the emerging economic center.   The perimeters of academic specialists' roles were defined by their dependence on the university when university managers and resource holders were quick to discipline them if they strayed too far to the right or left. But social science leaders were able to use their expert service to establish multiple resource exchanges with the corporate center, meliorating their dependence on specific academic institutions and particular sponsors. Their willing construction of an ideological center aligned with the emerging economic center set an expert role that institutionalized service to power. While this role is closely tied into the academic reward system, it does not govern all aspects of expertise.   Indeed, its careful placement is a guarantee to resource holders of predictable service to power, and its continuance allows individual teachers and researchers who are ideologically deviant to find some house room in higher education.

We begin by noting that the crisis of American ideology between the Civil and First World wars was marked by a struggle among at least three factions for normative and economic dominance. These were: (1) the leaders of the newly emerging, very large, national corporations, (2) the owners and managers of older, smaller, regional firms, and (3) the popular movements of the time: workers, family farmers, feminists and so on.[17]   Then, let us assume that old, new and radical social scientists could have entered into a resource alliance with any of these three factions.

What is of fundamental importance about the several possible alliances is that victory for each suggests a somewhat different twentieth-century role definition for the academic-based social scientists.   Thus, if an alliance between the old social scientist and the older, regional economic elites won the struggle for ideological domination within both U.S. society and higher education, then a "traditional" deductive, hand-crafted role would continue for academic social scientists.   If the new social scientist and the new corporate leaders won, then a "new and corporate centralist" high technology role would become established.   And, if the radical social scientists and popular movements could unite, intervene and win in the struggle between the economic elites, then a "radical and popular" role would be created for the modern social scientist (see Chart 1).   Given these several logical possibilities, how then do we account for the actual new social science expert role definition that occurred, one locating that role firmly in the middle of the concurrent ideological and economic centers?

From role theory we infer that (1) resources are essential for the execution of role performances, and (2) that persons in complementary roles are likely to supply resources for one another's role performances.[18] Accordingly, we suppose that academic and faction leaders would exchange resources with one another during this period to further the performances of each other's roles. Thus, the exchange of role resources can be used to account for whatever social science roles are institutionalized.

The central questions then become: (1) how did these new social science leaders seem to construct their own academic roles? (2) to what extent did they construct their roles in complementarity with (a) corporate leaders of the new firms, (b) traditional leaders of the older, regional firms, and (c) popular movement leaders? and (3) how did the university and the state organizationally mediate the construction of complementary roles with resource holders? To chart these exchange relationships between social scientists and resource holders, we explore, first, the activities of social scientists among themselves, particularly within their occupational associations; second, their relationships with university managers; and third, the manner in which the practice of social science expertise brought them into contact with political economic leaders active in the wider community.

Our use of an exchange framework to organize the data in this study might be read as bordering on a radical utilitarianism that assumes both individual and collective actors have a full sense of their objective situation and its exigencies. Accordingly, one might object, there is little possibility for symbolic mediation of perceptions and motivations to intervene between social science leaders and their environments. At the risk of being thought unfashionable, reductionistic, and even economistic, we do take a utilitarian position. Indeed, we stop short of radical utilitarianism only because perfect knowledge and information are inherently unattainable, especially in a world of rapid social and economic transition such as that occupied by the new social scientists.

Rather than radical utilitarianism, we take a position of reasonable pragmatic and materialistic utilitarianism, viewing the collective

Chart 1: Logically Possible Social Scientist Roles, 1865-1920

	Traditional and Sectional
Expert role	Publican: speaks from public platforms; seeks elected office; specifies public policy for regional gain
Possible resource suppliers	Smaller, regional capitalists and managers mobilizing funds and legitimacy in liberal policy assns., such as the Nat'l. Assn. of Manufacturers, Anti-Imperialist League
Education and Career	B.A., M.A. or professional degree degree but not Ph.D.; works in colleges as well as other cultural occupations
Self-conception	Teachers of future leaders; transmitter of established cultural standards adapted to new conditions
Method of discourse	Speculation within a natural law framework, validated by logical rigor and limited empiricism
Theory of social change	Political economy is understood in laissez-faire terms; only small-scale, fragmented social reform is possible; "the Manchester School"
Peer network	Amer. Social Science Assn. and local gentry; tent and town Chatauqua colleagues
Examples	W. G. Summer, D. A. Wells; F. B. Sanborn

18

New and Corporate Centralist	Popular and Radical
Advisor: provides data and advice for national policy makers, accepts intellectual and material advanced capitalism	Advocate: urges public policy which transcends the present in the name of the exploited everywhere
Larger national capitalists and managers centralizing funds and legitimacy in corporate liberal policy assns. such as the National Civic Federation	Oppositional leaders: populists, socialists, unionists, feminists creating radical action groups, as the IWW, socialist and populist parties
Ph.D., often in Germany, life's work at graduate schools created by, and managed for, corporate capital	Some post-graduate study; if Ph.D., often works in graduate schools and encounters difficulty for beliefs and actions; leaves for oppositional career
Creator of new ideas and knowledge reforming capitalism in a time of great unrest and promise	Social critic and activist in a society increasingly irrational and exploitative
Empiricism within an emerging positivist framework of value-free objectivity	Empiricism focused through a radical perspective and political program, modified by practical oppositional experience
Social evolution requires careful systematic state intervention and regulation; change is incremental; "the German Historical School"	Social conflict determines social order; widespread structural change inevitable; "Marxism," indigenous American radicalism
Amer. Econ. Assn.; Amer. Pol. Sci. Assn.; Amer. Soc. Society; AAUP; graduate department	Amer. Federation of Teachers; ad hoc oppositional mobilizations
E. R. A. Seligman, J. R. Commons, A. T. Hadley	S. Nearing; D. DeLeon; H. George

efforts of social scientists assembled in their associations as often compensating for all manner of informational and behavioral imperfections at the individual level. We take this position for two reasons. First, associations organizing occupations (like the new social scientists in the AEA) have the clear possibility and capability for creating more nearly rational plans for collective action than do their individual members. This occurs when occupational associations gather together experiences and analyses from all their members and then, through full, frank and candid discussion discern the proper joint actions required for success in their common enterprise. This is precisely what the new social scientists did over several decades. They used the AEA as an occupational forum to define collectively the expert role required to procure professionalizing resources from the industrializing American political economy. And while the leaders usually saw the main chance as the best chance, the long-run interests of their associations and their emerging professional sense of integrity and autonomy constrained their opportunism.

Second, as a group, the new social scientists themselves subscribed to and articulated a utilitarian, pragmatic view of their role and their science. In this they upheld and, in turn, were supported by the dominant American business ideology which, although varying with regional and industrial interest, espoused a utilitarian and materialistic approach to contemporary problems. And this dominant ideology also guided the exchange behavior of resource holders offering support to the new social scientists.

Of course, although the new social scientists worked collectively to develop their occupation along rational lines, there were all manner of cognitive, informational and behavioral imperfections at the individual level. Thus, one young economist saw Marx as a Christ-like figure, others worked with the social gospel movement, and another accepted an investment bank's commission for $100,000 for placing a Santo Domingan bond issue while on the island in the public service. But all eventually came to accept and act on the associations' collective definition of the expert role, finally perceiving theoretical Communism, militant Christianity and ad hoc greed as hindrances to sustained resource procurement and career development. Thus, rather than a radical utilitarianism assuming perfect knowledge and information on objective situation and environment, we posit imperfect individual knowledge and action with the reasonable possibility of collective utilitarian action by occupational associations of pragmatic materialists acting after considered discussion.

If we accept in principle the possibility of such a reasonably utilitarian exchange analysis, what data do we encounter when we consider the professionalizing new social scientists in their associations? First, reading the associations' journals of record fully and carefully, we find the dusty tomes filled with heat and light on the substantive questions before us: What is the proper role of the social science expert? Who and how should he serve? Second, in contrast with the fullness of organizational texts, we find a thinness of historical analysis both of the period and the central actors. For example, there is no schematic synthesis of social structure for the period. Instead, we find a richly contested historiography providing insightful chronological commentaries. But these chronicles rest more on sound judgments and intuitive leaps than on the details of abundant biographical and organizational analysis. For example, there is one solid, historical treatment of the ASSA, while its most important figure has no full biography and only a half-done autobiography. The new social scientists' lives are better recorded, but the coverage is still incomplete. Such material limits answers to questions about the exact social mechanisms--such as class, mobility and occupational status--working in the period. They also restrict the volume of actual exchange negotiations we can document fully. Nonetheless, by fitting together the associations' debates with their leaders' deeds and placing them against the available alternatives, we are able to trace many of the exchanges made to professionalize social science expertise in the modernizing university.

Thus at the heart of our methodology are the four major social science organizations: the ASSA, the AEA, the APSA and the ASS. These organizations are important, for they provided not only opportunities for reporting theoretical and empirical advances, but also forums for the full and frank discussion of the problems and promises surrounding the practice of social science expertise, be it old, new or oppositional. These debates raised significant and confronting issues: How should social science expertise be used? Whose interests should it serve? To whom is it accountable? And so on. Such debates about the role of the social science expert were fervent, lively and often heated, for the participants realized that the shape of the role--the expectations surrounding social science practice held both inside and outside the occupation--would inevitably mold the social theory and data developed by its practitioners. Thus, to debate the correct role for the social science expert was also to argue about the proper content of social science itself.

These debates went on elsewhere, of course, particularly in the graduate departments and schools preparing the newer social scientists for their calling. No doubt the class and common rooms at Johns Hopkins, Harvard, Chicago and Columbia reverberated with the long, and even loud, sounds of such arguments. But only the associations provided the national, cosmopolitan organization that focused, centered and orchestrated the more parochial department counter-points and school variations on these occupationally compelling themes of expertise and its exercise. And once some discipline-wide agreement on the expert role was achieved, the associations could become agents of that consensus, enforcing upon its membership the "quality control" necessary to stabilize the monopoly of knowledge upon which it was built.

To trace the debates on the social scientist's role, we have relied heavily on the published papers and proceedings of the four social science associations mentioned above. To situate such talk in the flow of the period's social life, we have linked those debates both to the biographies of the association's participants and to the large events--the history--of their times. To establish the biographical connections, we drew a sample of the leading lights of both the old and new social science associations. These leaders self-consciously organized and spoke for associations designed to shape social science use and point out its proper theoretical and empirical development. They aimed to create a sense of consciousness, cohesion and camaraderie--in short, a corporate sensibility--among their fellow social scientists. Accordingly, the words and actions of these leaders offer us instruction in how they sought to shape their period's expectations of the pragmatic and intellectual possibilities of the social scientist's role.

As a practical matter, we define the leading lights of each

association as its chief operating officers, those individuals who accepted the task of developing and sustaining the corporate sensibilities of each of the four social science associations. And since the old and new associations were somewhat different in their organizational forms, the exact posts defined as chief operating offices are slightly different.

The ASSA initially divided social science into four areas of study and established a department to attend to each. These departments were Education; Public Health; Economy, Trade and Finance; and Jurisprudence. In time, a fifth ASSA department emerged when Social Economy was separated from Trade and Finance. The five departments were intended as the major scientific organs of the ASSA. They were to gather and analyze data, as well as accept and present papers on their topics. The Department of Jurisprudence had as its additional task the perfection of legislation dealing with social issues. Working together, the several departments intended to discover the pertinent social science laws and transmute them into ameliorative legislation as the logical outcome of sustained scientific data and knowledge accumulation.

For our purposes--an investigation of the rise of the new social science--the ASSA's leading lights are, first, its general executive officers--the ASSA's president, treasurer and secretary; and second, the executive officers--the chair and the secretary—in four of the five departments. We are especially interested in the three departments that prefigure the later specialized social science associations: trade and finance (economics), jurisprudence (political science) and social economy (sociology). We are also interested in the Education Department, since its substantive concerns are central to the eventual content and practice of university-based new social science expertise. Further, the ASSA exerted its greatest influence shaping the role of social science expertise before the founding of the newer disciplinary associations, since it then had a virtual organizational monopoly over defining the theory and practice of social science expertise. Accordingly, we concentrate our analysis on the ASSA between 1865 and 1886 and draw our sample of its leading lights from this period.

From Haskell's recent histories of the ASSA, we drew 18 names. Of these 12 account for all the ASSA's presidents and general secretaries serving between 1865 and 1886. The other six were founding departmental officials.[19] To complete the leadership roster, we turned to the ASSA's _Journal of Social Science_. Here we found an additional 25 names of ASSA treasurers and departmental officials. This second listing of 25 is, however, incomplete, since the _JSS_ did not begin publication until 1869, and even then it inconsistently reported on ASSA office holding. In fact the _JSS_ covers 13 of the 17 possible years between 1869 and 1886, and therefore our additional 25 names represent perhaps three-fourths of the actual treasurers and departmental officials. Since, as Haskell notes, the ASSA left very little organizational residue--records, files and so on--this second list seems a reasonable one. Combining both lists results in a sample of 43 ASSA leaders active between 1865 and 1886.

Within the newer social science associations, we again identify leading lights by their organizational position. Since the AEA was more specialized and since the APSA and ASS copied the AEA's form, their organizational structures are somewhat more straightforward and near mirror images, with the central work of creating a corporate sensibility falling upon their presidents, vice-presidents, treasurers and secretaries. Lists of persons occupying these positions in the AEA, APSA and ASS were compiled from each association's publications of record. They yielded the names of 81 economists, 43 political scientists and 17 sociologists.[20] These listings are complete from the date of each association's founding until 1921; by then the modern social science expert role took enduring shape.

The organizational and intellectual service rendered by these leaders in the creation of this modern expert role is quite remarkable. They number 171 individuals, 11 of whom provided leadership in two associations and one who did so in three of the four. As a group, they held their key posts for a total of 506 years, or an average of about three years (See Table 1). Further, service in these top leadership posts is itself but a suggestion of their organizational contributions for they also helped staff the various executive boards and councils that guided the associations. Widening the definition of organizational leadership to include such executive bodies would greatly increase the number of posts held, the total years served and the number of individuals leading more than one association.

TABLE 1 Office Holding in Leading Social Science Organizations, 1865–1921

Organization	Leading Posts	Years Included in This Study	Number of Office-holders	Number of Years Posts Available	Average Years of Service
1. American Social Science Assn.	President, Secretary Treasurer; Chair and Secretary of Depts. of Trade and Finance, Jurisprudence, Social Economy and Education	1865–1886	43	162	3.77
2. American Economics Assn.	President, Three Vice-Presidents, Secretary and Treasurer	1886–1921	81	194	2.40
3. American Political Science Association	Same as AEA.	1904–1921	43	90	2.09
4. American Sociological Society	Same as AEA and APSA, except one less vice-president.	1907–1921	17	60	3.53
5. TOTALS			184	506	2.75
6. TOTALS, unduplicated*			171	506	2.96

*Eleven leaders held leading posts in two organizations, and one held by key office in three.

These organizational leaders were also intellectual leaders shaping the content of the new social science. We see this very clearly in their most striking over-representation among the knowledge producers publishing in the various associations' papers and proceedings. Table 2 reports the authorship of materials appearing in the principal publications of the four associations. Using data from several cumulative indexes, authorship is separated by office holding: officers versus other authors, with leaders of more than one association counted within the association sponsoring publication.

The ASSA's principal publication was the Journal of Social Science. Using Haskell's indexing of its articles,[21] we find that between 1869 and 1886 our leaders supplied 14.2 percent of the Journal's authors but 30.3 percent of its 234 articles. Here leaders out-produced non-leader authors by better than two to one. And the situation is even more compelling among economists. The AEA sponsored three series of principal publications between its founding and 1910 and published an index to them in 1917--its only indexing effort for the period.[22] Our sample of AEA leaders make up 16.0 percent of the authors, but accounts for 44.2 percent of the 1,068 titles published--monographs, articles, papers and discussion at the annual meetings as well as a very few author abstracts of work published elsewhere. In the AEA, then, the leader's over-representation of knowledge production approaches three to one.

The ASS's only official outlet was its Publications of annual meetings. The index[23] shows the ASS officers made up 10.9 percent of the authors and supplied 22.9 percent of the 201 papers and discussions published up to 1921, a two-to-one over-representation. After 1909, The American Journal of Sociology functioned as something of a tacit ASS journal of record, since the ASS mounted no other while its officers served as AJS's American advisory editors. In this period, 2.2 percent of the AJS's article authors were ASS officers. Yet they contributed 18.3 percent of the AJS's 437 titles; a ratio exceeding eight to one.[24]

Only among the political scientists do non-leader authors produce knowledge at anything like parity with association leaders. According to Iris's index to its annual meeting Proceedings, APSA leaders made up 20.2 percent of the authors and presented 23.4 percent of the 128 papers and discussions published.[25] In the journal of record, APSR, the key

Table 2 Officers as Knowledge Over-Producers in Their Associations' Publications

Publications	Officers			Other Authors		
	N	Items	Average Items	N	Items	Average Items
1. ASSA, Journal of Social Science, 1869-1886	25 (of 43)	71	2.84	151	163	1.08
2. AEA, all publications, 1886-1910	64 (of 81)	473	7.39	335	595	1.78
3. ASS, Publications (of annual meetings), v. 1 (1906)-v. 16 (1921)	14 (of 17)	46	3.29	120	155	1.29
4. ASS, American Journal of Sociology, v. 14 (1909)-v. 26 (1921)	7 (of 17)	80	11.11	314	357	1.13
5. APSA, American Political Science Review, v. 1 (1906)-v. 15 (1921)	29 (of 43)	72	2.48	210	482	2.30
6. APSA, Proceedings (of Annual Meetings), (1904-1913)	24 (of 43)	30	1.25	95	98	1.03
7. APSA, APSR, Substantive Articles, v. 1 (1906)-v. 15 (1921)	26 (of 43)	54	2.08	142	181	1.28

office holders amount to 12.1 percent of the authors, and their material comes to 12.9 percent of the 554 items listed in Janda's cumulative index.[26]

This near parity in political science knowledge production between leaders and non-leader authors should be seen in a somewhat special light. The political scientists of the period opened the pages of their Review to the events of the times in a unique manner. As Janda notes, "early volumes of the Review contain sections on 'legislative notes', 'current municipal affairs' and 'judicial decisions.'...These sections contain many entries ranging in length from one or two paragraphs to several pages."[27] Thus, the Review became something of a current events bulletin, one incorporating contributions from political scientists in all parts of the country. Since as much as half the pages of each issue published between 1907 and 1921 are made up of such items and since Janda's index contains all items greater than one page in length, the APSR figures undoubtedly reflect its association's unusual publication policies. Presumably, a similar policy was used in organizing its annual meetings and finds its way into the near parity noted in the Proceedings data reported above.

Confirmation of this interpretation comes when we look at the authorship of the leading substantive articles published in APSR. Considering only the several articles of analytical complexity and greater length appearing in each issue of APSR in front of the current, topical sections, we find a pattern closer to that in the other social sciences. APSA leaders were 15.6 percent of the substantive article authors and contributed 22.9 percent of the titles. This comes to an over-representation ratio of 1 to 63. This ratio is somewhat closer to the others and sufficient to suggest the leadership's hands shaping the role and content of their speciality's expertise.

Taken as a whole, then, our inspection of the association publications shows the leaders to be disproportionately high knowledge producers. This finding must be interpreted carefully. In no publication series do the leaders exhibit numerical domination--say, writing more than half the works printed. Yet, it must also be remembered that the vast majority of the associations' membership's were knowledge consumers, not producers, readers and not authors. Accordingly, the interpretation we advance is that the data leave no reasonable doubt that organizational leadership is strongly related to disproportionate and sustained efforts at knowledge production, and that these efforts have the inevitable result of molding the intellectual content of the fields and the social role of its practice. Further, given the high organizational position of these writers, we may safely suppose a certain effectiveness in their efforts to shape role and content.

Our interest in these samples of social scientists, old and new, is to help us situate the period's debate about social science expertise in the experiences of its participants. Using standard biographical sources,[28] we developed a uniform data collection detailing the lives of all but six of these leaders. This data collection allows us to compare, for example, the social origins of the old and new social science leaderships. Unfortunately, the loosely tied network of oppositional radical social scientists does not allow for any sort of systematic sampling. Accordingly, we are not able to accomplish any similar collective biographical analyses for the radical social scientists. Yet the odd lot of oppositional social scientists for whom we have located biographies--Scott Nearing and Daniel DeLeon, for example--are valuable beyond number.[29] For as important as collective biography is for an understanding of the relationship of knowledge and power, our work must confront the larger historical forces of the period--as indeed the association leaders were compelled to do. It is exactly where the actions of the associations' leaders must be connected to the period's structural developments that the oppositional biographies come into play. They illuminate resource relationships with their alternative views, casting light and sometimes heat with their unconventional comments and activities.

How did the association leaders shape the expert role? During the long period of structural change between the Civil War and First World War, historically unique opportunities existed for contacts between thinkers wanting to use their knowledge and expertise to try to influence American industrialization and political-economic leaders with both a sensitivity to the potential of social science and the ready resources to underwrite such expertise in action. As it happened, some social scientists did take advantage of some of these opportunities, establishing relatively enduring contacts with some political-economic leaders. Examination of how leading--and radical--social scientists dealt with some of these opportunities allows us to follow exchanges between men of knowledge and men of power, between holders of social scientific expertise and holders of resources sufficient to allow both its industrialization and use. In these exchanges we are able to see what academics in expert capacities offered political economic resource holders, what services they in fact rendered, and to what use social scientific knowledge was put. In this way, we are able to compare positions taken within the association's debate on the social role of knowledge with the actual ideational products delivered to the resource providers.

Our inspection of such historically unique opportunities and the way in which leading organizational social scientists entered them, allows us to connect both the leaders' biographies and the associations' debates with the larger structural forces of the period. And while we can make no claim to an exhaustive treatment of how all of the available opportunities were dealt with, we are able to document a considerable and representative volume of such exchanges within public policy forums, state and federal agencies, and at the largest grant-giving foundations. In short, then, our basic theoretical and methodological strategy is to locate the industrialization of social science at the intersection of the lives of those defining its expertise with the historically unique structural opportunities created by rapid post-Civil War economic development.

To begin exploration of the relationship between knowledge and power at this conjuncture of biography and history, Chapter 3 offers an account of how the ASSA came to grips with the early stages of accelerating post-Civil War industrialization. While the ASSA is usually seen as simply the key association of "traditional" or "old" social science, we prefer to see it as the site where American social science first came to grips with a quickened pace of economic development. Here we see a rudimentary formation of the modern social scientific expert's role developing in response to the ideological crisis generated by "early" post-Civil War industrialization (ca. 1865-1886). Discussion of this response continues in Chapter 4, which analyzes the new social scientists' further elaboration of this role as they developed careers as dependent intellectuals based in the modernizing university at the very middle of the emerging concurrent center.

32   Serving Power

NOTES

1. Burton J. Bledstein, The Culture of Professionalism (New York: Norton, 1977); James T. Carey, Sociology and Public Affairs: The Chicago School (London: Sage, 1975), pp. 27-37; Mary O. Furner, Advocacy and Objectivity (Lexington, Ky.: The University Press of Kentucky, 1975); Thomas Haskell, The Emergence of Professional Social Science (Urbana, Ill.: University of Illinois, 1977); David M. Grossman, "Professors and Public Service, 1885-1925: A Chapter in the Professionalization of the Social Sciences" (Ph.D. dissertation, Washington University, 1973).

2. Our use of the term "ideology" follows that of Kenneth M. Dolbeare and Patricia Dolbeare, in American Ideologies (Chicago: Markham, 1971). It is closer to the notion of Weber's "world-view" than Mannheim's "ideology" versus "utopia". More precisely, we mean by ideology a fairly coherent set of ideas explaining the problematic issues of the day and offering solutions to them. As such, ideologies help organize their adherents' beliefs and hopes about their world's present and future, giving structure to their perceptions in several ways. First, ideology outlines the operation of the political economy, clearly delineating who exercises power and on what grounds. This offers a framework for interpreting issues and conflicts encountered in everyday life, the media and in the political arena. Further, ideology outlines criteria for the moral evaluation of the ongoing political economy—on the fairness of who gets what, when, where and how. Finally, these descriptive and evaluative elements combine to supply an imperative for collective action, mandating defense of, or attack upon, the political economy. Ideologies thus either inhibit or inspire social movements.

3. For the relation of the Civil War to industrialization, see Charles, Mary and William Beard, New Basic History of the United States (New York: Doubleday, 1968); and Harold Faulkner, American Political and Social History (New York: Crofts, 1941).

4. For the effects of the war on ideological and social reorganization, see Karl De Schweimetz, Industrialization and Democracy (New York: Free Press, 1964).

5. See, for example, Jeremy Brecher, Strike! (San Francisco: Straight Arrow, 1972); Robert J. Goldstein, Political Repression in Modern America: From 1870 to the Present (Cambridge, Mass.: Schenkman, and New York: Two Continents, 1978); and Philip Taft and Philip Ross, "American Labor Violence: Its Causes, Character and Outcome," in A History of Violence in America, ed. Hugh David Graham and Ted R. Gurr (New York: Praeger, 1969), pp. 281-395.

6. Paul Studenski and H.E. Kross, Financial History of the United States, 3d ed. (New York: McGraw-Hill, 1963); Michael Meeropol, "W.A. Williams' Historiography," Radical America (July–August 1970): 24-49.

7. Robert Trattner, From Poor Law to Welfare State (New York: Free Press, 1974).

8. Joseph Rayback, A History of American Labor (New York: Free Press, 1966); Goldstein, Political Repression.

9. Samuel Hays, Response to Industrialism (Chicago: University of Chicago Press, 1957); Lewis Corey, The House of Morgan (New York: AMS, 1969).

10. See Robert Wiebe, The Search for Order, 1877-1920 (New York: Hill and Wang, 1967) and The Segmented Society (New York: Oxford University Press, 1975). But compare Wiebe's works to Frederick Lynch, "Social Theory and the Progressive Era," Theory and Society 4 (Summer 1977): 195-210.

11. The new historiography of professions neglects such oppositional thinkers, perhaps because they failed to "professionalize." For a sense of their ideas and impact, see Goldstein, Political Repression.

12. E. Greenwood, "Attributes of a Profession," Social Work 2 (April 1957): 44-55.

13. For a definition of professionalism specific to the Progressive era, see "General Report of the Committee on Academic Freedom and Academic Tenure," Bulletin of the American Association of University Professors 1 (December 1915): pp. 15-43. Compare this with modern definitions of professionalism offered by Wiebe, The Search for Order, and Wiebe, The Segmented Society.

14. On these points, compare Greenwood, "Attributes of a Profession," and Terrance Johnson, Professions and Power (London: Macmillan, 1972).

15. Max Weber, "Science as a Vocation," in From Max Weber: Essays in Sociology, ed. Hans Gerth and C. Wright Mills (New York: Oxford University Press, 1958), pp. 129-156. Quotes are on page 131.

16. The partial exception of this lack of attention to resource exchange and power is the work of Joseph Ben-David, "The Scientific Role: The Conditions of Its Establishment in Europe," Minerva 4 (Autumn 1965): 15-54, and those using his model, for example, Anthony Oberschall, "The Institutionalization of American Sociology," in The Establishment of Empirical Sociology, ed. Oberschall (New York: Harper & Row, 1972), pp. 187-251. Ben-David argues that a new scientific field cannot be institutionalized in the university without the support of outside resource holders who are in opposition to the established culture. Oberschall has used this model to analyze the rise of U.S. sociology. Although these writings do take resources into account, their treatments remained flawed. First, they do not work out in any detail the nature or conditions of the resource exchange. Thus, the effects of the resource exchange in shaping role expectations are hidden from view. Second, both hold that institutionalized sciences become autonomous and self-directing once established in academe. But, since the post-institutionalization terms of resource procurement remain unexplored, such statements of autonomy and self-direction

are theoretical, not empirical, assertations. For these reasons, the Ben-David position is part of the problem rather than a solution. Finally, Oberschall's analysis of the institutionalization of American sociology has its own additional flaw. His account depends heavily upon Hofstadter's reading of the period. Hofstadter's work, however, carries its own ideological freight, which Oberschall transships into his interpretation. Thus, not only does Oberschall's analysis keep the details of resource exchange hidden from view; it covers them over with Hofstadter's particular ideological concerns, for which see Lynch, "Social Theory and the Progressive Era."

17. For interpretations of conflicts between elites in the Progressive era, see William Appleman Williams, The Contours of American History (Chicago: Quadrangle, 1966) and Philip S. Foner, The Policies and Practices of the AFL (New York: International, 1964). On popular movements, see Linda Gordon, Women's Bodies, Women's Rights: A History of Birth Control in America (New York: Penguin, 1978) and Goldstein, Political Repression.

18. Ralph H. Turner, "Role: Sociological Aspects," in The International Encyclopedia of the Social Sciences, ed. David L. Sills (New York: Macmillan and The Free Press, 1968), pp. 552-557; Theodore R. Sarbin, "Role: Psychological Aspects," International Encyclopedia of the Social Sciences, pp. 546-552; Daniel Levinson, "Role Personality and Social Structure," in Sociological Theory, 3d ed., ed. Lewis Cosner and B. Rosenberg (New York: Macmillan, 1969), pp. 284-297.

19. Thomas Haskell, "Safe Havens for Sound Opinion: The American Social Science Association and the Professionalization of Social Thought in the U.S., 1865-1909," (Ph.D. thesis, Stanford, 1973), Appendix A, and The Emergence of Professional Social Science p. 104.

20. The numerical dominance of AEA leaders within the sample of new social scientists accurately reflects their centrality in creating the social content of the new expert's role. Not only did the

newer political science and sociological associations grow out of the AEA, but their leaders as well as their rank and file willingly accepted and operated within the role shaped primarily by economists. Indeed, these new political scientists and sociologists had often shared in its shaping as AEA members. This situation is not widely appreciated by sociologists commenting on their own social origins, and this flaws their otherwise often interesting work, as is the case with Oberschall, "The Institutionalization of American Sociology," and Herman Schwendiger and Julia Schwendiger, The Sociologists of the Chair (New York: Basic Books, 1974). Interestingly, Weber had no illusions in the matter, identifying himself as a "political economist" in "Science as a Vocation," p. 129.

21. Thomas Haskell, "Safe Havens," Appendix B.

22. "Index of Authors," American Economic Review 7, no. 4 (Supplement, December 1917): 24-56.

23. W.P. Meroney, "Index to the Sociological Papers and Reports of the American Sociological Society, 1906-30," Proceedings of the American Sociological Society, 25 (1931): 226-258.

24. Ernest R. Mowrer, Classified Index to the American Journal of Sociology Volumes 1-25 (Chicago: University of Chicago Press), supplemented by vol. 26 of AJS.

25. Mark Iris, Cumulative Index to the Proceedings of the American Political Science Review (Ann Arbor, Mich.: University Microfilms, 1970).

26. Kenneth Janda, ed., Cumulative Index to the American Political Science Review, Volumes 1-57: 1906-1963 (Evanston, Ill.: Northwestern University Press, 1964).

27. Ibid., p. xvii.

28. Data on all but 10 of the association leaders were found in three standard works: [Allen Johnson, Dumas Malone, Harris E. Starr, Robert Livingston Schulyler, Edward T. James and John A. Garrity, eds.] Dictionary of American Biography, 25 vols. (New York: Charles Scribner's Sons, 1928-1977); National Cyclopedia of American Biography, 91 vols. (Clifton, N.Y.: James T. White, 1892-1978); Who Was Who In America, 7 vols. (Chicago: Marquis, 1963-1976).

29. Scott Nearing, The Making of a Radical: A Political Autobiography (New York: Harper & Row, 1973); L. Glenn Seretan, Daniel DeLeon, The Odyssey of an American Marxist (Cambridge, Mass.: Harvard University Press, 1979).

3
Sound Opinion Shapes the Expert's Role, 1865-1886

Higher education did not always house monopolies of specialized knowledge, nor did the university always confirm the expert. Indeed, specialist associations pre-dated the rise of the graduate school: statistical, mathematical, natural and social science associations existed well before the Ph.D. was widely recognized as the capstone of our degree system. The men and women who peopled these associations and presented the results of their intellectual endeavors were the experts of their day. Often they had no connection with higher education; frequently their work in academies and colleges was but one face of a many-faceted career.

The American Social Science Association, organized in 1865, was such an organization of self-selected specialists. Its leaders' social position, published work and practical efforts in the field--not university certification--legitimated their claims to expertise. Since they were not dependent on the university for careers, they were able to move aggressively in fashioning an expert role that stressed social science as a policy science in the service of elite values. They emphasized the expert's service to society, focusing on two intellectual tasks. First was the job of technical rationalization of capitalism: devising schemes for the smoother management of a rapidly expanding economy and a limited welfare system to meet the demands of those exploited by industrial expansion. Secondly, ideological work was required to justify these technical rationalizations and their inherently unequal results: well-off capitalists and poor proletarians. To implement the technical and ideological policy they developed, ASSA leaders engaged in agitation, education and administrative service.

In this chapter, we view the ASSA as the organization from which the modern social science expert role emerged. We present the social origins and careers of 43 ASSA leaders, their ideas on social science expertise, and their practical experience as social science experts in the private sector and government between 1865 and 1886. We find that the ASSA was an organization whose leadership encompassed the educational, cultural, philanthropic and business interests of the New England mercantile and financial elite. Their social standing enabled them to use social science expertise to influence regional policy. However, their regional strength and social standing became organizational liabilities with both the rise of New York as the national center of industrial and financial activity and the rapid growth of the graduate school as an institutional home for specialists. For the most part, ASSA leaders continued to exploit their New England resource base and use their social science skills as independent experts unfettered by university career. By the turn of the century, they were outside the concurrent centers being defined by a nationally oriented corporate capitalism and a higher education geared to its service.

The ASSA, 1865-1886

The ASSA was perhaps the first general social science organization in the U.S.[1] It was certainly the most visible and important one in the early post-Civil War period.[2] Established in 1865, it was one of several organizations in different nations that took substance and form from the British Association for the Promotion of Social Science, founded eight years earlier.[3] The ASSA quickly placed itself in the forefront of the many movements of educated and articulate Americans seeking to comprehend and ameliorate the social consequences of rapid industrialization. These educated activists accepted as "sound opinion" the moral philosophy of capitalist political economic development. Social science would elaborate and extend their shared sense of "sound opinion" to cover these newer situations.

More exactly, the ASSA, in its constitution's Statement of Purpose, sought

to aid the development of Social Science, and to guide the public mind to the best practical means of promoting the Amendment of Laws, the Advancement of Education, the Prevention and Repression of Crime, the Reformation of Criminals, and the progress of Public Morality, the adoption of Sanitary Regulations, and the diffusion of sound principles on Questions of Economy, Trade and Finance. It will give attention to Pauperism and the topics related thereto; including the responsibility of the well-endowed and successful, and the wise and the educated, the honest and respectable, for the failures of others. It will aim to bring together the various societies and individuals now interested in these objects, for the purpose of obtaining by discussion the real elements of Truth; by which doubts are removed, conflicting opinions harmonized, and a common ground afforded for treating wisely the great social problems of the day.[4]

In substance, the ASSA wanted to gather together all those willing to apply scientifically the sound political and economic opinion current in reform circles. In 1865, these sound opinions included hard money, a revenue tariff, free trade, civil service reform, all within a fundamental commitment to a continually expanding American capitalism.[5]

In form, the ASSA, like its British model, was divided into four departments--Education; Public Health; Economy, Trade and Finance; and Jurisprudence. This organizational structure was designed to define major problem areas for systematic investigation. The Education Department considered proper instruction and curriculum in formal institutions and popular forums. Public Health treated all aspects of social hygiene, from epidemics and vaccination to drainage and housing. Economics, Trade and Finance explored issues such as the national debt, tariff and taxation as well as questions of social economy, including the labor question, pauperism, prostitution, and intemperance. The fourth department, Jurisprudence, had a dual purpose. It was to deliberate on legal science and to bring legislation in accord with the social science developed in the other departments.[6] The ASSA, then, was internally organized to mobilize knowledge according to scientific principles and solve what its membership saw as pervasive social problems. The departments were to gather data, circulate information, accept and present papers on pertinent subjects. In this way, social science would develop out of sound, received principles of moral philosophy and provide a rational basis for ameliorative reform.

The ASSA, by gathering to itself all manner of reformers, meant to coordinate the technical and ideological tasks of social amelioration in the period. It desired to be something of a clearinghouse and testing ground for social scientific knowledge and practice. Its success is indicated by the lines of social science organizations issuing from it. On the one hand, it fathered a series of health and welfare groups, such as the American Public Health Association, a National Conference of Charities and an American Prison Association. On the other hand, it mothered scholarly organizations, notably the American Historical Association and the American Economics Association. These younger associations in time took up many of the aims and tasks of the ASSA. But during the decade or two before their birth, the ASSA's in-gathering of social science knowledge and practice allowed it to give decisive shaping to its period's definition of the social science expert.

The ASSA Leadership, 1865-1886

Although the ASSA had national aspirations, its leadership's social origins and careers suggest that it was more nearly a regional enterprise. Its leaders seem quite simply to have been a self-selected segment of the New England socioeconomic elite that grew out of Boston's post-revolutionary mercantile and financial strength and came, by 1830, to dominate its region's cultural organizations.[7]

Standard biographical sources supplied data on 40 of the 43 ASSA leaders (Appendix, Table 1). Analysis of these data make clear their deep regional roots. Of the 40, 73 percent were born in New England (Appendix, Table 3), most to families settling in North America before 1700 (Appendix, Table 2). Most of those who earned a college degree did so at a New England school (Appendix, Table 5), almost all from one of the region's pre-revolutionary institutions. Most (72.5 percent) chose New England as the main location of their life's work (Appendix, Table 4). And almost all are buried in their section's rocky soil. Thus, their biographies are undoubtedly part of New England's history.

The standard sources also illuminate the socioeconomic status of these leaders. Again a collective reading seems unequivocal. They are a very active cultural fraction of their region's upper ranks. Consider their families of birth. At a time when the bulk of New England's labor force was engaged in either farming or manual work, only eight (20 percent; see Appendix, Table 8) ASSA leaders were born into families working the land and only one (2.5 percent) had a father who was a laborer. More of the ASSA leaders came from "professional families." Some 35 percent of their fathers were clergy, doctors, lawyers or journalists. Almost as many--32.5 percent--of the fathers were in business, manufacturing or commercial lines. A final 5 percent were public officials. In sum, the ASSA's leaders were born well into their region's middle and upper social reachers.

Further, the evidence of their own lives shows them operating in their region's higher circles. For example, since perhaps 1 percent of the period's youth attended college, we may consider educational attainment as an indicator of both socioeconomic status and cultural aspirations. Of the 40 leaders 32 for whom we have data (80 percent, see Appendix, Table 5) attended college. Eleven went to Harvard, an institution "more expensive for the paying student than any other American college . . . because it had never abandoned the English tradition that a university student should be both a gentleman and a scholar."[8] Another ten went to Yale, a school sharing Harvard's traditional tuition policy. Of the 29 (72.5 percent) finishing the bachelor's degree, 22 (55.0 percent, see Appendix, Table 7) went seriously beyond that attainment, entering professional and graduate institutions. Fourteen (35 percent) completed advanced degree work. In the arts and sciences, four earned doctorates while two gained master's standing. Three others won theology degrees; another three, law degrees. Two took MDs.

As might be expected of a well-born and remarkably educated group, most of the ASSA leaders pursued careers as elite cultural workers. Fourteen (35 percent, see Appendix, Table 9) spent at least half their adult work lives as college professors, and six of these did turns as college presidents. About the same proportion (37.5 percent) had careers in the other learned professions, mainly as clerics, lawyers and doctors but also as editors, librarians and the like. Smaller proportions found their principle adult occupation in business, manufacturing and commerce (17.5 percent) or as public officials (5 percent). The remaining two leaders (5 percent) were women, well-off and outside the labor market, yet active in educational and philanthrophic affairs. Interestingly, ten of those who found their main careers outside higher education were nonetheless involved in college and university work. Five were college professors; three were college presidents; and another two served as both. These ten "part-timers" in higher education make up a quarter of the ASSA leadership and, of course, linked the colleges and universities into their wider, extra-curricular circles. Thus, by educational attainment and career achievement, the ASSAers qualify as leaders within their region's elite cultural apparatus.

Beyond this, our biographical sources contain some clues as to the lives led by the ASSA leaders. Most (72.5 percent) show some sort of aesthetic activity, ranging from personal musical and theatrical involvement to founding and directing museums, libraries and other community enterprises. A majority (57.5 percent) engaged in various philanthropies, supplying material and social support for all manner of sociocultural organizations. Such charity suggests independent means of fortune well beyond the 25 percent who enjoyed extended periods abroad or at leisure, and the 22.5 percent who are reported as having family wealth. Finally, about a third (35 percent) of these leaders have a kin cross-listed in the biographical sources, showing family connections into wider networks of cultural, political and economic leadership.

Over all, then, these ASSA leaders clearly constituted an active intellectual segment of their region's socioeconomic elite. And what of those they led, the ASSA membership? The ASSA's social base was in its region. In 1878, 48 percent (of 441) members resided in New England; in 1880, 45 percent (of 423) did so. But its fellows shared more than geography. Of its 1877 members, one-half had business connections.[9] Further, in the words of the ASSA's historian, "most members . . . had a basis for convivial interaction quite apart from any shared interests in a particular occupation or field of knowledge," be it social science, applied or other. "The men who attended ASSA meetings typically knew each other socially and often were related by blood or marriage. They came primarily as gentlemen and concerned citizens; their connection was . . . their common membership in the gentry class."[10]

In sum, the ASSA was an organization whose leadership encompassed the educational, cultural, philanthropic and business interests of New

England. Its leaders were rooted in the region's established socioeconomic elite, being the sons and daughters of its middle, upper and professional strata. They shared a social background intensified by kinship and social bonds. Their uncommon educational level marked them as learned men and women in the public eye, and their careers as intellectual workers validated that claim. The ASSA served as an arena in which they, as self-selected representatives of their elite, might legitimately seek solutions to its social problems within the received wisdom of the day. And those members attending to the ASSA easily understood these solutions, for they shared the leader's elite social position and world-views. In their search for such regional solutions, the ASSA leadership shaped the emerging content of the social scientific expert role and disseminated it to the association's membership and beyond.

The ASSA Leaders and the Definition of Social Science Expertise, 1865-1885

During the first two decades after the Civil War, there were other social science associations. The ASSA, however, "was the best organized and had the most distinguished personnel of all these groups."[11] Accordingly, they were well positioned to define the period's understanding of the social science expert, and they did with considerable self-consciousness and vigor. First, they spent time and thought exploring the meaning of a social science and thereby the role and practice of the expert. Second, they took up the actual tasks of social science expertise, working to apply the lessons of their science to what they saw as the pressing problems of their period. Third, they developed ideological and material resources for themselves, resources that were also useful to later social science experts.

Papers exploring the purpose and method of social science were frequently read at annual meetings and appeared in the ASSA's Journal of Social Science (JSS). Between 1869 and 1886, at least 16 such articles were published, 11 of these by leaders.[12] Henry Villard, writing as ASSA general secretary in the Journal's first issue, clearly set down the guidelines followed by future authors. Social science was the "science of society." It studies "man as a social being" in exactly the way any other science treats its particular subject matter: "collecting facts, applying principles and reaching general laws which govern social relations."[13] Such laws would then allow rational solutions to the social problems of the day.

Of course, social science must be carefully set apart from a number of other enterprises that might be misidentified with it. As might be expected of a future railroad robber baron speaking for a regional socioeconomic elite, Villard cautioned that social science was not the same as certain popular ideologies then contesting the sound opinions current among the ASSA's leadership. Social science was neither socialism nor radicalism. It was "constructive," not "destructive," conservatively cultivating the good in society rather than uprooting the established order. Further, Villard insisted that social science was not philanthropy. Unlike intellectually undisciplined and inefficient alms-giving, social science did not "treat symptoms" but instead acted from "convictions based on careful inquiry and enduring principle."[14] The ASSA's social science was thus more than facts collected and arranged by objective scientific methods. It had a clear normative element, one consistent with the interests of its regional political economic sponsors: conservative reform vigorously deployed in support of accelerating capitalistic industrialization.

Villard's notions were shared by many other writers in JSS. F.B. Sanborn, the ASSA's long-term general secretary, repeatedly underlined the ASSA's enduring commitment to the scientific method, to collecting and interpreting facts as a means to the "sound" solution of social problems. Thus, after 1877's massive labor unrest, Sanborn advanced a test for social science's expert practice. Is it based on sound opinion: on "proof drawn from experience"? Does it thereby improve the "general social condition"?[15] As Benjamin Pierce, the Harvard-based natural scientist in charge of the U.S. Coastal Survey, put it in the same year: the ASSA's social science was meant "to survey and mark out the safe channels for society to navigate," and thus to bring out and avoid "the dangers which may be hidden from superficial investigation."[16] Then, too, consider W.T. Harris, the noted Hegelian whose St. Louis had been briefly under worker rule during the 1877 strikes. He wrote in 1879 that social science studies man in institutions but considers "both the history of society and its ideal."

This necessarily combines scientific and normative judgments. "We interpret both the present and the past by the future." Then, using society's ideal, "we have the means of comprehending and remedying imperfections that we may discover in society."[17] And the future United States commissioner of education did not consider that society's ideal might be other than the sound opinions held by his ASSA fellows.

Finally, the 1885 ASSA presidential address of John Eaton affirmed the association's collective commitment to science. The then United States commissioner of education asked for more complete governmental statistical services so that social science could more easily establish broad empirical generalizations and social "truths." Social science, by establishing such truths would help correct "errors" in societal organization and "the evils which flow from them."[18] Once again, the leader's position assumed a fundamental political consensus on ends underlying the use of the scientific method as a means of policy clarification and selection.

In sum, the ASSA's idea of social science was accurate factual knowledge about social conditions, carefully collected and scrutinized, used to maximize sound values--a social science supporting the continued social domination of a New England-based socioeconomic elite. What was wanted amounted to a policy science geared to practical use, particularly the shaping of solutions to pressing public problems. Within this science, the role of the expert is straightforward. The expert is the policy scientist and the action intellectual who blends together scientific method and elite values to create the blueprints for the emerging society. We see this expert role most clearly in the actual scientific applications advanced by ASSA leaders.

ASSA Leaders as Social Science Experts, 1865-1886

The ASSA held that the general use of social science was the amelioration of social ills along the lines of their region's "sound ideas." To suit their social science to the times, ASSA leaders developed fairly specific ideas and applications for its practice. In short, they created a role definition for social science experts. Franklin B. Sanborn's 1881 address, "The Three-fold Aspect of Social Science in America," identifies the key role obligations of ASSA social science experts. Sanborn argued that ASSA social science in practice involves agitation, education and administration.[19] Exactly how the ASSA worked at the tasks of technological rationalization and ideological construction is found in its leaders' words and deeds in these three areas.

AGITATION

Agitation amounted to far-flung propaganda efforts in support of the sound opinion shared among the ASSA's membership. ASSA leaders gladly became outspoken publicans. They engaged in policy influence attempts in full view of the adult citizenry, trying to mobilize the responsive middle strata to social action. As a cultural edge of their region's elite, they eagerly articulated their region's preferred positions on currency, tariff, civil service and all other reform issues of the day. For example, to agitate for "sound money" in the post-Civil War period was to side with creditors against debtors, and to argue for New England's financial interests against Western and Southern agrarians.[20] Again, to favor "freer trade" meant supporting established New England manufacturers, merchants and shippers against rising mid-Atlantic industrialists seeking a few years' "protective tariff" isolation from overseas competition. Exploiting their abundantly available opportunities brought them before legislative committees, town meetings, lecture audiences, and public forums of all sorts, not the least of which were their own annual meetings.

Further, when some potential existed for establishing voluntary associations supporting sound and scientific ameliorative charities and social reforms, the leaders offered social and material encouragement. As might be expected, we find the ASSA leadership at the birth of the National Civil Service Reform League as well as many organizational expressions of the "sound money movement." And since the ASSA was a generalized social science organization, its leaders linked it to other agitational vehicles capable of focusing more exactly on the public issues of the day. Most often these affiliates were "health, education and welfare" organizations: prison associations, public charity conferences, boards of public health, committees of provident institutions and public education.

Another set of affiliated associations reflected the ASSA's commitment to agencies interested in data development and management. They participated in the planning of the Ninth U.S. Census, attended International Statistical and Standardization Congresses, and supported the efforts of state labor bureaus to gather information on the intensity of the capital-labor struggle. Finally, the ASSA helped agitate for the creation of the means of sociocultural conservation, elaboration and dissemination. It affiliated with the Boston Museum of Fine Arts, the Concord School of Philosophy, the Massachusetts Historical Association and the YMCA.[21] Taken together, these many inter-organizational connections forged by ASSA leaders reveal the broad and generalist sense of their agitational social science. It also makes clear the leaders' continuing willingness to enter the public lists of social action and do ideological battle with competing social reformers.

Indeed, the leaders' willingness to engage in public agitation extended even to the ballot box. They entered the political arena of party politics when it seemed useful. They energetically sawed party planks and carpentered platforms, supported correctly disposed statesmen while opposing outrageously unsound opportunists, contested nominations and even sought election. At least 14 (35 percent) of the leaders were active in electoral politics. C.F. Adams, May and T.S. Woolsey held local posts. G. Bradford, G.W. Curtis and both David and John Wells attended party conventions and sometimes ran for office. H.A. Hill and F.J. Kingsbury were state legislators as were A.D. White and C.D. Wright. E. Washburn served in state and federal legislatures. G.S. Boutwell and A.H. Rice were virtually professional politicians holding party, local, state and federal positions.

In short, the ASSA's leaders were publicans speaking everywhere for sound opinion. Their sense of agitation meant linking social science expertise into a wide phalanx of organizations seeking solutions to the social issues of the day. And it also meant becoming involved in the formal political apparatus when necessary to lead the way toward proper state policies. By using such agitational devices, the leaders hoped to advance their agenda of the day's social issues along with their preferred solutions. Such efforts were part and parcel of their regional role as experts.

50   Serving Power

EDUCATION

The educational aspect of the ASSA's sense of the social scientist's expert role is most clearly seen in the leaders participation in formal organizations and agencies. The career educationists among the leaders were well positioned to disseminate sound opinion. Two served as U.S. commissioners of education. Two were trustees at Harvard; another two, at Yale. They professed widely: four at Harvard, four at Yale, two at MIT and others at Cornell, and the Universities of Iowa, Michigan and Pennsylvania. They managed large educational enterprises. William Barton Rogers organized the Massachusetts Institute of Technology (MIT). Andrew D. White molded Cornell. Edmund Jane James restructured the Wharton School at the University of Pennsylvania. Thomas Hill and Charles W. Elliot presided over Harvard. William T. Hammond headed law schools at Iowa and St. Louis's Washington University. T.D. Woolsey shaped Yale, as did Daniel Coit Gilman before he turned his hand to the University of California and Johns Hopkins. Such posts offered magnificent opportunities to further approved attitudes and sound opinions within established and emerging institutions.

There is a second, less obvious, facet of the ASSA's educational sense of social science expertise. It involved designing popular instruction to broadcast sound ideas to unschooled workers, ill-tutored capitalists and even pre-school children. In 1869, Charles Francis Adams, speaking to the ASSA, noted the dangers of widespread suffrage in an industrializing political economy drawing to itself laboring immigrants uneducated in American democracy: "Universal suffrage can only mean in plain English the government of ignorance and vice . . . it means a European, and especially Celtic, proletariat on the Atlantic coast, an African proletariat on the shores of the Gulf, and a Chinese proletariat on the Pacific."[22] Adams proposed a two-edged solution: widespread easily available popular education coupled with literacy tests for votes.

In 1871 Samuel Eliot discussed the labor question before the ASSA and proposed a similar schooling for industrial workers. His curricula would provide "social education, training in the laws of society, in the relations of class to class and of man to man in the questions of production and consumption, wages, exchanges and wealth."[23] In 1874,

William Graham Sumner likewise spoke for the broadest sort of popular education, saying "popular agitation and discussion, unmethodological as it is and little adapted to satisfy a scientific thinker, is a great good," for it educates the public and influences legislation. Sumner, however, sounded a characteristically cautionary note, for educating "millions of voters to sufficient knowledge" of the ASSA's sound notions of social science and economics "involves the severest test to which popular institutions have ever been put, one which hitherto they have never endured."[24]

But the force of events required the ASSA social science expert to attempt even more. Thinking out loud about 1877, the raucous year of violence between labor and capital,[25] Sanborn concluded there was "missionary work" to be done educating both industrial workers and their employers, particularly the "powerful and corrupting centralizers of capital and controllers of legislatures."[26] And by 1880 future Commissioner of Education W.T. Harris and Emily Talbot announced their expert views of reforming primary education by bringing it to three-year-olds. "Social science.......is interested in any device that will reach the proletariat and neutralize the seeds of perverseness and crime in their earliest growths. No device promises fairer results in this direction than the kindergarten."[27]

Of course, the ASSA's expertise in popular and primary education involved deeds as well as words. Some, like Samuel Eliot and C.F. Adams, led school reform efforts in Quincy and Boston[28] and others such as Abby W. May and W.G. Sumner served on school boards. In short, then, the educational role of the ASSA social science expert involved designing "devices," curricula and organizations to disseminate better those sound ideas reflecting the interests of New England's socioeconomic elite to all needing much instruction.

The ASSA and State Administration

But the ASSA's most important contributions to the modern social science expert role pivoted about its leaders' participation in state administration. There they played very active roles in the creation and perfection of state agencies that went well beyond the minimal monopoly of legitimate violence: the policeman and the judge. They thus established, and defined as legitimate, the modern social science expert advancing elite interests via state service.

By the 1880s, Sanborn saw the administrative aspect of social science expertise as the "execution and practical illustration" of sound "principle" in local, state and federal agencies.[29] This amounted to defining the social science expert role as routinely linking together the higher reaches of the class structure and the state bureaucratic apparatus. In 1886 Sanborn noted how the ASSA had come to see its 20 years of collective effort at administration. Sanborn first listed with approval the post-Civil War state expansion into public education, public health and fiscal planning; factory and bank inspections; tariff and tax commissions; the partial regulation of railroads and utilities; census data collection; parks and museums. Then he affirmed:

> our association, at its very outset, seems to have contemplated just this expansion of powers and interests. . . . But we also contemplated our own more special work, the combination of private initiative and associated activity with whatever governments might undertake.[30]

Even discounting these remarks for the self-congratulatory tendencies usual to associational stock-taking, there is no mistaking the role model being delineated. The social science expert mediates between private power and the activist state. And given the ASSA's notion of science in the service of sound elite opinion, the expert acts in the interests of a socioeconomic elite: as a class-biased intellectual in state's clothing.

The ASSA's social science expert in state service acted in two ways. First, leaders were public administrators, creating and heading up new state agencies, casting as best they could the future direction of state action as well as establishing the state as a primary service area for later experts. Second, they supplied language and labor for the civil service reform movement, creating and institutionalizing the ideology of the nonpartisan, and thus disinterested, expert as the ideal servant of society's collective interests. This ideology masked the expert's service to society's elite sectors.

The administrative work of ASSA leaders in the state sector was varied and impressive. Between 1865 and 1886 they held numerous state and federal posts. There they pioneered and restructured agencies to meet popular demands without eroding elite privilege. They essentially rationalized and centralized government agencies, perceiving this work as the best way of using the facts and generalities discovered with the social science methods continuously affirmed in their ASSA discussions. And the ASSA served as a continuing forum wherein practical experience was shared, administrative actions coordinated and information for further efforts gathered.

Given the ASSA's roots in New England, it is not at all coincidental that Massachusetts became an exemplar of conservative state intervention in American capitalistic enterprise. Moving well beyond previous ad hoc ameliorative efforts organized by unsystematic philanthropists, Massachusetts pioneered state intervention schemes with the ASSA in the fore. Thus Samuel G. Howe and F.B. Sanborn helped organize the Massuchusetts Board of State Charities. Sanborn served as its secretary from 1865 to 1869, while Howe was its chairman from 1865 to 1874. Another ASSA leader, Boston businessman Hamilton A. Hill also served on this board, which sought to supervise and coordinate previously decentralized public charity efforts within the Commonwealth. It also engaged in data collection to identify scientifically the causes of pauperism and other social ills. At nub, the board attempted to rationalize the state's increasing welfare burden by centralizing such efforts to meet what Sanborn in 1869 termed the three tests of "economy, humanity and efficiency."

By 1874 nine other states had instituted agencies modeled on Massachusetts, and the ASSA-sponsored Conference of Public Charities elected Sanborn as its secretary to guide cooperative efforts to standardize statistics and prevent pauperism. Building on these experiences, the ASSA hosted similar national conferences for state public health and prison agencies.[31] All these efforts at centralization and rationalization were continued and elaborated by later social science experts. These latter-day experts also accepted the tacit ideology of such agencies: (1) that individuals received the rough-and-ready social justice they deserved in capitalistic development, in a sense blaming the victims and not the process creating them, and (2) that experts were essential to maximize the economy and efficiency of the welfare state's administrative apparatus.

Massachusetts also created the first state labor bureau in response to worker agitation and reform demands. After briefly allowing laborites to run it, the agency was placed in ASSA leader C.D. Wright's able hands. He shaped it into a statistical agency since data collection would yield generalities for policy makers as well as stilling public uncertainties stirred by industrial disputes. Wright's views were entirely consistent with the ASSA position on science in the service of power, and his future service included administering perhaps the first technically adequate state census in the United States, heading the nation-wide association of state labor bureaus and reproducing the Massachusetts Labor Bureau at the federal level as first United States commissioner of labor, a post again created in response to laborite agitation.[32]

Charles Francis Adams, Jr., reshaped New England railroad commissions and set a precedent for the national regulation of America's first big business. Before the Civil War, railways were individually state chartered and thereby held responsible one by one for specific service: public transit. By the 1860s popular discontent with railway management and service was widespread and their regulation continuously on the political agenda. Many, especially Westerners, demanded lower fares via public regulation or ownership. Adams educated himself and established his own expertise in a series of publications all pointing toward state regulation of the industry rather than state ownership. When Massachusetts created its Railroad Commission in 1869, he became its chairman and spokesman, shaping a regional New England policy of general and routine incorporation, one encouraging industrial consolidation and capitalistic control rather than a Western, Grangerite policy of public service transit at the lowest fare. The commission fostered even larger combinations and inter-line pools, and "reasonable" rates of return: a "just profit" rather than a "just fare." Clearly rejecting laissez-faire notions of unlimited competition among lines as unduly chaotic, the Commission established an ideology and practice of state regulation between the two menaces of unchecked monopoly and popular control. In this, Adams and his commission anticipated academic doctrines in railroad and public utility economics. They also set the example for other New England state agencies and federal regulatory bodies like the Interstate Commerce Commission. So well did Adams express corporate railway interests that in 1879 he joined fellow ASSA leader David Wells as two-thirds of the private industrial arbitration board regulating the several pools among the nation's rail lines.[33]

In shaping such early efforts at state amelioration, the ASSA leaders expressed and affirmed their shared sense of social science soundly preserving the best features of their social order. As Sanborn once put it: "We have steadily sought those modifications of the existing order, and the correction of present evils and abuses, which tend most to the good of society as a whole."[34] It was as socially concerned, self-selected intellectual agents of a regional socioeconomic elite that they acted as the initial organizers of basic state bureaucracies--welfare, labor, rail, education and so on--designed to cope conservatively with the most pressing problems of rapid post-Civil War, capitalistic industrialization.

Through this administrative work, they effectively demonstrated one dimension of the social science expert's role. They showed that the state was a service sector for expert employment. But they also went beyond deeds to author and establish an ideology of expertise in the widest public service. Their clearest and most important contributions to the ideology of expertise for the common good is seen in the ASSA leaders efforts at civil service reform. The ASSA leaders' civil service support was partly a result of their own experiences in creating and shaping state agencies to ameliorate some of industrialization's social ills. But these efforts were also based on sentiments widely shared by the period's most vocal reformers and were rooted, in part, in fears of an enfranchised emerging "political proletariat." At nub, the ASSA leaders feared that recent immigrants whose labor powered the rapidly industrializing economy would organize and displace their kind in socioeconomic power. To counter this threat, they developed schemes to control these immigrant industrial workers and rhetoric to justify the schemes. Their rhetoric styled the emerging working class as potentially a "close combination of vice, ignorance and brute force, wholly inaccessible to reason or the dictates of public virtue."[35]

Schemes like popular and adult education (mentioned above) sought to control these industrial workers indirectly through indoctrination in "sound ideas." But civil service reform directly attacked a specific organizational form that industrial workers might use to gain power: the political party. The rhetoric here saw parties as political machines run by bosses who bought votes with cash and other timely favors, including supplying government jobs via patronage appointments. For the civil service reformer, patronage was the critical fuel that powered the political machine and, as such, a "huge ogre . . . gnawing at the character, honor and the life of the country."[36] Thus, the first point of civil service reform was to abolish the "spoils system." And since the ASSA was a constructive reform group of social scientists, it suggested a variety of positive alternatives. In these we find a nascent and growing definition of the expert role in state administration, one that emerges as an enduring ideology in subsequent decades.

First, the ASSA, along with the broader civil service movement, took a nonpartisan position, insisting that political truth and justice was not to be found within the parties themselves. Accordingly, the state bureaucracy must not be in any sense dominated by this or that political party. While parties might well legitimately contest for legislative power, they should not have influence in executive or administrative matters. This, of course, raised the question of how administrative recruitment should occur. The basic ASSA--and reform--answer was that certified experts should staff the state apparatus, thus putting their decisions "beyond party politics."

Accordingly, the ASSAer who was dean of Yale Law School asked for permanent nonpartisan commissions staffed by experts to "hear" proposed legislation and corps of trained draftsmen to write the bills, which would then move into the legislature for representative consideration.[37] Another--a leading editor--thought experts themselves might be certified by tests measuring "the comparative general intelligence of all applicants and their special knowledge of particular official duties."[38] A third ASSAer argued for a national social science-oriented training school for experts modeled on West Point or Annapolis.[39] And a fourth, the U.S. commissioner of labor, urged agencies to use certified and tested experts who would have an ability to make decisions "mathematically and scientifically correct and morally just to all."[40]

It is important to add that ASSA leaders did not require merit testing and certification for all political posts. Their sympathies probably were with those civil service reformers who would exempt elected officials, mainly legislators and chief executives: "all those higher officers who really represent that policy of a party and those principles of a campaign which the people have approved."[41] They also exempted top policy-making positions: cabinet and agency executive posts like those they themselves held from time to time. Baldy put, extending merit criteria to the very top of the bureaucratic ladder infringed on elite privilege. Or, in the charming rhetoric of Samuel Eliot, the ardent civil service reformer who desired a social science West Point: "Many men who are the best qualified for our high offices would feel it a humilation to have their qualifications demanded of them. Nor could they be examined, even if they would, by commissioners of probably inferior abilities to themselves."[42]

Thus, the ASSA's civil service reform was designed to check the emerging political proletariat. But it also sought to permit the continued policy perogatives of entrenched and threatened socioeconomic elites and their experts, like those leading the association and linking the state and class systems. Finally, it crystallized a vocabulary of merit, testing and certification all useful in ideologically defending the expert's role.

The ASSA and New Social Science Expertise

From their practical and ideological experiences as state administrators and early social science practioners, the ASSA leadership became increasingly sensitive to the uses of expertise. This awareness was widely shared. As John Eaton, United States commissioner of education, remarked to the association in 1885, "Investigators are becoming experts, and they are more in demand."[43] For their part, while the ASSA leaders welcomed the rise of newer forms of social scientific expertise and used their region's resources to offer it hospitality, they came to understand the differences between these newer experts and themselves.

One way to claim avant-garde social science expertise in the 1880s was via training at a German graduate school. The ASSA opened its meetings and publications to those so certified. Its annual meetings heard addresses and its journal printed papers by "new social scientists" elaborating the latest historical methods,[44] exhibiting the fruits of those methods in fully footnoted studies,[45] and exploring the latest theory and tactics for containing "unsound" socialist and radical ideas.[46] Furthermore, the ASSA opened its ranks to German-trained experts, selecting Henry Carter Adams, Henry W. Farnum and Edmund Jane James as departmental officials in the early 1880s. For their part, the new experts seemed to have accepted the hospitality of the ASSA for some time thereafter.[47] Finally, the ASSA's leaders' high positions within the educational apparatus were usually used to help ease newer forms of graduate social science education into place. All save the Rev. Thomas Hill and the senior Woolsey as presidents of Harvard and Yale encouraged the rapid and distinctive development of the new social science expertise in America.

The ASSA's admiration and support for the university-based new social science was necessarily limited. As an organization, it was committed to its own definition of social science expertise, one involving--as we have seen--intellectuals of elite status and sound opinion engaged in education, administration and agitation, but without the impersonal certification of specialized advanced degrees. Sensing the challenge to this role implicit in the new social science's use of university certification, the ASSA in 1878 offered to merge itself into the period's rising graduate school par excellence, Johns Hopkins.[48] Such a merger would have given a semblance of graduate university recognition and near certification to the ASSA's definition of social science expertise. And, in exchange, a financially troubled university then selling off depressed Baltimore and Ohio (B & O) Railroad stock might have gained a new income-producing division.[49]

The merger offer was considered carefully by Hopkins' founding president, Daniel Coit Gilman. Gilman was very well acquainted with the ASSA's sense of expertise, having counseled and attended its birth, and served it as both director and long-term vice-president. Indeed, Gilman served as ASSA president while considering the merger proposal. Gilman refused the merger, using his 1880 ASSA presidential address to urge the ASSA to rework its sense of expertise.

In a masterwork of polite and sympathetic criticism, Gilman

underlined the distinctions between the ASSA's and the newer, university-based senses of expertise. The essential difference was one of means and not ends. Thus, Gilman as spokesman for the new social sciences at Hopkins found no difficulty in affirming the aims of the ASSA. He readily endorsed the ASSA's continuing sense of social science as "the ascertainment of principles and laws" using the methods common to all other sciences. Experiment and obsevation yielded facts. "Reflection upon these facts" followed "until the laws were discovered from which . . . rules and methods of management might safely be deduced." And he certainly supported the continuing normative thrust of the ASSA to study scientifically the "conditions which tend to make a perfect state of society where 'each is for all and all for each'" and to enact legislation furthering these conditions.

While Gilman endorsed the ASSA's continuing goal of a policy science furthering class harmony and the interests of a socioeconomic elite, he suggested some alternative and more industrialized means toward this end. He thought the ASSA might organize more systematically planned investigation and research within its departments. These departments could also report their findings more completely with detailed reviews of the recent literature. He also proposed another department, one specializing in "historical sociology." The ASSA should also consider publishing more purely scientific articles, promoting fuller scientific discussion at its meetings, and forming more "local institutions" for the further promotion of its social scientific work.[50] In essence, Gilman was asking the ASSA to adopt the specialized apparatus of new social science as a more efficient tool toward its well-appreciated ends.

The ASSA did not follow Gilman's suggestions for more specialization. To do so would have required it to pattern itself along the industrial lines taken by the new social science. This the ASSA could not do and still maintain its own definition of generalized, if regional, social science expertise. Indeed, the ASSA's organizational response to Gilman's considered refusal to merge it into Hopkins was a reaffirmation of its older role. In the 1880s, the ASSA worked to enter its own course of social science into the nation's college curriculum. Emily Talbot and the Education Department canvassed higher educational institutions on their offerings. Sanborn, James, Harris, and Francis

Wayland, Jr., dean of Yale Law School, outlined a proper course based on the ASSA's understanding of social science expertise. Sanborn actually taught such a course from 1885 to 1888 at Cornell, under the sponsorship of Cornell president and ASSA leader A.D. White. The ASSA also began to structure more discussion and debate into its annual meetings, devoting, for example, part of its 1890 session to the "single-tax" issue and its 1895 assembly to the "free silver" question.[51]

These several innovations reveal the limits of the ASSA's interest in reworking its role definition of social science expertise. Its collegiate curriculum was designed to teach sound principles and administrative practices of ameliorative reform, schooling its students for generalized volunteerism in later life. These undergraduate courses were but a new means to transmit the established ASSA version of social science expertise, not a mechanism to further the specialized social science expert role that Gilman had in mind. And while the ASSA's leaders were greatly pleased to host well-publicized festivals of popular education, filled with the fury of agitation, advocacy and values in conflict and clarification, these discussions were not the specialist scholarly ones Gilman had suggested to them.

Viewed in the larger context of the industrializing nation, the ASSA's merger offer and Gilman's rejection reveal a regional intellectual leadership contemplating its past, present and future. The ASSAers had been linked by sponsorship to New England's resources all through the nineteenth century. As part of its region's intellectual elite, the ASSA leadership had long opposed alternative sectional idealogies, notably the Southern sociologies that had legitimated slave-based agrarian capitalism, and the protective-tariff economics produced in the more industrial mid-Atlantic states. Tied to resources and definitions of social economic problems through well-established cohort, friendship and kinship networks, the ASSA's leadership was faced with crisis when its region was. The post-Civil War rise of the mid-Atlantic states, especially New York, as a center for emerging national industrial and finance capital forced New England's ASSA intellectuals to face the choice of supporting its region's relatively immobile merchant and industrial capital or forging extra-regional alliances.

The ASSA's early leadership had not been insensitive to the

possibilities of building links outside New England. But given its essentially sectional character, its efforts at extra-regional expansion were disastrous. Affiliate associations were established in other cities--Albany or Detroit--only to vanish under pressure of local events.[52] In 1879, Baltimore's Johns Hopkins provided something of a new opportunity. As a graduate university, Hopkins could provide a useful data factory for the ASSA's sound opinion. Furthermore, its newness meant the ASSA's previous ideological commitments had not built up a residue of antagonisms. Finally, Gilman was clearly sympathetic to the ASSA's sound opinion and the general thrust of its social science as policy science, and he had a proven track record in resource procurement outside New England.

When Gilman rejected the ASSA's merger offer, he stressed the new social science's specialization in tacit opposition to the ASSA's generalist predilections. Gilman's Hopkins required academically contained careers quite different than those known by most ASSA leaders. For example, Sanborn could combine his broad intellectual training and experience with familiarity of his region's material and cultural infra-structure to fashion and market ideational products personally. He could translate classics, write biographies, author articles on social issues, found secondary schools, teach at a university--all the while providing leadership for the ASSA. By stressing the organizational requirements of academic specialization, Gilman underlined conditions of dependent intellectual production that were unacceptable to generalists, such as the ASSA leadership. Indeed, the generalist's ability to address a broad range of tasks was rooted in a certain anarchy of intellectual production. But, if the ASSA leader's were to forge an extra-regional alliance with Hopkins--or elsewhere--they had to bring these individualistic tendencies under career control. This, of course, they were unwilling to do. As a result, they maintained their ongoing style of intellectual production and their regional networks. In so doing, they cut themselves off from acting as intellectual guides and legitimators for those rising mid-Atlantic industrial and finance capitalists creating the present day's economic center.

Nonetheless, the ASSA leadership did fashion the role of the social science expert in the first two decades after the Civil War. Those like

Gilman, who created the newer graduate school-based social science expert role, necessarily built upon the ASSA's handiwork. First among the ASSA's contribution was its example as action intellectuals. Like later specialists, they solved politically explosive technical and ideological problems that would enter academic textbooks as scientific truths: witness Adam's railway economics. To this we may add their definition of education as a means of popular control and indoctrination; the establishment of the states as a site for expert employment; the formulation of a vocabulary using terms like "nonpartisan," and "economy . . . and efficiency," to defend expert (rather than popular) decision making in public agencies; and the guarded recognition of graduate education as a mechanism of expert certification.

These contributions amount to a rudimentary shaping of the modern expert's role and a sizable first step toward its present-day form. And while there is some merit in seeing the ASSA leaders as an older generation of social science experts replaced by a newer one, this view does not capture the fullest understanding to be seen from their collective biographies. More telling are the long-term continuities between the ASSAers and their immediate successors to the mantle of expertise, continuities mediated by the newer social scientists' need to house their careers and knowledge in graduate and modernizing universities. The shift in expertise, then, is not so much from an older generation to a new and younger one. Rather, it is from a regional set of generalists to a more nearly national collection of specialists accommodating themselves to the emerging economic and ideological concurrent centers.

NOTES

1. Thomas L. Haskell, The Emergence of Professional Social Science: The American Social Science Association and the Nineteenth Century Crisis of Authority (Urbana, Ill.: University of Illinois Press, 1977).

2. Luther Lee Barnard and Jesse Barnard, Origins of American Sociology: The Social Science Movement in the United States (New York: Crowell, 1943), p. 558.

3. Similar associations were formed in Belgium, France, Germany, Italy, Russia and Switzerland reflecting reformers' concern with the consequences of industrialization throughout the Western world. See Barnard and Barnard, Origins of American Sociology, p. 539 and Henry Villard, "Historical Sketch of Social Science," Journal of Social Science 1 (June 1869): 6.

4. Constitution, Address and List of Members of the American Association for the Promotion of Social Science (Boston: Wright and Potter, 1866), p. 3.

5. Ari Hoogenboom, Outlawing the Spoils: A History of the Civil Service Reform Movement, 1865-1883 (Urbana, Ill.: University of Illinois Press, 1968), pp. 55, 167-197.

6. Constitution, Address and List of Members, pp. 15-16; Barnard and Barnard, Origins of American Sociology, pp. 543-544.

7. Philip Hall, "Four Families in Economic Enterprise: The Rise of a Massachusetts Elite, 1760-1830" (Ph.D. dissertation, State University of New York, Stony Brook, 1967); and Oscar Handlin and Mary Flug Handlin, Commonwealth: A Study of the Role of Government in the American Economy: Massachusetts, 1774-1861, rev. ed. (Cambridge, Mass.: Harvard University Press, 1969).

8. Samuel Eliot Morison, Three Centuries of Harvard, 1636-1936 (Cambridge, Mass.: Harvard University Press, 1936), pp. 201; John S. Brubacker and Rudy Willis, Higher Education in Transition: A History of American Colleges and Universities, 1636-1976, 3d ed. (New York: Harper & Row, 1976) note the high cost of higher education at "older colleges" in this period, p. 40.

9. Barnard and Barnard, The Origins of American Sociology, pp. 549-550; Edward C. Kirkland, Dream and Thought in the Business Community, 1860-1900 (Ithaca, N.Y.: Cornell University Press, 1956), pp. 15-16.

10. Haskell, The Emergence of Professional Social Science, p. 174.

11. Barnard and Barnard, The Origins of American Sociology, p. 558.

12. Given the ASSA's purpose of promoting social science, virtually all papers read at its meetings or published in its Journal of Social Science (hereafter: JSS) contain or imply something about the purpose, method and possibilities of social science. However, 16 papers contain some titular reference to these matters, suggesting a deeper and fuller treatment than that found in the other 218 papers published between 1869-1886 in vols. 1-21 of JSS. The papers by non-leaders are H.B. Adams, "New Methods of Study in History," JSS 18 (May 1884): 213-263; E.L. Godkin, "Legislation and Social Science," JSS 3 (1871): 115-132; H. Greeley, "Method of Diffusing Knowledge," JSS 1 (June 1869): 88-90; E.M. Hunt, "Health and Social Science," JSS 18 (May 1884): 29-43; and W. Strong, "The Study of Social Science," JSS 4 (1871): 1-7. The papers by leaders are J. Eaton, "A Word on the Scientific Method in the Common Affairs of Life," JSS 21 (September 1886): ix-xxiii; D.C. Gilman, "The Purposes of the ASSA, and the Means That May Be Employed to Promote These Ends," JSS 12 (December 1880): xxii-xxiv; W.T. Harris, "The Method of Study in Social Science," JSS 10 (December 1879): 28-34; B. Pierce, "The National Importance of Social Science in the U.S.," JSS 12 (December 1880): xii-xxi; F.B. Sanborn, "The Work of Social Science in the U.S.," JSS 6 (July

1874): 36-45, "The Work of Social Science, Past and Present," JSS 8 (May 1876): 23-39, "Social Science in Theory and Practice," JSS 9 (January 1878): 1-13; "The Three-fold Aspect of Social Science in America," JSS 14 (November 1881): 26-35, "The Commonwealth of Social Science," JSS 19 (December 1884): 1-10, "The Social Sciences: Their Growth and Future," JSS 21 (September 1886): 1-12; H. Villard, "Historial Sketch of Social Science," JSS 1 (June 1869): 5-10.

13. Villard, "Historical Sketch", p. 6.

14. Ibid., p. 9.

15. Sanborn, "Social Science in Theory and Practice," p. 4.

16. Pierce, "The National Importance of Social Science," p. xiii.

17. Harris, "The Method of Study," p. 29-30.

18. Eaton, "A Word on the Scientific Method," p. xx.

19. Sanborn, "Social Science in Theory and Practice."

20. Horace Samuel Merrill, Bourbon Democracy of the Middle West, 1865-1896 (Seattle, Wash.: University of Washington Press, 1967).

21. Sheila S. McVey, "Social Control of Social Science Research: The Development of the Social Scientist as Expert, 1875-1916" (Ph.D. dissertation, University of Wisconsin, 1974), p. 297.

22. Charles F. Adams, "The Protection of the Ballot in National Elections," JSS 1 (June 1869): 111.

23. Samuel Eliot, "Relief of Labor," JSS 4 (1871): 137.

24. W.G. Sumner, "American Finance," JSS 6 (July 1874): 182.

25. For the details of the widespread disorders, see Robert V. Bruce, 1877: Year of Violence (Chicago: Quadrangle, 1970).

26. Sanborn, "Social Science in Theory and Practice," pp. 7-8.

27. W.T. Harris and E. Talbot, "Report on the Kindergarten Schools," JSS 12 (December 1880): 9; see also W.T. Harris, "Moral Education in the Common Schools," JSS 18 (May 1884): 122-134.

28. Michael B. Katz, Class, Bureaucracy and Schools: The Illusion of Educational Change in America, expanded ed. (New York: Praeger, 1971) details the reform role played by Adams, Eliot and W.T. Harris, among others.

29. Sanborn, "The Three-fold Aspect of Social Science in America," p. 30.

30. Sanborn, "The Social Sciences: Their Growth and Future," pp. 1-2.

31. Barnard and Barnard, Origins of American Sociology pp. 535-536; F.B. Sanborn, "The Supervision of Public Charities," JSS 1 (June 1869): 80, 85; "Conference on Boards of Public Charities," JSS 7 (September 1874): 210-250.

32. James Leiby, Carroll Wright and Labor Reform: The Origin of Labor Statistics (Cambridge, Mass.: Harvard University Press, 1960).

33. Edward C. Kirkland, Charles Francis Adams, Jr., 1835-1915: The Patrician at Bay (Cambridge, Mass.: Harvard University Press, 1965), pp. 34-64; and Men, Cities and Transportation: A Study in New England History, 1820-1900, 2 vols. (Cambridge, Mass.: Harvard University Press, 1948), 2: 230-267; Charles Francis Adams, Charles Francis Adams, 1835-1915: An Autobiography (New York: Russell and Russell, 1968), pp. 172-175.

34. F.B. Sanborn, "The Commonwealth of Social Science," p. 7.

35. Adams, "The Protection of the Ballot," p. 111.

36. G.W. Curtis, "Civil Service Reform," JSS 14 (November 1881): 51.

37. F. Wayland, Jr., "Opening Address: On Certain Defects in Our Method of Making Laws," JSS 14 (November 1881): 1-25.

38. Curtis, "Civil Service Reform," p. 46.

39. Eliot, "Civil Service Reform," JSS 1 (June 1869): 119.

40. C.D. Wright, "The Scientific Basis of Tariff Legislation," JSS 19 (December 1884): 26.

41. "Report of the Civil Service Commission," JSS 5 (1873): 141. For a sense of shared ideas among reformers see Hoogenboom, Outlawing the Spoils, pp. 123-134, who places this "Report" in its historical context.

42. Eliot, "Civil Service Reform," p. 116.

43. Eaton, "A Word on the Scientific Method," p. xxi.

44. H.B. Adams, "New Methods of Study in History": 213-263.

45. Edward W. Bemis, "Local Government in Michigan and the Northwest," JSS 17 (May 1883): 49-69; and Henry Carter Adams, "The Financial Standing of States," JSS 19 (December 1884): 27-46, are early examples.

46. Henry W. Farnum, "The German Laws of October 21, 1878," JSS 13 (March 1881): 36-53; and E.W. Bemis, "Socialism and State Action," JSS 21 (September 1886): 33-68.

47. For example, J.W. Jenks delivered a paper to the 1891 annual meeting and headed the Finance Department in the mid-1890s.

48. Haskell, The Emergence of Professional Social Science, pp. 144-167.

49. Hopkins' common shares of B & O had a par value of $1.5 million. Their sale value is often quoted as twice that amount. See Daniel Coit Gilman, The Launching of a University (New York: Garrett Press, 1969), p. 30. But they were sold in 1878, 1892 and 1895 for half that amount: $774,126. See Abraham Flexner, Daniel Coit Gilman (New York: Harcourt, Brace and Co., 1946), p. 99. On the fiscal problems created by the stocks, see Hugh Hawkins, Pioneer: A History of Johns Hopkins University (Ithaca, N.Y.: Cornell University Press, 1960), pp. 3-5 and 316-322.

50. Gilman, "The Purposes of the ASSA."

51. Haskell, The Emergence of Professional Social Sciences, pp. 195-202.

52. Indeed, the ASSA's only strong continuing affiliate was in Philadelphia. Its linkage to the ASSA resulted from Villard's kin connections there. With the ASSA's decline in the 1890s and the concurrent rise of the American Economic Association, the Philadelphia group transformed itself into the American Academy of Political and Social Science. See Haskell, The Emergence of Professional Social Science, pp. 116-119, and issues of the academy's Annals.

4
Modernizing Managers and Dependent Intellectuals

By 1885 the ASSA's regional role for social scientists centered on technical rationalization and production of ideology. Its expert practice proved unproblematic. Well-placed ASSA leaders enjoyed close, informal relations with New England's established seats of learning. They shared occupational and sometimes family ties with the region's mercantile and industrial elite. Their easy access to policy makers and regional resources made impersonal credentials and university careers unnecessary. As generalists in regional matters, they had little collective need to define social science narrowly. Indeed, their broad social science gave them wide scope to practice their expert role through education, agitation and service in the varied administrative posts evolving to answer industrial New England's social problems. However, the ASSA's regional role definition and resources were ill suited to meet the needs of both the industrializing economy and the increasing numbers who wanted to practice a more national social science.

New social science organizations--the American Historical Association and the American Economic Association--launched at the ASSA's annual gatherings were able to establish a more nearly national role but endorsed a further division of intellectual labor. Increased specialization called for more routine cultivation of resources, closely linking the success of these new organizations to the transformation of regional colleges into a nationally integrated network of graduate universities. These new associations' connections with higher education modified the expert role established by the ASSA. In the American university the institutionalization of social science was its industrialization: the hierarchical organization of knowledge production based on specialized roles requiring greater resources than the individual could command. The role of social science expert became available to larger numbers through the development of specialized academic careers, but the associations' work in defining the expert role was now mediated by donors, trustees, political leaders and university managers. As university careers became necessary to support increased specialization, associated experts became dependent intellectuals.

In this chapter, we are concerned with determining the role modifications and limitations that occurred during the process of locating and industrializing social knowledge in the graduate university. We look at the ways university managers, guided by a vision of a reorganized and expanded system of higher education, used certification of specialists to dominate an emerging ideological center aligned by extensive resource needs with an economic center controlled by large, national corporations. We note the proliferation of specialists' associations and focus on the emergence of the AEA, examining its leaders interaction with university managers, established experts and resource holders in shaping a social science expert role. We look especially at the part AEA leaders played in resisting or adapting to the dependence inherent in academic industrialization, thus finding the outside limits of the academic expert role. We see, then, the way the ASSA's regional role was transformed to a more national role serving the newer power centered in the rising corporate sector.

University Managers: Resources for a Vision

Although the ASSA as an organization made no firm commitment to creating expertise for the graduate university, individual leaders devoted their lives to this task. In his 1880 presidential address Gilman had outlined[1] another means of producing and disseminating social science expertise. His speech captured a vision of industrialized knowledge production and distribution becoming institutionalized in the graduate university. It was shared by a handful of ASSA leaders and innovative educators outside the association. Thus, Gilman of Johns Hopkins was understood by fellow ASSA leaders such as President Andrew D. White of Cornell and Harvard's President Eliot. And similar perspectives were shared by non-ASSAers like Michigan's President Angell, Chicago's President Harper and President David Starr Jordan of Indiana and Stanford Universities.[2]

At the heart of these educational managers' vision was specialization. Systematically organized, specialized knowledge would place university-based experts in a position of advantage in answering the full array of technical and social questions facing industrial America. Legitimate monopoly would follow successful solution of problems and the university—not regional culture, traditional religion or corrupt party politics--would develop "scientific" criteria for national decision making.

Although social science expertise had an important place in the intellectual architecture of university builders like the ASSA's Gilman, White and Eliot, it was only one wing of a larger design. These leaders sought to create institutions housing all manner of experts who would command technical and ideological credibility via legitimate monopolies of theoretical knowledge and its practical application. Their institution building was informed by their understanding of how older knowledge monopolies operated. Accordingly, they reformed, and thus strengthened, established professional schools.[3] In addition, they built graduate schools--programs for the pursuit of liberal studies beyond the baccalaureate--to parallel the professional schools. The graduate school placed a "fourth faculty"--liberal studies--alongside the older learned professions of theology, medicine and law.[4] Graduate school faculties would do for the newer knowledge specialists what divinity, medical and law schools did for ministers, doctors and lawyers. It would certify its graduates as credible experts to the community-at-large.

However, expert certification required the reform of collegiate education. Managers gradually replaced the broad classical curriculum disseminated by generalists at regional colleges with the elective system. Experts in narrowing fields dispensed specialized knowledge to undergraduates, preparing them to enter strengthened professional schools and new post-graduate centers. These educational reformers shared their vision of the potential of new knowledge generated by academic specialization with audiences across the nation.[5] They were heard and encouraged both by resource holders anxious to solve the pressing problems of capitalist industrialization and by parents hoping that careers certified by the graduate school would provide their progeny with social security in a boom-and-bust economy.

These new university managers were more nationally oriented than the majority of the ASSA leadership. Men like Eliot, Gilman and White, although themselves distinguished representatives of New England's cultural traditions, became increasingly impatient with the association's enduring commitment to a regional "sound opinion" on currency, national debt, tariff, civil service and other issues crucial to the well-being of New England's socioeconomic elite. Since "sound opinion" mirrored this elite's practical and material concerns, it failed to reflect the wider and national nature of rapid industrialization. Seeing Boston as the permanent hub of an internal empire of manufacture and commerce, ASSA leaders gave scant attention and insufficient analysis to the rise of a system of competing cities and universities spreading production and distribution across the country. They also ignored the growing centralization of national corporate decision making in New York-based trusts.[6] Thus, new university builders and managers found the ASSA's regional focus increasingly inadequate for defining the nation's social problems, for centralizing their solutions and exploiting the seemingly inexhaustible vein of resources found in more nearly national fortunes.

And the men who built and managed the modern university system were extremely sensitive to the resource requirements of their task. They could have hardly been otherwise. The objective demands for resources were obvious. Significant capital funds were needed to pay for the physical plant, the land, bricks and mortar necessary to house the new expertise. Substantial operating expenditures were required to maintain well-stocked libraries, laboratories with up-to-date equipment, and a supporting army of secretaries and custodians, research and teaching assistants.

Moreover, the subjective experience of managers both before and after assuming university presidencies underlined the pivotal role played by resources in academic life. President Eliot's wealthy father was ruined in the panic of 1857 and forced to pay debts with his wife's holdings. Eliot himself, in 1863, reluctantly suspended a promising academic career when Harvard found it could not advance two chemists.

As Eliot put it at the time: "The essential difficulty was a lack of money to maintain two professors, and they chose [Walcott] Gibbs for the one."[7] During Eliot's presidency (1869-1909) at Harvard, he found himself often faced with similar financial limits. For example, in 1887, the department of political economy had to choose between F.W. Taussig and James L. Laughlin. Taussig was retained, eventually headed the department and its Quarterly Journal of Economics, and became an AEA leader. Laughlin was let go and suffered a nervous breakdown. After working in the insurance industry, he rallied sufficiently to chair the economics department and edit the Journal of Political Economy at Harper's University of Chicago.[8]

President White was the son of a banker who left him a sizable fortune. In 1863, as chairman of the New York Senate Committee of Education, he became interested in that state's 1 million-acre land grant under the recent federal Morrill Act. Fellow senator and telegraph financier Ezra Day Cornell agreed to match that grant with land and funds. Together White and Cornell founded the upstate New York university that bears the financier's name. White became its president and guiding spirit for two decades. But resources proved difficult to find, particularly when Ezra Cornell's personal fortune declined with the panic of 1873. After Cornell's death the next year, White increasingly dipped into his own purse and dunned fellow trustees "to meet debts and finish buildings."[9]

Gilman's father, like Eliot's, experienced major financial reverses, skidding from presiding over an iron-making plant in Norwich, Connecticut, to representing such manufacturers in Brooklyn. Gilman's first academic post, after touring Europe with his college friend Andrew White, was raising funds for Yale's Sheffield Scientific School. He subsequently became assistant librarian at Yale, resigning when President Woolsey, an ASSA leader, confessed that the corporation could not afford to pay for the expansion of library services that Gilman desired. In 1866 Gilman became secretary of Sheffield's governing board and continued to seek funds for a school "ill endowed and . . . for years on the point of fading out."[10]

Like White, Gilman presided over a precariously funded new university. Johns Hopkins had left his estate and 15,000 shares of B & O common stock. But the enormity of the estate's worth, perhaps $2 million, limited its marketability, and until it was finally sold to the city of Baltimore, its upkeep drained rather than supplied resources. Likewise, the stock could not be easily sold for its estimated $1.5 million value because of its size: selling off large blocks might well depress its price. Accordingly, Gilman was forced to rely on B & O dividends. But Hopkins' death removed a major support of the B & O's economic viability—his ability to pledge his bank and personal fortune to prop up the railroad when it was pressed by creditors during economic depressions. Without such support the railroad's dividends cycled in its industry's usual exaggeration of the economy's boom-and-bust rhythms, creating extreme problems for Gilman's academic planning and expansion.[11]

For other university presidents, the situation varied in biographical detail and organizational degree. But all of the modernizing educational managers had to deal with resource procurement as a serious and continuing problem. For Angell, there was Michigan politics to be considered. For Harper at Chicago, it was the New York-based Rockefeller organization. For Jordan, it was Stanford's widow. University building depended on an unpredictable economy, the fortunes of elected officials and the caprice of capitalists and their heirs.

When academic social scientists began to make stronger claims to a monopoly of social knowledge and elaborate the university-based expert's role, they were guided and supported by these educational managers, and their role was informed by the university's resource needs. Educational managers, as university builders seeking resources, self-consciously subscribed to conservative explanations of wealth production and use which were routinely—but not exclusively—reflected in academic economists theories of production and distribution. Thus, social scientists became an increasingly important source for building a national ideology dedicated to the conservation of capital that fueled the industrializing university.

But managers also wanted social scientists to offer technical--pragmatic, not merely ideological--solutions to the social and material problems of industrialization. Technical amelioration aided university managers in their endless quest for resources and furthered the university's instruction of the public in its need for all types of expertise. For example, academic economists as expert social scientists were expected to improve the national production and distribution system, stabilizing the seemingly inevitable cycle of boom-and-bust. Such stabilization would convince resource suppliers of the university's worth and also demonstrate to the general citizenry the value of university-based knowledge. In this manner, the economists' specialized expertise not only would give the nation a technically more perfect economic system but would better guarantee the stability of the university's present resources and the prospect of continued funding for the fourth faculty as a whole.

Proliferation of National Specialist Networks

Like educational managers, academic experts in the modern university were ardent in their search for material and symbolic resources to establish and maintain legitimate monopolies of specialized knowledge. Learned societies or disciplinary associations were key elements in the resource strategies of both managers and faculty. Members collectively defrayed some of the costs of knowledge production and dissemination at the same time they generated the expertise necessary to demonstrate the modernizing university's links to a developing industrial economy. Academics formed national networks holding geographically scattered specialists together as well as affirming the corporate sensibilities and purpose of expertise through annual meetings and sponsorship of serial journals and monographs. These associations also solicited funds and received direct subsidies in support of expert endeavors, sometimes acted as brokers between private funding agencies and individual members and worked to build ancillary agencies that aided academic effort, such as the National Archives. And through these activities they wrought symbolic resources for specializing fields by creating an image of experts dedicated selflessly to science and the pursuit of knowledge.

Of course, national networks of subject matter specialists existed well before the rise of the graduate school. For example, the American Statistical Association was founded in 1827 by Bostonians like ASSA leader Edward Jarvis, who had a continuing interest in the accuracy of the U.S. Census.[12] But the rise of the fourth faculty led to a marked proliferation and standardization of such associations. And through these learned societies, specialists began defining what was expert knowledge and practice, what was the content of the expert role and who indeed was an expert.

University managers usually aided and rewarded faculty active in the creation of national networks. Consider the philologists, who were the first sizable bloc of American students to seek specialized overseas training and certification from the German Historical School.[13] In 1883 they formed the Modern Language Association (MLA), setting the pace for university-based experts. Johns Hopkins Professor A. Marshall Elliott was a catalyst for the MLA and became its first secretary. He was supported by Gilman, who knew something about specialist groups, since he had helped bring about the first annual convention of American librarians in 1853 and had served as a secretary of the American Orientalist Society in the 1860s. For Elliott's work with the MLA, Gilman promoted him to associate professor even though he had previously been regarded as a marginal scholar in danger of losing his job. Elliott used the resources he had concentrated to good advantage, helping to found Modern Language Notes in 1886 and constructing at Hopkins the department to which "most Romance-language scholarship in American traces."[14]

The first university-based national network that had important implications for the role of social science expert was the American Historical Association (AHA). The founders of the AHA acknowledged their interest in American social science expertise and resources by holding their organizational meeting in 1884 under the sponsoring umbrella of the ASSA. Many ASSA leaders had published extensively on historical topics and were sympathetic and supportive of the notion of a national specialists' organization. In fact, the AHA's call was signed by the ASSA's current president and secretary along with historians from Gilman's Hopkins, White's Cornell, and Angell's Michigan.[15]

At the founding meeting, ASSA president and U.S. Commissioner of Education John Eaton offered the AHA a permanent and semi-autonomous department in the ASSA. At the same time he warned historians against the excessive specialization that separate organization might bring. But as the ASSA leadership had spurned Gilman's earlier advice to curb their generalist predilections for a more specialized mode of knowledge production, the historians turned aside Eaton's warning. They were committed to specialization.[16] The historians saw the ASSA as a welcome resource base and tapped the historically active and committed amateurs among its membership and audience, spreading the word of their new association along the ASSA's established network. For its part, the ASSA was more committed to solving problems in the present than excavating the past. It did not seriously attempt to hold historians in the social science fold.

Like other emerging specialist associations, the AHA sought a role definition that would enhance opportunity for academic careers, and augment role resources through creation of an autonomous national network able to develop, coordinate and rationalize the tools of industrialized historical research in precariously funded universities. Its constitution provided the initial point for their role definition. Six short paragraphs simply name the organization and define membership classes, official dues, modes of election and constitutional amendment and finally the aim of the association: "the promotion of historical studies."[17] Unlike the ASSA, the AHA charter contains no claim to mobilize data in the service of reform. It intends no ameliorative interventions and harbors no explicit theory of social justice. Moreover, the narrow definition of role did not accentuate differences between American historians practicing without benefit of a degree and those trained in the German Historical School. Together they were to create a newly national past and celebrate a future manifest destiny, unconstrained by the details of immediate reform.

Historians were extremely successful in securing resources. Their organization, with its narrowly defined constitutional emphasis on specialization, was quickly granted a federal charter. Congress paid association publication costs amounting to $8,000 a year, at the time an enormous subsidy for a learned society. The AHA also secured government assistance for compiling and printing the papers of national heroes and won the willing cooperation of state and local historical societies.[18] The AHA, then, demonstrated that a narrowly specialized expert role could facilitate the national mobilization of resources. When economists could not agree on the part reform would play in the social scientists' role, the historians' definition was at hand.

Economists Organize to Define National Social Science Expertise

Philologists and historians were not the only fourth-faculty specialists forming national resource networks. Efforts were being made by political economists who found the ASSA's regional role unsatisfactory in view of their increasingly national perceptions of economic problems. The specialists returning from Germany were particularly active. However, the centrality of economics to social issues surrounding industrialization caused heated conflict over role, and made initial organization difficult. The Political Economy Club was proposed in 1882, and drafts of constitutions for a national economic association were circulated by German trained Ph.D.s in 1884. The next year, the American Economic Association (AEA) was successfully organized. These three organizational efforts offered competing definitions of the expert role, each describing different reformist roles. But broad, substantive definition of the content of the expert's role seemed only to engender controversy and impede resource support. By the late 1880s the AEA retreated to the formula established by the AHA.

The Political Economy Club was to be an association of leading academics and men of affairs. In Gilded Age style, these men agreed to meet periodically over dinner to share their expert appreciation of the pressing issues of the day. Although the Political Economy Club was active from 1883 to 1897, it failed to offer a viable alternative to the ASSA's role definition. While successful in bringing together university men and persons of considerable resources, it did not emphasize specialization and chose to present itself in less than national terms, thus disqualifying the club from decisively molding the new social science. Although it broadened its membership base somewhat beyond the ASSA's New England, it was socially selective and recruited almost exclusively from the East Coast, neglecting leaders from the Western and Southern hinterland where much of the nation's economic, educational and ideological ferment was occurring.

Something of its East Coast collective sensibility is captured in the details of its formation. J.L. Laughlin, the Harvard economist, became its secretary-treasurer and guiding light. Its first president was Simon Newcomb, a specialist in mathematics and physics, who gave expert service at the U.S. Navy's nautical division in Washington and Baltimore's Johns Hopkins University. Its first choice for major speaker was Yale's William Graham Sumner, who offered the club his words at Delmonico's, the exclusive New York eatery.

Like the ASSA, the club welcomed German-trained economists, but its implicit commitment to an East Coast version of New England "sound opinion" limited its attractiveness as a forum for the full and frank exchange of economic opinion. The club's leaders, men like Newcomb and Laughlin, were quickly drawn into open conflict with reforming new social scientists on the labor question, the proper intervention of the state, and the money problem. Finally, the fact that many of the club's members commanded significant resources inhibited the unfettered exploration of economic ideas that challenged sound opinion. Thus, the club broadened regional horizons beyond the ASSA and narrowed its focus to political economic issues. But it was still guided by a sound opinion that saw economic reform as the financial problems of an East Coast segment of the upper ranks. In short, it failed to qualify as a national resource network for career economists.[19]

Successful efforts to create an economists' association began when E.J. James and Simon Patten in 1884 circulated their constitution for a "Society for the Study of National Economy." James had just secured a position at the University of Pennsylvania's School of Finance and Commerce endowed by protectionist Joseph Wharton. Patten had not yet found a university job. Although inexperienced in American intellectual circles, they had a clear conception of the uses of economic expertise, modeling their society on a German economic association, Der Verein für Social-politik. This association brought together business, government and academic spokesman favoring ameliorative reform by the state. Indeed, many of the German professors who had instructed Patten, James and other new social scientists had been members of the association and urged their American students to found a similar organization.[20]

The society's constitution encouraged specialist economic investigation, association publication and popular discussion of the "special problems" of American industrialization. This sequence of expert investigation, association publication and citizen discussion had a decidedly reformist end in view: to combat laissez-faire ideology and shape state policies toward "the best utilization of our resources" while securing for "each individual the highest development of all his faculties."[21]

The James-Patten constitution argued at length for an active and ameliorative state, locating sovereignty in "the people" and linking true economy in government to good administrative design. Further, it identified problems and proposed solutions to issues presented by industrialization. First, educational reform supported by federal funds and guidelines was required, since selfish and incapable local officials had failed to maintain the nation's "standard of intelligence" and "industrial efficiency." Second, the industrial capital-labor question was to be answered by asserting the general community interest against the shorter run interests of both owners and workers. The state would identify and express this general interest in laws dealing with both working and residential conditions, with hours and wages legislation as well as sanitation laws. Finally, it would prevent the inefficient accumulation and deployment of capital, and encourage balanced regional development. Accordingly, the closing sections proposed state action against "transport companies" (railroads) whose policies distorted economic development; land reform preventing exploitative tenancy by absentee landlords, and national planning for the "symmetrical development" of all sections.[22]

Except for its nationally oriented, university-based specialist emphasis, the James-Patten constitution proposed an association that defined an expert role quite close to that of the ASSA. Technical rationalization is guided by a clearly articulated normative position. Political economy is a policy science. The academic expert is active in popular education, state administration and continuous agitation. Indeed, at the same time that the society's constitution was circulating among university-trained economists, James was helping the ASSA write its model college course instructing students in precisely such uses of social science expertise.[23]

While the conduct of the expert role was similar to the ASSA, the content was quite different, embodying elements of its German model and containing, incongruously, a strong, populist Midwestern flavor. Like the _Verein_ it assumed an already active state. However, James and Patten viewed the American state as pursuing policies that benefited individual rather than collective ends. They saw the laissez-faire rhetoric of the minimal state as masking exploitative accumulation and cloaking unbalanced development. The economic specialist would correct this in service to an activist state democratically responsible to the people. The role set out by James and Patten was national in scope. It called for trained experts to conduct economic studies that detailed the problems of the day, suggested remedies, and identified academics as economic activists. This broad and explicit role definition made the James-Patten constitution an unacceptable document: it could accommodate neither the regional interests of established experts in the ASSA or the Political Economy Club, nor the special interests of the men who supplied university resources.

The response to the Patten-James role model was swift. Hopkins Professor Richard Ely, himself a German-trained reform advocate from the Midwest, authored a narrower definition of social science expertise. He identified a single problem--the conflict between capital and labor--as the primary question facing economists, but offered no detailed line of inquiry, nor suggested any clear line of action. However, he too saw economics as a policy science, assumed an activist state, and saw utilization of specialized experts as necessary to guide intervention. And avoiding a broad condemnation of laissez-faire ideology, he identified the speculative, pre-industrial methodology of established economists as a substantial part of the problems attending American industrialization.

Ely's definition of expertise thus advanced the claims of young German-trained specialists and their sympathizers whose work, like his own, had been badly reviewed by economic conservatives such as Political Economy Club President Simon Newcomb. He spoke too for self-taught experts such as Francis A. Walker who felt that laissez-faire ideologues--Sumner in particular -- had made his academic advance at Yale impossible. By pointing out the fit between students of the German Historical School's science and the problems of the day, Ely advanced the interests of new specialists and he avoided the James-Patten emphasis on broad popular political economic reform, with its clear and present danger of offending resource holders, and established experts defending regional interests.[24]

Economists with national interest were more easily able to come together over Ely's draft than the James-Patten proposal. Accordingly,

Ely's draft constitution became the basis for the AEA organizational meeting held in September 1885. Like the founding of the AHA, this meeting was held in the shadow of the ASSA's annual meeting. Such shared location enabled the AEA, again like the AHA, to claim symbolic legitimacy from the ASSA as well as recruit members and announce its own birth. The ASSA made no attempt to bring the AEA into its fold. Perhaps seeing the emergence of fourth-faculty specialist associations as inevitable, its general secretary welcomed AEA members and wished economists well in their separate association.[25]

Although Ely's constitution narrowed the specialist role, some economists at the founding meeting urged its modification. Henry Carter Adams feared the AEA might be tarred with Germanic statism and was loath to criticize laissez-faire analysis too harshly. E.R.A. Seligman also worried about the AEA's being misconceived. While agreeing with Ely's rejection of ungrounded laissez-faire speculation, he also shared Adams's fear that the AEA would be seen as over-committed to statism. In his words, "modern economics has, however, not yet attained that certainty in results that would authorize us to invoke increased governmental action as a check to the various abuses of free competition." And, like Adams once again, he felt a greater appreciation should be given the received work of older economists. The unorthodox E.B. Andrews too urged modification on similar grounds.[26]

To meet these and other objections, a committee of five--including James, Adams and Andrews--revised Ely's draft. The result was a constitution less aggressively statist and less sharply critical of established economists' work. When objections were still voiced, a footnote was attached proclaiming that even the revised version was not binding on members. The revision of Ely's draft became the AEA's founding constitution.

Article IV's Statement of Principles most clearly articulates the AEA's definition of the expert role.

1. We regard the state as an agency whose positive assistance is one of the indispensable conditions of human progress.

2. We believe that political economy as a science is still in the early stage of its development. While we appreciate the work of

former economists, we look not so much to speculation as to the historical and statistical study of actual conditions of economic life for the satisfactory accomplishment of that development.

3. We hold that the conflict of labor and capital has brought into prominence a vast number of social problems, whose solution requires the united efforts, each in its own sphere, of the church, of the state, and of science.

4. In the study of industrial and commercial policy of governments we take no partisan attitude. We believe in a progressive development of economic conditions, which must be met by a corresponding development of legislative policy.[27]

While the experts' technical rationalization of the economy was guided by a vaguely progressive ideology, the final draft was quite conservative compared to the James-Patten constitution. The activist state is linked to human progress, not popular democratic reform. Substantive criticism and the imperfect economic system justified by laissez-faire ideology becomes an attack on the methodological flaws in previous economic analysis. The monopolistic claims of specialized academic experts are strengthened by paralleling the narrowed authority of their university-based science with that of the church and the state. Finally, the social scientist is a nonpartisan educator without substantive theory and an activist without a constituency.

But even this narrowed version could spark controversy, create factions in the economic community, and impede resource support. In the interests of presenting a united professional front to the community-at-large several of the associations's early leaders worked to jettison the Statement of Principles. As Walker wrote to Seligman, "it is highly desirable to bring into the AEA all classes of American economists or at least to give none a valid excuse for remaining outside."[28] For a specializing field intent on claiming a legitimate monopoly of knowledge, consensus among credible practitioners had to be attained. The appearance of unity was a symbolic resource as important as direct subsidy in initial attempts to create a national network of economic specialists.

The formula resorted to was the narrow specialist definition established by the AHA. In 1887 the AEA's always controversial Statement of Principles was dropped from its constitution. In an echo of the AHA, the purposes presented by the AEA constitution became simply:

1. The encouragement of economic research.

2. The publication of economic monographs.

3. The encouragement of perfect freedom in all economic discussion.

4. The establishment of a Bureau of Information designed to aid members in their economic studies.[29]

All reference to specialists' role in shaping reformist national economic policy was dropped. Future social scientists would use this narrow role definition as a proven formula.

As Seligman later explained to Ely, abandoning the statement was not a final or real rejection of the intent it expressed--"I do not think, nor did anyone suppose that the change could be interpreted as . . . a change in the sentiment which dominates the association." Instead, dropping the statement was a strategy for resolving impossible differences over the kind of reform in which the expert economist would engage. As he put it, "the idea was simply that the association should meet chiefly in the lines of method--and that the emphasis of the historical and statistical method would be sufficient."[30] But refusal to grapple with the problems posed by the uses of expertise made reform in aid of the existing center inevitable.

In 1892 to mark clearly the end of any rift between German-trained Ph.D.s and American economists schooled in regional roles, the AEA unanimously chose Charles Dunbar as its second president. A former journalist, he headed the Harvard economics department and occupied a chair gifted by Boston businessmen concerned with subsidizing "sound opinion." His election celebrated new-found unity and minted symbolic wealth for the association. Thus, a more nearly national and highly specialized role slowly evolved from the interaction between university-trained specialists and regional social scientists. However, a routine supply of resources for this role had yet to be firmly established.

Dependence and Labor Market Dynamics

Whether through the "fourth faculty" or rigorous professional schooling, university modernizers used specialization as a strategy for procuring resources. Creating a knowledge monopoly meant cornering the market in a particular occupational line. And when such specialization was useful in solving social problems, the managers were better positioned in their unending quest for capital and operating funds. Yet intellectual workers participating in such monopolies became occupationally dependent on the university. Commitment to a specialized field reduced their opportunities outside academia. Thus, as the modernizing managers were sensitive to robber barons and railroad presidents, so aspiring professors became attuned to the resource opportunities controlled by university administrations.

These managers directly controlled allocation of scarce positions, thereby shaping the development of academic careers. At the time of the AEA's founding, there probably were more trained economists than specialized academic jobs. Chairs of political economy emerged slowly: Williams (1854), Harvard (1872), Yale (1874), Columbia (1876), Minnesota (1885). Few institutions offered an array of political economics courses, and articulated programs centered in specialized departments and schools were virtually nonexistent in the 1870s and 1880s. The younger political economists who studied in the German Historical School had differentiated themselves from a host of other cultural workers in hopes of increasing their marketability. But they anticipated academic demand. Specialized training was not even a prerequisite for an academic post. For instance, Minnesota's Folwell had taken advanced training in Germany, but it amounted to a few courses in comparative philology. His actual qualification for the chair of political economy was his past service as University of Minnesota president, not a doctorate.

University managers operating in this labor-surplus situation had ample opportunity to hire and advance political economists holding correct views and practicing an acceptable expertise. Given the vagaries of statistics for the late nineteenth century, it is difficult to show the impact of these labor-market dynamics upon the fourth faculty generally and on political economists in particular. However, if we look at the career pattern revealed by the biographies of the 34 AEA leaders active between its founding (1885) and the emergence of its two supplementary organizations, the American Political Science Association (APSA) and the American Sociological Society (ASS), 1904, we can begin to assess the structural potential for intellectual dependence when managers control a critical resource--jobs.[31]

We should first note that these early AEA leaders were without the solid regional resources that underwrote the ASSA's expertise in action. Lacking the concentrated status, wealth and power of a regional elite, they were much more vulnerable to the role expectations held by educational managers. Thus, while the AEAers usually came from families of respectable middling and better social location (Appendix, Table 8), their families tended to have settled somewhat later (Appendix, Table 2) and more nationally (Appendix, Table 3) than did the ASSAers. Furthermore, the AEAers were schooled much more widely and longer. After attending a wide regional range of colleges (Appendix, Table 5), most went to graduate school, often overseas, and two-thirds earned doctorates (Appendix, Tables 6 and 7). And they used their specialized learning to secure jobs. Thirty-one (91.2 percent) of the early leaders held appointments at some time or another in a university or college. Twenty-eight (82.4 percent) were academic careerists, spending at least half their work lives in higher education (Appendix, Table 9), holding posts across the industrializing nation (Appendix, Table 4). Indeed, 6 of the 28 careerists learned managerial lessons well enough to become university presidents themselves.

How the labor market instructed these leaders in the scarcity of specialized positions and the prerogatives of educational managers is seen in the length of time it took the 28 to find academic posts. In the 1870s 11 leaders looked for specialized jobs, professorial appointments devoted mainly to modern political economic topics. Five held doctorates. One found specialized work immediately, teaching in a university. A second and third waited a year, doing language instruction and assisting professors. The fourth taught high school and did hack-writing for six years. The fifth helped work the family farm for ten years before an academic opportunity opened.

The three without degrees but with some specialized German training faired about as poorly. One found proper work at once, but he had been promised that job before his two years overseas. A second, son of a distinguished Ivy League professor, was a foreign language tutor for four years, after which he secured a post in political economics at his father's university. The third was a professor-of-all-trades at a smaller school who suffered and recovered from a mental breakdown while waiting six years for work suiting his specialized skills. And as if to underline management prerogative in times of labor over-supply, three leaders were appointed to chairs on the basis of their general experience in the cultural sector, without ever having stepped through the seminar door.

In the 1880s, eight careerists found proper work. Of the six Ph.D.s, only one secured a job immediately. The next two needed a year. The last three took three, four and five years respectively. In contrast, two leaders without advanced preparation were called to specialized chairs. In the 1890s, all nine leaders who found specialized jobs had advanced training. The sole non-Ph.D. found his position immediately, as did seven of the eight doctorates. The last Ph.D. taught philosophy for a year until his promised political economics post opened.

Of the 28 careerists, 13, most of whom held doctorates, were forced to delay practice of their chosen specialization, sometimes for a significant period of time. For several, delay caused such anxiety that standard biographical dictionaries record nervous illnesses and breakdowns. Since trained economists unable to find posts participated in the early AEA, even those who quickly located suitable positions were aware of labor surplus in their field and the fragility of an academic career during the transition to industrial knowledge production. This lack of opportunity underlined and legitimated educational managers' definitions of the expert role, for they controlled its availability. Thus, the specialized intellectual experienced his structural dependence on the resources of the industrializing university.

Discipline and the Academic Freedom Cases

Encounters with labor-market vulnerability may have accentuated political economists' awareness of their occupational dependence, but it did not offer explicit instruction on the limits of expertise. However, the academic freedom cases of the 1880s and 1890s offered on-the-job training in dependence to those involved and object lessons to the field as a whole. These cases began to define the boundaries that resource holders saw as appropriate for university-based social knowledge.

Since political economists were encouraged by their university managers and were themselves eager to show their social usefulness, they frequently offered expert opinion outside academia. Given the substance of their knowledge, they could not avoid taking positions on the issues of industrialization. But as they intellectually positioned themselves in public forums, their right to give expert advice was often challenged by donors and trustees who disagreed with their conclusions. Too often university managers refused to rescue political economists thus tossed on the rough seas of public controversy. Instead, they used these instances to discipline economic experts whose substantive arguments and public actions complicated efforts at resource procurement.

Of the many well-known academic freedom cases occurring between 1885 and 1904, three involved early AEA leaders. Henry Carter Adams, Richard T. Ely and Edward Alsworthy Ross each tried to practice the active, if restricted, expert role offered in the AEA founding constitution. But each unwittingly crossed an as yet undefined boundary between seemly and unacceptable agitation. In essence, each directly and critically addressed the public on capital's domination over labor. Each was sharply disciplined by his university managers for utterances ignoring the vested interests of sponsors and trustees.

Adams was AEA first vice-president from 1886 to 1891 and president in 1896 and 1897. In 1886 he held a split appointment, teaching one semester at Cornell and the next at Michigan. Enamored of the Knights of Labor and disenchanted with capital, Adams' outspoken concern with social justice had already caused President Angell to request him to make a formal statement clarifying his position on private property, inheritance and socialism. After Chicago's Haymarket incident, Adams wrote an article defending anarchists' First Amendment freedoms and in a widely reported lecture argued that workers should demand a share of capital's proprietary rights. Capitalist Henry Sage led fellow Cornell trustees' attack on Adams and pressured President Charles Kendall Adams to fire him.

When the economist's contract was not renewed by Cornell's Adams, his dependence on Michigan's Angell doubled. He made no public protest but worked to preserve his Michigan position, disavowing all he had written in support of the Knights. President Angell thereupon secured for Adams a permanent Michigan position. Adams then advised his economics colleagues to avoid public utterance on controversial topics and "confine their attempts to influence policy to behind-the-scenes work as technical experts advising legislators or operating government regulatory commissions."[32]

In another widely observed case, AEA architect Richard T. Ely was tried for economic heresy by a special commission of the University of Wisconsin Board of Regents. Ely was AEA secretary from 1886 to 1891, first vice-president in 1893, second vice-president in 1894, and president in 1900 and 1901. In the year of the Pullman strike (1894) a maverick regent, Oliver E. Wells, charged Ely with corrupting the university's youthful students by supporting union leaders during a local printing strike, removing a printing contract from a non-union shop, and generally speaking and writing in support of socialism and social violence. Ely was eventually acquitted. Faculty solidarity and managerial support worked for him as did personality and political clashes within the board of regents. However, equally important was his own testimony disavowing any strong commitment to workers' movements and stressing his past services strengthening the technical and ideological foundations of the industrializing economy. In effect, he gave public evidence that he had learned the limits of the new social science expertise.[33]

E.A. Ross followed Ely as AEA secretary in 1893. He found rapid academic advancement through prolific scholarly publication coupled with solid teaching. First hired by Indiana's President David Starr Jordan from Ely's Hopkins seminar, he then followed Jordan to Stanford University. Several years of speaking and writing in favor of inflationary bimetalism and organized labor aroused Mrs. Stanford's ire toward Ross, and she insisted that Jordan fire him. Doing what he could to slow and soften the blow, Jordan followed Mrs. Stanford's command. In 1897 Jordan began negotiating Ross's resignation and in 1900 removed Ross from Stanford's classrooms.

Ross was well prepared for his firing. He released letters in which Jordan admitted that Mrs. Stanford's dislike forced his dismissal. He managed a press campaign against the university and accepted the faculty's solid support, complete with principled resignations from senior as well as junior staff. Ross insisted that he had not spoken on issues outside his specific scientific competence and that his statements were not mere popularizations. Ross carefully defended his role as a professional scientific expert, one with certified access to a legitimate monopoly of knowledge, while denying popular agitation. He then moved to a pre-arranged job at the University of Nebraska.[34]

The AEA, for its part, used the Ross case to attempt to resist arbitrary discipline by university trustees. Ross's detailed preparation of his own defence on professional grounds made it a likely case for collective action. The AEA appointed three leaders as an investigating committee. In a month it had reported for Ross, over the signatures of 15 prominent social scientists, of whom 8 were AEA leaders. Hundreds of copies of the report were sent to college presidents and economics professionals everywhere.

The AEA tried to convince the academic community to draw limits that would protect experts. The message was clear: college-based specialists productively occupying the ideological center have a shared interest with university managers in resisting resource suppliers' attacks on the expert role. However, managers committed to the hierarchy of industrial knowlege production were unwilling to offend trustees and donors by making common cause with faculty. The AEA's efforts did not result in Ross's reappointment at Stanford, nor did the AEA make its investigatory body achieve standing committee status. The concept of academic freedom had not yet found organizational form in the scholarly community.

These three academic freedom cases illuminate the dynamics of fourth faculty discipline during the AEA's first two decades. While not representatively sampled, the cases do show that managers and trustees acted to limit the emerging social science expert role. And they do suggest an estimate of the extent to which other political economists were similarly treated. Since 3 of the 34 early AEA leaders were disciplined directly, perhaps some 9 percent of all political economists were likewise instructed by their managers. At any rate, these cases capture only the most extreme and negative forms of what Ross might call the techniques of academic social control. Managers' manipulation of working conditions, promotions and pay increments provided further opportunity for role enforcement. Consider, for example, Columbia University's handling of Daniel DeLeon and E.R.A. Seligman, two young political economists waiting for their first promotions.

In 1886 both DeLeon and Seligman were appointed to post-doctoral prize lectureships. Both lecturers were publicly active in the debates surrounding Henry George's single-tax scheme. DeLeon supported George's 1889 campaign for the New York mayoralty, chairing and speaking at meetings on and off the campus. Seligman opposed the single tax, publicly debating George at the 1890 ASSA meeting. Despite warnings from Columbia managers, DeLeon continued working for George. President Barnard offered his trustees a resolution immediately dismissing DeLeon for being "an active champion of a movement which is regarded by this body as menacing the destruction of the existing order." But Columbia's trustees refused to martyr him. Instead, they advanced Seligman to a professorship while offering DeLeon a third three-year term as lecturer. DeLeon understood the career mobility implied and refused. He left academia and became a central figure in the American Socialist Labor party, editing their weekly, providing for decades a continuous critique of the industrializing economy and university. Seligman remained to help shape the university-based expert role and became an indefatigable rationalizer and defender of American capitalism.[35]

Industrialization of social knowledge modified the expert role delineated by the ASSA. The growth of the graduate university made the expert role more routinely available to specialists through the development of predictable academic careers. The new experts transformed the ASSA's regional, generalist and self-selected role to one that was national, specialized and emphasizing certification as a condition for entry.

However, political economists became institutionally dependent intellectuals, and this made it more difficult for them to act freely as experts. Specialization increased their marketability but only in the industrializing sector of knowledge production. Once in the modernizing university, their knowledge was channeled by organizational hierarchy. Mediation on the part of donors, trustees and managers fashioned an ideological center aligned with the emerging economic center. Thus, economists were compelled to shape an expert role that fit within parameters set by the university's resource needs. Even new experts with strong consensus on their narrow role found that occupational organization in specialist associations did not counter-balance such institutional mediation. By the turn of the century, political economists were still unable to resist arbitrary discipline of performance in a role already strongly shaped by resource suppliers' expectations.

While academic industrialization fostered specialists' careers, it inhibited political economists incorporating into their field those ideas contrary to or even critical of the university's resource base. For example, the James-Patten notion of an expertise that served the popular will was untenable as was the ability to engage freely and independently in a dialogue between expert and public as did Adams, Ely, DeLeon and Ross. Although the early economists' strong criticism of capitalism was excluded from the expert role, reform remained a key component of their work. But reform unguided by full discussion of the ends of amelioration became expert service to the emerging corporate center. Only as advocates of the existing system would social scientists be able to persuade resource holders of their objectivity.

NOTES

1. D.C. Gilman, "The Purposes of the ASSA and the Means That May Be Employed to Promote These Ends," JSS 12 (December 1880): xxii-xxiv.

2. See Burton J. Bledstein, The Culture of Professionalism (New York: W.W. Norton, 1977) for brief biographies and a general statement of the world-view of the modernizing university presidents, although Laurence R. Veysey, The Emergence of the American University (Chicago: University of Chicago Press, 1965) remains the best overview.

3. For example, upon assuming Harvard's presidency in 1869, Eliot turned first to reforming the professional schools. See Hugh Hawkins, Between Harvard and America: The Educational Leadership of Charles W. Eliot (New York: Oxford University Press, 1972), pp. 58-61.

4. Daniel Coit Gilman, The Launching of a University, with a New Forward by Francesco Cordasco (New York: Garrett Press, 1969), p. 7, argues that "the complete university" includes four faculties: law, medicine, theology and philosophy.

5. For example, Harvard's Charles Eliot was a major figure in college reform as well as secondary school reorganization. See Hawkins, Between Harvard and America, pp. 224-262.

6. On the rise of the system of cities, see Howard P. Chudacoff, The Evolution of American Urban Society (Englewood Cliffs, N.J.: Prentice-Hall, 1975), and on the centralization of decision making see Lewis Corey, The House of Morgan (New York: AMS, 1975).

7. Hawkins, Between Harvard and America, pp. 19-29, quote at p. 27.

8. Robert L. Church, "The Economists Study Society: Sociology at Harvard, 1891-1902," in Social Sciences at Harvard, 1860-1920, ed. Paul Buck (Cambridge, Mass.: Harvard University Press, 1965), pp.

32-33.

9. Dictionary of American Biography (DAB), s.v.   "White, A.D.," by George Lincoln Burr, quote at p. 90.

10. Abraham Flexner, Daniel Coit Gilman: Creator of the American Type of University (New York: Harcourt, Brace and Co., 1946), pp. 3-15, quote at pp. 13-14.

11. Hugh Hawkins, Pioneer: A History of the Johns Hopkins University, 1874-1889 (Ithaca, N.Y.: Cornell University Press, 1960), pp. 3-5 and 316-332.

12. DAB, s.v. "Jarvis, Edward," by William B. Leonard.

13. Carl Diehl, Americans and German Scholarship, 1770-1870 (New Haven, Conn.: Yale University Press, 1978).

14. On Marshall, see Hawkins, Pioneer, pp.   109 and 160-161, with Hawkins's judgment on romance-language scholarship at p. 161. See also T.L. Haskell on Marshall, The Emergence of Professional Social Science (Urbana, Ill.: University of Illinois press, 1977), p. 171. Haskell at pp. 171-177 reports Gilman's role in the American Orientalist Society while Flexner, Daniel Coit Gilman, p. 8, tells of his helping the librarians' needs.

15. Haskell, The Emergence of Professional Social Science, pp. 168-177.

16. Ibid.

17. "Constitution of the American Historical Association," Papers of the American Historical Association (1885): 20-21; and James Harvey Robinson, The New History with a New Introduction by Harvey Wise (New York: Free Press, 1965).

18. J.F. Jameson, "The American Historical Association, 1884-1909," American Historical Review 15 (October 1909): 1-15.

19. Alfred W. Coats, "The Political Economy Club: A Neglected Episode in American Economic Thought," American Economic Review 51 (September 1961): 624-637; Haskell, The Emergence of Professional Social Science, pp. 179-180; Joseph Dorfman, The Economic Mind in American Civilization, Vol. 3, 1856-1918 (New York: Viking, 1949), p. 272.

20. Haskell, The Emergence of Professional Social Science, pp. 180-181; Benjamin G. Rader, The Academic Mind and Reform: The Influence of Richard T. Ely in American Life (Lexington, Ky.: University of Kentucky Press, 1966), pp. 34-35; Daniel M. Fox, The Discovery of Abundance: Simon N. Patten and the Transformation of Social Theory (Ithaca, N.Y.: Cornell University Press, 1967), pp. 37, 108; Richard A. Swanson, "Edmund J. James: A 'Conservative Progressive' in American Higher Education" (Ph.D. dissertation, University of Illinois, 1966).

21. "The Constitution of the Society for the Study of National Economy," Appendix III, in Richard T. Ely, Ground Under Our Feet: An Autobiography (New York: Macmillan, 1938), pp. 296-299.

22. Ibid.

23. Haskell, The Emergence of Professional Social Science, p. 196; JSS 21 (September 1886): 13-20.

24. Ely, Ground Under Our Feet, pp. 132-137; Rader, The Academic Mind, pp. 35-38; Haskell, The Emergence of Professional Social Science, pp. 181-186.

25. F.B. Sanborn, "The Social Sciences: Their Growth and Future," JSS 21 (September 1886): 1-12.

26. "Report of the Organization of the American Economics Association,"
     Publications of the AEA 1 (1887): 5-46, quote at p. 40.

27. Ibid.; Constitution of the AEA (New York: Philip Cowan, 1885), pp.
     4-5.

28. F.A. Walker to E.R.A. Seligman, September 24,   1887, in Joseph
     Dorfman, ed., "Seligman Correspondence, 1," Political Science
     Quarterly (PSQ) 56 (March 1941): 108-109.

29. "Report of the Organization of the American Economics Association,"
     p. 40.

30. E.R.A. Seligman to Richard T. Ely, January 29, 1899, Ely Papers,
     State Historical Society of Wisconsin, Madison.

31. Biographical data are drawn from standard biographical sources; see
     Chapter 7 for a fuller analysis. The APSA was organized in 1903,
     the ASS in 1905; we have designated 1904 as the year best able to
     represent the organization of both.

32. The fullest discussion of the Adams case is in Mary O.   Furner,
     Advocacy and Objectivity (Lexington, Ky.; The University Press of
     Kentucky, 1977). On Adams's later career, see David M.   Grossman,
     "Professors and Public Service, 1885-1925: A Chapter in the
     Professionalization of the Social Sciences," (Ph.D.   Thesis,
     Washington University, 1975), pp. 37, 69; and DAB, s.v. "Adams,
     Henry Carter."

33. Rader, The Academic Mind, pp.   150-151; Furner, Advocacy and
     Objectivity, pp.   164, 187, and "Report of the Committee of
     Education," American Teacher 12 (November 1927): 12.

34. Edward Alsworthy Ross, Seventy Years of It: An Autobiography (New
     York: Appleton Century, 1936), pp. 64-68; Julius Weinburg, Edward
     Alsworthy Ross and the Sociology of Progressivism (Madison, Wisc.:
     State Historical Society, 1972), pp. 43-55; Furner, Advocacy and

Objectivity, pp.   252-286.

35. On DeLeon, see L.   Glen Seretan, _Daniel DeLeon_ (Cambridge,   Mass.:
     Harvard University Press, 1979); on Seligman, see his _DAB_ entry and
     Scott   Nearing,   _The   Making   of   a   Radical_   (New   York: Harper
     Torchbooks, 1973), p.   117.

5
"Not With Students But With Statesmen . . . in the Leadership of an Organized Body Politic"

The academic freedom cases of the 1880s and 1890s helped define and clarify the role expectations developing among university managers, social scientists and resource suppliers. During these decades, the AEA provided an invaluable forum for the full and frank discussion of the university-based political economists' continuing ambitions to create a policy science shaping the nation's future. At the AEA's annual meetings, role expectations, resource exchange strategies, and the imperatives of policy advice became the stuff of presidential addresses and heated debate.

Shaping the Expert Role

In disciplining Adams, Ross, Ely and others, university trustees and managers indicated what sorts of behaviors were intolerable to resource holders interested in building universities. At the same time, since the industrialized university did not generate profits, its trustees and managers expected gains to be made from an increasingly refined division of academic labor if they were to make legitimate funding claims on private fortunes and the public purse. Indeed, they wanted social scientists to act as entrepreneurs for both the modern university and their specialization by demonstrating the social utility of their expertise. Thus, social scientists, while discouraged from critical exploration that challenged industrial capitalism, were encouraged to develop knowledge that would reform that system.

Academic social scientists accepted the limits set on expertise by managers and resource holders. As institutionally dependent intellectuals, they had little choice. Yet they furthered their own interests, working within these parameters to create an expert's role that would expand their influence in public affairs, enhance the prestige of their careers, and secure resources for their profession. Dropping the AEA's constitutional Statement of Principles meant calming methodological conflicts and achieving a minimal consensus on role within the circle of certified academic specialists. It did not mean abandoning ambitions to act as national policy advisors. But both the academic freedom cases and association's constitutional controversy instructed the specialists in the need for a sound strategy to reach policy consulting positions. Over two decades, a wider AEA consensus emerged urging the expert policy advisor to avoid ideological extremes, to build a constituency outside the university, and to locate an area of service where he could act without fear of reprisals.

By avoiding ideological extremes, AEA leaders began to construct a new normative center for America's industrial era. They carefully defined a middle way between laissez-faire anarchism on their right and state socialism to their left. Instead they offered conservative reform that recognized emerging corporate capital as both the vital center of the political economy and the harbinger of evolutionary progress in a "complex, modern industrial state."[1] They attempted to build two constituencies for this new ideological center. First, they sought reform opportunities where they could demonstrate their ideological prowess and technical skills to progressive businessmen and politicians who could envision the uses of a centralist social science in solidifying the emerging economic center. Second, they developed the rhetoric of "the public." Here they meant the ill-defined "respectable," "enlightened," "well-educated" middle strata who might be attentive to certified academic experts offering policy advice on the disquieting issues of the day. And they began to identify the fledgling state bureaucracy as an arena where they could serve without entangling themselves in popular controversy.

Relying on this three-pronged strategy, AEA leaders remained committed to creating the role of policy advisor as first articulated in their constitution. They continued to see their public mission as solving the problems raised by "the conflict of labor and capital" through the "positive assistance" of the state.[2] They developed this expert policy advisor role while accepting the role limits set by university managers and resource holders. Pursuing this strategy to gain access to policy advisor positions decisively shaped the substance of academic social thought. Thus, the conflict between labor and capital became split into "the trust question" and the "labor problem," each requiring a separate solution that preserved and rationalized the emerging corporate center that was providing resources for the modernizing university. Since consideration of alternative economic structures was precluded by their role's resource needs, the ideological and technical tasks of academic social science expertise in policy-making settings outside the university became clear. At nub, the expert was to create a convincing rationale and suitable mechanisms for maintaining industrial corporate capital. And this was to be done in "the first new nation," whose constitutionally enfranchised and armed citizenry were increasingly uneasy about industrialization's patent effects: greater economic inequality and increasing political corruption. Exactly what shape this expert role should take was the subject of a 20-year discourse among AEA leaders. Because the answers offered by AEA leaders continued to involve state-administered ameliorative reform, the critical questions for developing their role as experts were: what degree of reform? which branch of government? and how does one gain routine access to policy making posts?

In this chapter and the next we focus on the AEA's understanding of the expert role by examining its presidents' addresses from the association's founding in 1885 until 1904, the point at which political scientists and sociologists formed separate specialist associations. In its early years, the AEA did not always meet annually, nor was the elected president always able to deliver his address. We look then at the words of eight presiding officers who gave thirteen speeches. Francis A. Walker, the first president, spoke in 1889 and 1891. Vice-president William Watts Folwell filled in for the ailing Dunbar in 1893. In 1894 and 1896, John Bates Clark addressed the AEA, in 1897 it was Henry Carter Adams. Franklin Giddings substituted for Adams in 1898. Arthur Twining Hadley gave his presidential addresses in 1899 and 1900; Richard T. Ely in 1901 and 1902; Edwin R.A. Seligman in 1903 and 1904. These eight presiding officers represent 23 percent of the AEA's 34 "early leaders" heading the association between 1885 and 1904.

We also analyze association debates surrounding these presidential addresses. Thus, we get some sense of the degree to which presidents' positions on role were accepted by other leaders as well as followers. To gauge the difference between the rhetoric surrounding role and actual practice, we look briefly at presidential careers to see how these chief officers executed the expert role. And we present contemporary critiques of the role. In the first of these two chapters, we focus primarily on presidential attempts to define role content, constituency, and strategies for gaining access to expert positions in policy settings outside the university. In the second, we concentrate more heavily on association efforts to put the role into action, noting the resources used to field AEA expertise and contrasting this with the rhetoric used by presidents to legitimate the role.

Presidential Ambitions and Policy Role Expectations

The presidents of the AEA saw themselves as spokesmen for the newly specializing field of economics and used their annual addresses for "gathering up and giving expression to . . . common sentiment of the Association."[3] When speaking about the problems and possibilities of economic theory, they also addressed the place of the economist in public affairs. And they held no mean amibition for their new science. At the least, they saw university-based economists as having a strong voice in shaping public policy. At most, they saw themselves and their students as future philosopher kings of a modern industrial state, determining the nation's destiny with their knowledge.

They thought that the AEA was organized at a time exceedingly favorable to the development of such a role, for the chaotic economy demanded a national economic policy. In 1891, Walker, the first AEA president, stressed that the "revolution" in "industrial relations" transforming the last quarter of the nineteenth century meant "no class of questions now take precedence, in the public thought, of economic questions."[4] There were false prophets--socialists, nationalists, anarchists, single taxers--and unschooled competitors--articulate citizens, journalists, politicians. But their sudden rise to prominence and eager audiences only pointed to the opportunity for professional economists if they were able to create an economics adequate for what

Seligman styled "a new industrial order."[5]

As the steady increase of specialized positions after 1893 began to provide a secure academic base for a growing number of AEA leaders and members, they turned outward, seeking extramural outlets for their social science. By seeing national economic policy through W.W. Folwell's eyes, as "issues which science ought to decide for all," they advanced their professional claims to monopolistic possession of legitimate social knowledge.[6] In turn, their increasingly successful work outside the university—whether giving expert advice to legislative bodies on tax and money questions, developing the technical capacity of regulatory agencies like the Interstate Commerce Commission or working for the Bureau of Labor—made viable their claims to a monopoly of social knowledge.[7]

Such public service was seen as more than a building block for the profession. Social scientists' subject matter was society; it compelled them to try their hand at influencing public policy formation. As President Hadley put it in 1899:

> If we fail in our influence upon public life we fail in what is the most important application of our studies, and in what may almost be said to constitute their fundamental reason for existence. . . . I do not say that the opportunity to become advisors and leaders of national policy should be sought by economists as their sole duty, or to the neglect of their other public responsibilities. . . . But I believe that their largest opportunity in the immediate future lies not in theories but in practice, not with students but with statesmen, not in the education of individual citizens, however widespread and salutary, but in the leadership of an organized body politic.[8]

In their capacity as experts, social scientists would be able to link modernizing industrial and knowledge production systems. If they were able to become leaders of the "organized body politic," it would be due to the social utility of their field. If this could be demonstrated, then knowledge would rightfully shape industrial production and its attendant social organization.

Like Hadley, President Seligman saw policy making as the birthright of social knowledge. In 1903 he looked to the future of a new century and prophesied an economics that would put "put us in a position to control . . . and mold" the material forces of social progress. As the economist developed greater predictive capacity, he would be acknowledged as "the real philosopher of social life" and have public "deference paid to his views."[9]

Although Hadley and Seligman spoke of transforming experts into reigning philospher kings, power and influence were not sought as ends in themselves but as the prerogatives of men equipped by professional training and discipline to make wiser public policy decisions than others. Ambition for national leadership was seen as an attribute of expertise rather than a drive for self-aggrandizement. Accumulated knowledge demanded use. Although Hadley and Seligman addressed more fully than other presidents the ambition and consequent power social scientists might strive for, they did no more than confirm the Declaration of Principles in the AEA's 1885 constitution, where economists saw themselves as partners with the church and the state in solving the "social problems" of a newly industrial nation.[10]

The professional ambition of AEA leaders was unbounded but not blind. Even if economists fell short of leading the body politic, some form of public policy role was necessary. Each of the AEA's presidents understood what the academic economist did as a specialist outside the university was as critical to the development of the discipline as teaching and research inside the university. Direct and successful service to the emerging industrial state gave credence to their professional claims. If a significant number of economists were able to demonstrate the immediate social utility of their discipline in a public leadership or policy advisor capacity, the expansion of a university base sustaining routine academic careers for growing numbers of economists was more likely. If their claims to exclusive expertise were publicly vindicated, they would attract students, identify career opportunities and bring private patronage and state support for further study and research.[11] The expectations voiced by AEA presidents for economists working in the public sector were sometimes excessive but emphasized all the more strongly the importance of such a role.[12]

The AEA'S Discourse Defines Its Policy Expertise

The AEA's emerging ideological center had room for significant differences. It contained a variety of role expectations ranging around its own ideological mid-point. We find some of this ideological range in addresses by Francis A. Walker, who spoke in 1899 and 1891, and Vice-president William Watts Folwell, filling in for an ailing President Dunbar in 1893. Both Walker and Folwell, as experienced university managers, lent legitimacy to the policy aspirations of their fellow economists. But Walker's words reflected a biography steeped in Eastern establishment experiences, while Folwell's indexed a life shaped by more Midwestern environments. Taken together, their addresses illuminate the right and left sides of the AEA's image of the expert policy advisor in a democratic society undergoing rapid industrialization.

The association's first president, F.A. Walker, bridged the gap between ASSA social scientists and early AEA leaders. Although not an ASSA leader, Walker had been active in its affairs. Like many ASSAers, he lacked specialized academic training. After Civil War service, he learned political economy by aiding his industrialist father in the preparation of a widely acclaimed economics text. He went on to play a notable role in public affairs. He assisted ASSA leader and national director of the revenue, D.A. Wells, in the reorganization of the Federal Bureau of Statistics. He headed the U.S. Census in 1870 and 1880 and occupied a chair of political economy at Yale while representing U.S. presidents at international monetary and statistical conferences. During his term as AEA chief officer, he was president of an expanding Massachusetts Institute of Technology and the American Statistical Association.[13] In securing Walker's services, specialized social scientists selected an uncertified economist who had made his reputation through his public role.

In 1889 Walker's first presidential address celebrated a new unity of political economy. The AEA was the American manifestation of an international "Communion of Economists," responding to the problems of the industrial revolution. "The working class had 'come of age' and called their late guardians to render an account of their stewardship." Accordingly, economists had to turn their attention to the problems raised by an increasingly militant and more fully enfranchised working class.[14] They had to meet wide-spread popular "demand for a thorough treatment of the questions of distribution, in all their bearings upon human welfare." For an example, he turned to public finance. He argued that laissez-faire principles of taxation were no longer socially adequate: taxes could no longer fall finally on consumption. Industrialization had altered the structure of society, and the burden of taxation now fell too heavily on "individuals and classes who are at a disadvantage in the unceasing struggle over the product of industry."[15]

Accordingly, the public role for the new economist was to offer technical assistance to the tax-writing legislator. Together they would determine where the community's fiscal burdens should first and finally fall. In this policy capacity the new economist was a heroic figure who "with all his senses alert, his very soul in strain . . . sounds and tests the public body" to locate those unable to bear the pressure of the system and offer them relief.[16] The required theoretical analysis and empirical research that would inform the legislator would also provide a secondary benefit: the economist would be able to offer theory and data to educators for their classroom instruction. The policy role of the economist, then, was to help revise laissez-faire's outmoded formula of distributive justice with one more appropriate for the newly emerging national economy and one that could also be incorporated into the legal system and taught in the schools.

Having thus positioned the AEA's expertise to the center of laissez-faire, Walker, in his second presidential address, was more intent on identifying the AEA's competitors farther to the left. He was alarmed by the great gains alternative economics had made among the "cultivated classes." Blaming laissez-faire for building "such a record for opposing wholesome measures of reform" that trained economists were "able to do little in stemming the tide of socialism," he urged the AEA to serve as "the economic drill sergeant," recapturing and constructively channeling middle-class reform energies.[17] While Walker was offended by "the public adhesion of large numbers of respectable and responsible citizens" to Bellamy's Nationalism, he thought the excitement _Looking Backward_ had generated would pass. But single taxer Henry George could not be dismissed as an "economic absurdity," since he inspired a political party as well as offered potential AEA resource suppliers a competitive interpretation of American economic life.[18]

Walker attacked George on technical grounds and called his audience's attention to an ASSA debate on the single tax that had taken place the previous summer. The debate was offered as an example of the way economists could assume a public role in shaping middle-class opinion. In an open forum attended by the "cultivated classes," AEA leaders like Seligman, Clark and James engaged in debate with single taxers, most notably Henry George, as well as with advocates of laissez-faire like ASSA official W.T. Harris. The AEA leaders offered a competitive middle-way interpretation of American economic reality and succeeded in "getting a hearing."[19]

Like Walker in his presidential address, AEA leaders participating in this ASSA debate sought to discredit George by attacking him from a superior knowledge base and exposing his technical weaknesses. Seligman, for example, faulted the single tax as theoretically inadequate for an industrial society: machines, not land, produced wealth. He belittled George's tax reform as simplistic and naive, stressing that single taxers were "without thorough training in economics, without a conception of the necessary complication of all modern revenue systems." Instead he advocated an income tax that would adjudicate the issue of distributive justice by burdening everyone's relative ability to pay.[20]

In his response to Seligman, George went beyond the details of public finance to put forward a critique of the policy role sought by the AEA leaders. First, he raised the issue of the expert in a democratic society. He attacked the claim of the specialist to more authoritative knowledge than the average citizen. He argued if the people could not comprehend the economics of their daily lives, "whose laws lie at the bottom of questions we are called upon to settle with our votes, then democratic republican government is doomed to failure, and the quicker we surrender ourselves to the government of the rich and the learned, the better." Second, he accused the professoriate of belonging to or "consciously or unconsciously being influenced by the very class who profit by the wrong" perpetuated by gross inequities in the distribution of wealth.[21]

Seligman had the last word. He denied all charges of class bias on the part of trained social scientists, heralding them, as had Walker, as international agents of reform. However, he did not deal with the question of how professors retained their intellectual autonomy while depending on political and economic elites for institutional funding. Nor did he resolve the contradiction raised by the knowledge monopolizing expert in a democratic society. Instead, he accused George of "vulgar error" and spoke further about the technical differences between nominal and real capital. Like Walker in his 1891 presidential address, Seligman tried to reach the educated middle class by undermining George's professional credibility while demonstrating his own.[22]

In his two addresses, Walker sounded many themes other AEA presidents would replay. He positioned trained economists in an emerging ideological center by identifying extremist enemies: socialists and uncertified reformers like Bellamy and George on the left hand and adherents of an out-dated laissez-faire on the right. Economists were to translate this centralist ideology into practice through a public role that involved aiding legislators and educating the public. The public consisted of "respectable and responsible citizens" who were the natural constituency of social science experts: they could not be lost to popular prophets. By capturing and channeling the reform energies of the middle classes, it was possible to exert pressure on the legislators social scientists were so eager to aid. Furthermore, as the Henry George debate suggests, teaching the "cultivated classes" to accept the discipline of experts was critical to development of a public role. In short, Walker thought the most profitable strategy for the expert was to hold middle-class attention while advising prudent and cautious reform.

Second Vice-president Folwell spoke to the association in 1893, substituting for the ailing President Dunbar. Like Walker, Folwell had no specialized economic training but had seen military service, practiced law and managed a university. He was the University of Minnesota's first president and afterwards its first professor of political science.[23]

While agreeing with much of Walker's centralism, Folwell was somewhat to his left on the problems presented by corporate capital. Thus, Folwell positioned the AEA between laissez-faire and socialism. He echoed Walker on the part played by laissez-faire in discrediting economics as a field; it had caused the "average citizen" to see the discipline "as an empty and useless pseudoscience." However, he was more willing than Walker to see some justice in the socialist critique of industrial society. He valued the centralized, cooperative model of society put forward by socialists, but could not see a world without competition. He asked economists: "to gain for society all the advantage of brotherhood without sapping and withering manhood."[24]

To blend cooperation with competition and thus create an alternative to laissez-faire and socialism, Folwell called "for the recognition and development of a science of public economy." He asked that the AEA's experts, supported by the universities, answer questions of public policy. The role of the economist in treating these questions was two-fold. First, the economist had to put his science between party politicians and the voter. Party platforms, whole campaigns rested on economic questions--"immigration, taxation, railways, telegraphs, roads, pauperism, corporations"--that science should decide. Using the press, economists would reach "the great unthinking public." Second, economists should give advice to legislators as well as implement reform through serving the administrative branch of government. Thus Folwell, like Walker, stressed shaping middle-class opinion and assisting an interventionist state as the public role of the economist.[25]

Yet Folwell's sense of issue was different. Most pressing among the many problems demanding the economist's attention were "public land policy" and the "labor policy of the nation." Using language reminiscent of the early proposal for an American economic association developed by James and Patten, Folwell asked for the formation of a land-use policy that maximized national planning and minimized the role of the Eastern speculator. With regard to labor, he argued that "the arrival of large production, and the massing of vast capitals through exploitation," combined with the increase in immigrant workers, had moved the labor question beyond the realm of private contractual arrangements and made it instead a public policy issue. "The changed condition of our industrial state" called for administrative regulation of both capital and labor.[26]

Although Folwell selected somewhat different problems than did Walker and gave them a slightly populist emphasis, they were agreed on the main aspects of the expert role. Specialized economists were trying to find a middle road; they wanted the "serious thinking public" to follow and support them in their search. In return, social scientists would use their knowledge to shape more equitable public policy without resorting to ideological extremes that would unduly alter the existing order.   And most importantly, Folwell refrained from reiterating Henry George's critique of the political illegitimacy of university-based social science expertise in an industrializing capitalist political economy. Folwell thereby demarcated a leftish policy expert's role, while Walker outlined a rightish one. But both were well within the AEA's self-defined ideological center of social science theory and practice.

The Capital-Labor Question Is Debated as a Policy Issue

In 1894 and 1896 John Bates Clark addressed the AEA as its president.   In 1897 it was Henry Carter Adams. Spurred by two decades of boom-or-bust coupled with seemingly endless industrial violence, these first-rate minds explored the policy possibilities presented by the capital-labor question. Both presidents assumed that the expert policy advisor should devise technical schemes to create a more socially responsible industrial order. And both understood that such technical amelioration depended on noneconomic philosophical premises expressed in theoretical analysis. Thus, both knew that ideological presuppositions underpinned the technical schemes advanced by social engineers such as themselves. Speaking in the after shock of the nation-quaking Pullman strike, their words offer a sense of the political limits that the AEA accepted in its eagerly sought policy advisor role. With Clark we see something of the right-ward limits of the role, while Adams explains some of the roles' left-most potential. Taken together, they offer us a measure of the substantive width contained within the AEA's centralist ideology.

John Bates Clark was the first German-trained economist and first career academic to hold the AEA's presidency. Moving from the relative obscurity of Carleton College by dint of perserverance and publications, he won posts at Smith and then Columbia.[27] He represented the successful fourth faculty specialist. Clark saw the central question of academic economics as determining the social system best suited for an industrial society such as that emerging in the U.S.   This broad question necessarily subsumed many pragmatic issues, forcing the theoretician to engage society at several points. In addition to advancing the science of economics, the answer would determine "what type of legal action will perfect the industrial system" and quell social unrest by revealing "a line of public policy that is safe and efficient."[28] The exact theoretical problem that Clark set himself to answer in his 1894 address was "whether socialism has a right to exist." He was very clear as to why he chose the problem. Rampant social discontent found expression in two powerful movements, anarchism and socialism. Anarchism was "self-terminating" and not worthy of intellectual attention, but socialism posed a serious theoretical challenge to the existing order. Tacitly addressing the Marxist theory of surplus value, Clark thought if socialists could prove that capitalist society defrauded workers of their product, then all good men should and would join them.[29]

Said Clark, "I wish to test the power of recent economic theory to give an exact answer to this question." To do so, Clark assumed competition was a natural force, that private property was the basis of industrial society, and that the entrepreneur was the active agent in social progress. Accordingly, the concrete questions he tried to answer became, how does competition adjust the rate of wages? and was industrial competition still active? By diagraming market forces, he showed to his satisfaction that pricing mechanisms gave workers their just due while allowing capital its fair profit.[30] He thus refuted the socialists' thesis of objective labor exploitation.

Of course, certain theoretical conditions had to be met before competition could do its lawful work of distributive justice--the work force had to be fully mobile, there could be no reserve labor force, and monopoly could not be allowed to influence the general rate of wages. Clark granted that all these conditions were not yet met. Here the economist as policy scientist found his role. But the economist "is not, in his proper capacity, an advocate," since any interventionist action exceeding the natural limit of competition was doomed to failure.[31] Accordingly, economists advised policy makers on the pragmatic possibilities of the moment by monitoring natural competition so closely that they could "predict what measures will of necessity be adopted and retained." Fitting practice to theory he offered a tentative sketch of model legislation regulating the labor market to a nation pondering the implications of the Pullman strike.

Clark thus proved to his own satisfaction that industrial "mastership and plutocracy, in a good sense, yield by natural law a democratic result; for it is by the wealth that these ensure that the productive power of labor must rise." Capitalism was not guilty of "industrial fraud." Socialism, therefore, was not justified to reasonable men.[32]

In his 1895 address Clark continued to test modern economic theory's ability to define an appropriate social system for an industrial order. He argued that the key to such a system was its "power always to progress." And the force behind such a system was competition. The central question became whether the trust impeded competition. Clark answered "no," since latent competition held the trust in check. He further argued that gains in efficiency and economy justified the trust, that "accumulations of capital afford the ultimate guarantee of industrial progress," and finally, that if the trust exacted a social cost from the public that was greater than that taken by other forms of business organization it was off-set by its contribution to progress.[33]

Clark realized the present system was not perfect, that trusts sometimes acted in a "predatory way . . . crushing competitors unjustly or illegally" but preferred not to "resort to legal forces" unless absolutely necessary. Indeed, he saw labor as a potential check on destructive combination. Strikes were one way of adjusting industrial claims until the system was perfected. As such, industrial disorder was preferred to legally constrained competition. Labor, even though belligerent, would find "the undetected harmony of interest between itself and honestly increasing capital. It will fight over distribution; but it will protect capital as such."[34]

Clark positioned the trained economist between anarchism and socialism and like Walker and Folwell before him, tried to define an ideological center that would hold the middle classes steady. His addresses made clear the ideological function of economic theory in explaining the imperfect but progressive nature of capitalism to the "better classes." Yet the public role he assigned economists did not permit technical amelioration independent of the natural law of competition: that law made the entrepreneur rather than the economist the lead actor in the modern industrial drama. Thus, Clark saw the expert more as policy advisor than policy maker. In this vision, the economist's public role reflected Clark's theoretical assumptions and a deductive methodology relatively unschooled in historical analysis. Clark assumed on a priori philosophical grounds that corporate capitalism was an exceptionally rational, efficient and productive economic system. Given this assumption, then its abundance would solve all disputes about distributive justice. Thus, the capital-labor question was solved by insuring some minimal (even latent) competition among firms. Within this theoretical framework, the reformist energies of policy advisors went into curbing the competitive abuses of "bad trusts" and working with the progressive management of "good trusts" and "responsible" labor organizations. Clark's elegant theory and policy analysis echoed other, more popularly phrased critiques of corporate capitalism.[35] But, unlike competing anarchists and socialists, Clark's policy advisor did not show "reasonable men" a way to take economic production into their own hands.

In both his AEA presidential addresses Clark reveals the discipline's right-wing answer to the capital-labor question then stalking North America. Concentrated capital in its trust form was extremely rational, efficient and productive. Accordingly, only those corporations that abused the trust form must be controlled. In his subsequent career, Clark continued to be an advocate for "good trusts," for example, upholding them at the 1898 Conference on Trusts sponsored by the Chicago Civic Federation. And from 1910 until his retirement from Columbia in 1923, he headed the historical division of the Carnegie Endowment for International Peace. There he lent his expert legitimacy and management skills to developing the cultural consequences of a good corporate fortune.[36]

When Henry Carter Adams addressed the AEA in 1897, he already had solid experience as an extramural policy expert, having served for a dozen years as head of the statistical section of the Interstate Commerce Commission while teaching economics at Michigan.[37] Like Clark, Adams was a successful fourth-faculty academic. His address reveals the left-ward limits of the AEA's emerging ideological center.

Like Clark, Adams also addressed the question of what social system best suited an industrial society. He, too, thought that socialism was a competitive alternative to a socially irresponsible capitalism. However, he saw the economist's public role as more actively analyzing industrial tension and designing larger scale interventionist measures in response to structural imbalances. His analysis argued that business corporations had evolved so far beyond labor organizations that serious competitive imbalance existed. Indeed, the problem of industrial order could not be solved unless labor was given a more recognizable stake in the capitalist economy.

Adams theorized that current industrial discord--such as the Pullman strike--was the result of the failure of jurisprudence to keep pace with economic development. Considered historically, Anglo-Saxon jurisprudence embodied the ethical consensus of the community. Its genius was a flexibility permitting it to evolve with changes in political and industrial relations. In this tradition, legal evolution was usually the result of widespread popular "agitation" stemming from fundamental changes in the economy. Current disorder arose from a disjuncture between the legal and economic systems. Since this agitation had structural roots, it could be met only by legal evolution or forceful repression. But, as sustained repression was not a real alternative in a political democracy, Adams asked for the formulation of a new jurisprudence shaped in part by economists holding a position between state socialism and laissez-faire anarchism.

He then moved into direct disagreement with Clark's presentation of the proper relationship between labor and corporate capital organized in trusts. For Adams, corporate capital had transcended a "bourgeois conception of private property." It had evolved beyond the limits of personal liability, human mortality and common virtue. In so doing, it escaped as well Anglo-American jurisprudence and classical economic theory. In essence, the corporation institutionalized property rights in a newer, more powerful business form without a parallel evolution in labor rights. The resulting labor agitation was an effort to bring about the evolution of these legal rights. Since economics had not clarified such historical developments, its sound opinion supported the suppression of worker's aspirations, not their expression in legal evolution. Consequently, society was on the brink of "industrial warfare."

Moving from theory to policy advice, Adams proposed that economic experts champion a new industrial property for workers. Like a corporation's charter, it would be a state-sanctioned intangible right, akin perhaps to citizenship. Its existence would give labor a responsible stake--a property interest--in the new corporate form of business enterprise. For example, the state might legislate a worker's property that could be combined in guild-like labor trusts and then offered to capital in contracts subject to courts of arbitration.

Unlike Clark, Adams saw the economist in his public role as an expert advocate, articulating a new philosophy of social justice. He saw theory as wed to action and ideology, issuing a new theory of prosperity that would "express the rights of individuals associated together in an industrial unit" and "express the duties of these units to the public at large." At present,

The role of the economist should be to analyze the situation so as to express these suppressed labor rights, and to prepare the way for bringing this period of industrial warfare to a close; and this should be accomplished, not by the enslavement of labor, but by imposing upon labor the responsibility without which liberty is but a name.

Further, he must work on the "legislative enactment" of corporate regulation that would make possible the "attainment of a just price and the preservation of industrial mobility."[38]

In sum, Adams acknowledged that articulating the suppressed rights of labor was a task to which "communism, collectivism and socialism" had set themselves. But he argued these suppressed rights be incorporated into the Anglo-Saxon tradition of jurisprudence as a "conservative solution" to the problems faced by capitalism. Like Clark he was deeply concerned with preserving a system based on private property and fueled by competition. However, Adams saw industrial order as depending on more than natural competition monitored by experts. It hung on the system's willingness to counter-balance the power of corporate capitalists by evolving legal rights to ensure labor's willing participation. And, unlike Clark again, Adams's sense of the policy advisor's role was clearly that of the action intellectual combining specialized analysis with aggressive agitation for ameliorative reform. At root, Adams's address was a definition of the policy scientist as a university-based expert operating outside academia as a public philosopher and social engineer.

The debate following Adams's address argued the substance of his proposed "new rights" for labor, ranging mainly to Adams's right. Arthur T. Hadley, a Yale political economist, AEA second vice-president in 1895 and president in 1899 and 1900, argued for a more tightly circumscribed ideological center. Agreeing that Adams expressed "many things we have all been thinking," Hadley found fault in the new legal rights proposed for labor. He held that the "fundamental character of industrial and economic conditions" had not changed as sharply as Adams thought. Accordingly, there was little need for the legal counter-balancing Adams proposed. Rather, industrial peace would be secured by "going forward along old lines; not by going backwards to the starting point and then beginning anew in a different direction." And in any case, labor needed to show more "responsibility" rather than have more "rights."[39]

Hadley's criticisms of Adams were elaborated by fellow Yaleman H.W. Farnam and Harvard's Edward Cummings. Farnam, who was AEA second vice-president in 1893 and president in 1911, thought new labor rights would not bring industrial peace since older rights--like the right to employment--had not. Rather, he held that collective bargaining was now within labor's rights and urged contractual negotiations as the proper treaty-making mechanism in industrial warfare.[40] Cummings also found no need for new labor rights. Instead, union leaders needed to become more "business-like," and--echoing Hadley—more "responsible." Cummings added that since capital bore more of the costs of "constant industrial reorganization," capital might well merit a legally superior status over labor.[41]

Adams's position was supported by Franklin W. Giddings, AEA first vice-president in 1896-1897, and later a leader in the American Sociological Society. Giddings found Adams's analysis of industrial warfare correct. Leo S. Rowe, who later rose to leadership of the American Political Science Association, also pronounced Adams's historical analysis sound.[42] But Giddings thought Adams's solution too abstract and urged an expansion of specific state-guaranteed social security rights, such as severance pay for faithful service.[43] Giddings's desire for material benefits--for bread not legalisms--was seconded by Professor C.S. Walker of Masschusetts Agricultural College and disputed by political journalist George Gunton.[44]

Adams himself had the final word. He simply insisted that his thesis of evolving Anglo-Saxon jurisprudence with its related role of policy advocate expressed, "in language pertinent to the present situation the principles which have proved themselves adequate to every social crisis sustained by the English speaking people since the thirteenth century."[45] While Adams's address drew some ideological fire, all debaters agreed that one of the central questions facing economists was how to end industrial warfare while preserving private property. And even Clark in his previous addresses accepted the rhetoric of the economic expert as policy architect of a more socially responsible corporate order through carefully designed, albeit minimal, state intervention.

In practice, however, the expert was very often a draftsman rather than an architect as Adams's later career reveals. In his early years at the Interstate Commerce Commission (ICC) he saw himself as able to influence policy and shape ameliorative reform as a behind-the-scenes technical expert. Emphasis on technique did not preclude concern with substance. As an ICC technician, he treated issues such as capital valuation and fair profit, hoping to generate data that would clarify "suppressed labor rights" as well as gain a just fare for railway users. However, by accepting the corporate sector as the legitimate keystone of the economy—an ideological position clearly articulated in his presidential address and necessary for continued service with the ICC—he limited his own policy-making autonomy. In the course of his career, he moved from concern with the "conflict of labor and capital," to the "labor problem," to an exclusive focus on the technical problems of railroad regulation, finally working directly for the roads. In 1911 he was retained as an accounting consultant by the New York Central lines and paid a princely $15,000 per year, plus an equal amount of expenses--while continuing to hold his Michigan professorship.[46] He ended his career advising Chinese railroads and their American financiers. Unable to shape policy bearing on labor's suppressed rights through the ideology he accepted as necessary to sustain an academic career, he eventually abandoned the problem as a policy issue. The reality of expert service denied the rhetoric of the economist's role as policy scientist balancing the claims of capital with the rights of labor. Capital's resources tipped the scales.

At the time Adams gave his presidential speech, the consequences of centering the expert role on administrative service to the state might have been difficult to foresee. However, at least one trained social scientist pointed to the likely consequences of the role and in a highly visible career offered an alternative way of shaping policy. Daniel DeLeon, who was not promoted at Columbia's School of Political Science after supporting Henry George in the New York mayoralty race, left academia altogether. Concluding that policies adequate for popular needs would not be shaped by academic economists dependent on the university, DeLeon sought another resource base as leader of the American Socialist party. Addressing an audience of striking textile workers at approximately the same time Adams was addressing the AEA, DeLeon characterized social science experts as servants of power "at the command of our plutocracy" and explicitly cautioned labor to ignore the deliberate mystification of economic questions by "capitalist professors."[47]

DeLeon's views remained outside the academy. Indeed in the late 1890s AEA leaders were intent on translating their growing consensus on role into practice. In 1898 Giddings, as first vice-president filling in for the absent Adams, once again called on economists to treat pertinent public issues. He noted with pleasure that the program was "imminently practical" and opined that future economic work would focus more strongly on "problems of production, exchange and distribution; of capital, price, rent, interest, wages and profits." And "with many other members," he thought political economists might well take "a more prominent stand on questions of public policy, making an increased effort "to bring before the public a strictly scientific view on such great matters as the currency and taxation." Thus, beyond the "scientific study" of the "objective world of business affairs," Giddings saw the economist actively engaged in policy analysis and public opinion formation. Giddings remarks were brief and direct.[48] In effect, they simply restated the AEA's crystallizing collective sense of the modern policy expert's role without dwelling on possible problems, such as Henry George's egalitarian critique of the expert in a democratic polity or DeLeon's laborite labeling of the expert as servant of power.

Addressing the Question of Access

By 1898 AEA presidents and debaters had consistently defined the economic policy expert as guiding government intervention aimed at producing a form of state capitalism rather than a variety of state socialism. And although prior AEA leaders had exhorted their fellow economists to seek wider policy influence, they offered little instruction as to how this could be accomplished. In his 1898 presidential speech, Hadley turned to the problem of how expertise could be brought to bear on policy making. Since the AEA's definition of the expert pivoted on state intervention, he outlined a strategy for gaining access to state power arguing that the field could fulfill its potential only when practical politicians regularly asked and took economists' advice "as an incident of the workings of government machinery."[49]

Hadley spoke with some authority. He had been an expert witness before the Cullum Commission, which framed the legislation for the Interstate Commerce Commission, and had served as Connecticut commissioner of labor statistics. And, as president-elect of Yale, his words carried weight with both his professional colleagues and other university managers.[50] After blaming laissez-faire for economists' loss of public influence, he turned to locate that point of governmental structure at which economics would be able to regain policy-making power. He considered in turn the judiciary, the legislature and the administration.

The judiciary was quickly dismissed. In tacit rejection of Henry Carter Adams's views on Anglo-American jurisprudence, the courts were seen an unlikely point of access. A conservative judiciary guided by precedent was unlikely to use new technical knowledge. Indeed, attempts to provide the judiciary with technical expertise—through railroad, labor, tax and similar commissions—had either proved extraneous to legal development or simply antagonized the courts. Nor was the legislature the point at which economists could win influence. Given its present level of political corruption, it was incapable of making sound public policy. "Instead of cooperation for the general interests we have log rolling for the particular interests." Further, representative government was based on each legislator's loyalty to his district while the economist "is trying to pursue collective interests." Thus, "the economist is at a disadvantage in influencing members of the legislature, because his ends are different from theirs."[51]

The executive branch, free from "judicial conservatism" and "legislative particularism," was theoretically the point at which economists should seek influence. However, there were several barriers. The chief executive was hemmed in by constitutional checks, forcing the president to depend on his party rather than the advice of experts. And economists could not penetrate the party structure because their encouragement of independent voting antagonized politicians who needed predictable behavior at the polls.[52]

However, recent developments held out some hope for economists seeking to exert influence through the executive. First, municipal reform movements were overcoming local party power and giving "real authority" to the executive, who in turn utilized the "advice of economic experts." Indeed, it was "increased centralization of administrative power which gives the expert a fair chance."[53]

Second, although Hadley regretted the Spanish-American War and imperial expansion as a policy, he could not overlook the chance it offered experts. Imperialism would create the same need for a strong central administration at the national level as municipal reform had at the local. As he saw it, imperialism:

> brings new problems of administration upon us as a nation . . . the need of an efficient army will of itself make it necessary to give more independence to the administration and more opportunity to its expert advisors . . . with no colonies and a small army we could do what we pleased with our revenue bills. With larger possessions and larger necessities for defence, they must be framed by a responsible administration on a sound economic basis.

Imperialism, by strengthening and centralizing the administration, provided economic experts with their point of access. Regardless of his reservations about imperial policy, Hadley urged his colleagues to take advantage of a conjunction of political and economic circumstances that would increase their influence. Said Hadley, "Here is the opportunity for the younger economists of the country."[54]

Hadley's remarks brought forth both affirmation and dissent over the strategy outlined. E.R.A. Seligman supported Hadley, refining his analysis. Surely times of crisis--such as wars of imperial expansion--allowed expert economists their chance to "exert more influence." But crises aside, "the more democratic the community, the slighter has been the influence of economic theory on practical life." However, economic experts in democratic societies could achieve lasting influence by holding a centralist position in the ideological spectrum. In a democracy, policy was always "the result of compromises between warring class interests." By ideologically aiming "at a point midway between the extremes of undue conservatism on the one hand and of undue radicalism on the other" economists could avoid siding with any particular class. They could thus shape policy in service of the whole society as self-proclaimed spokesmen of the normative center.[55]

John Rogers Commons disagreed with both Seligman and Hadley. He argued that economists gained influence only when they represented class interests. Adam Smith's expertise shaped history because his arguments were directed against the declining aristocratic and agricultural classes and in harmony with the interests of the commercial classes then coming into power. "Economists have not lost influence as a whole--only those who stand for a class which has passed the day of its political power." Economists like Henry George and Karl Marx had great influence because they "represented the radical classes that are acquiring political power." Indeed, even if economists would, they could not represent society as a whole. Such claims really meant the economist wished to perpetuate the existing order.[56]

Hadley's rebutal rebuked Seligman for introducing the issue of class and rejected Commons's interpretation of economic knowledge in the service of power.[57] But his rejoinder did not settle matters. In the wake of Hadley's provocative suggestion of imperial service as the profession's main chance, Seligman had inadvertently raised Henry George's question of the place of the expert in a democratic society, while Commons, like DeLeon, had accused economists of holding an ideological bias that served the existing order. Hadley's explication of the Spanish-American War as opportunity knocking had opened the AEA's door to popular and widely appreciated challenges to their experts' claim to a monopoly of useful social and ethical knowledge. Unexpectedly, the AEA now faced both imperial expansion as an opportunity structure and further debate on the expert's role. How the AEA's handled imperialism's opportunities and the unanticipated ideological challenges to its policy aspirations is explored in the next chapter.

The AEA'S Shaping of Expertise, 1885-1900

Upon organization as specialists in 1885, AEA leaders had defined an expert role calling for economists to act as policy makers providing answers to the ideological crisis of their era. But as specialized intellectuals dependent on the university, they could not offer public answers to economic questions that challenged their institutions' resource base without incurring sanctions. Thus, they began to devise a strategy for accommodating their role to a resource network capable of sustaining academic careers.

Their strategy simultaneously shaped their role as experts and the content of modern social science. Thus, the socialist's project of revolutionary struggle over "surplus value" became academic debate about Clark's theory of the "good trust" and its monitoring social engineer versus Adams's evolutionary disjuncture with its action policy scientist. By eschewing ideological extremes to avoid confrontations with resource holders, they identified the construction of a new normative center as the focal task of social science. They not only blunted the cutting class edge of social science, but within the confines of the center were quick to acknowledge the primacy of the corporate sector in economic policy formation. In choosing the middle class as part of their constituency outside the university, they banked on the reform energies of such enlightened strata to stimulate demand for ameliorative intervention. Indeed, they offered scientifically biased and profoundly conservative answers to questions about the normative content of competing economic theories. They thus demonstrated their ideological utility to resource holders at the same time they schooled the middle class to rely on expert judgment in matters of social reform. In selecting an area of service they looked for one where they could act without fear of reprisals. Following civil service reform formulas common to ASSA leaders, they readily identified public administration as correctly nonpartisan. Given AEA leaders' own proclivities toward a positive state, and the national scope of their policy-making ambition, this helped them see the executive branch of the federal government as a highly appropriate policy setting.

In developing a strategy to implement the expert role, AEA leaders attempted to align themselves with those groups best able to provide a resource network capable of sustaining policy making within the context of an academic career: the corporate sector, the reform-minded segment of the middle class, and the emerging federal bureaucracy. To tap these resources, they formulated policy on the labor and trust questions suited to conservative reform and the long-term perfection of corporate capitalism. The function of the expert was ideological and technical: he offered the "middle way" as a normative path with scientific grounding and devised technical apparatus for engineering the road--regulatory bureaus, commissions, state agencies.

By aligning themselves as they did, they rejected alternative social science roles and resource alliances. They turned away from the popular economics of Henry George, the socialism of Daniel DeLeon, and the role of advocate for the rising working class suggested by John Rogers Commons. The AEA's lack of serious consideration of a popularly based role is understandable in light of their status as dependent intellectuals. The resources at the command of popular groups depended on the uncertain prospect of future political victories. Moreover, the leaders of popular movements had little stake in the production of specialized knowledge and questioned the authority of experts based in the industrial university.

In their alignment with resource holders, the AEA not only rejected a popularly based role but also broke step with the ASSA's sense of expertise. The New Englanders had served as intellectuals for a regional political economic elite. The AEA had national ambitions. Accordingly, the AEA modified the role expectations of intellectuals serving power. Like ASSA leaders, AEAer's continued to see the work of the expert as tripartite: education, agitation and administration. However, these categories were altered to meet the national needs of modern social science. Education was increasingly confined to an emerging network of graduate universities and colleges. Agitation narrowed to influencing middle-class public opinion. Administration emerged as a key facet of the expert role. And, by the Spanish-American War, the executive branch of the federal government was identified as the area most appropriate for academic economists to serve as extramural experts shaping national policy. Although AEAers had yet to achieve routine policy access in significant numbers, by the turn of the century they seem resolved to implement their expertise in roles working "not with students, but with statesmen."

NOTES

1. E.R.A. Seligman, "Social Aspects of Economic Law," Publications of the American Economic Association (PAEA), 3d series, 5 (February 1904): 65.

2. Constitution of the American Economic Association (New York: Philip Cowen, 1885), pp. 4-5.

3. W.W. Folwell, "The New Economics," PAEA 8 (January 1893): 22.

4. F.A. Walker, "The Tide of Economic Thought," PAEA 4 (1891): 18.

5. E.R.A. Seligman, "Economics and Social Progress," PAEA, 3d series, 4 (February 1903): 67.

6. Folwell, "The New Economics," PAEA 8 (January 1893): 33.

7. Prior to Hadley's 1899 address, 14 AEA leaders for whom we have biographical information served the federal government as experts. Three served on the U.S. Industrial Relations Commission, three in the Bureau of Labor, two in the Interstate Commerce Commission and two on the Senate Finance Committee, while the other four held a variety of positions in different agencies.

8. A.T. Hadley, "The Relation between Economics and Politics," Economic Studies (ES) 4 (February 1899): 9, 27-28.

9. E.R.A. Seligman, "Economics and Social Progress," PAEA, 3d series, 4 (February 1903): 69-70.

10. Constitution of the AEA.

11. For Hadley's views of the importance of public service to the "prosperity" of economics, see "The Relation between Economics and Politics," ES 4 (February 1899): 9-10.

12. For the presidential role expectations of those not mentioned in the text, see John B. Clark, "The Modern Appeal to Legal Forces in Economic Life," PAEA 9 (October, December 1894): 11; Henry C. Adams, "Economics and Jurisprudence," ES 2 (February 1897): 33, 35; F.H. Giddings, "Address of Welcome," ES 2 (February 1898): 56.

13. Dictionary of American Biography (DAB), s.v. "Walker, Francis Amasa" by Jeanette P. Nichols.

14. F.A. Walker, "Recent Progress of Political Economy in the United States," PAEA 4 (1889): 23, 35.

15. Ibid., pp. 31, 39. For a standard presentation of laissez-faire principles of taxation, see David A. Wells, "Rational Principles of Taxation," Journal of Social Science (JSS) 6 (July 1874): 120-133.

16. Walker, "Recent Progress of Political Economy," p. 40.

17. Walker, "The Tide of Economic Thought," p. 21.

18. Ibid., p. 24. For support for the single tax on the part of sponsors of AEA projects, see DAB, s.v. "Shearman, Thomas Goodell" by Edward Conrad Smith.

19. Walker, "The Tide of Economic Thought," p. 20. For the ASSA debate, see "Social Economy Papers: The Single Tax Debate," JSS 27 (October 1890): Part I.

20. "Address of Professor Edwin R.A. Seligman," JSS 27 (October 1890): 44.

21. "Remarks of Henry George," JSS 27 (October 1890): 85, 84.

22. "Remarks of Professor Seligman," JSS 27 (October 1890): 95.

23. DAB, s.v. "Folwell, William Watts" by Solon J. Buch.

24. W.W. Folwell, "The New Economics," _PAEA_ 8 (January 1893): 21, 40.

25. Ibid., pp. 30, 34, 31.

26. Ibid., pp. 34-36.

27. _DAB_ (Suppl. 2), s.v. "Clark, John Bates" by Alvin Johnson.

28. J.B. Clark, "The Modern Appeal to Legal Forces in Economic Life," _PAEA_ (October-December 1894): 10-11.

29. Ibid., p. 9.

30. Ibid., p. 10.

31. Ibid., p. 28.

32. Ibid., p. 29.

33. J.B. Clark, "The Theory of Economic Progress," _ES_ 1 (April 1896): 6, 15.

34. Ibid., pp. 21, 22.

35. For example, the distinction between "good trusts" and "bad trusts" was made popular by Henry Demarest Lloyd in _Wealth versus Commonwealth_, published the same year Clark gave his first presidential speech. Lloyd knew and corresponded with many early AEA leaders, particularly those involved with the social gospel movement. See Chester McArthur Destler, _American Radicalism, 1865-1901: Essays and Documents_ (Connecticut College, 1946; reprint ed., New York: Octagon Books, 1965), pp. 135-161.

36. _DAB_ (Suppl. 2), s.v. "Clark, John Bates" by Alvin Johnson.

37. _DAB_, s.v. "Adams, Henry Carter" by William Bristol Shaw.

38. Henry Carter Adams, "Economics and Jurisprudence," ES 2 (February 1897): 7-35, quote at p. 26.

39. A.T. Hadley, "Discussion of the President's Address," ES 2 (February 1897): 36-37.

40. H.W. Farnam, "Discussion of the President's Address," ES 2 (February 1897): 41-42.

41. Edward Cummings, "Discussion of the President's Address," ES 2 (February 1897): 43-45.

42. Leo S. Rowe, "Discussion," ES 2 (February 1897): 40-41.

43. F.H. Giddings, "Discussion," ES 2 (February 1897): 38-39.

44. C.S. Walker, "Discussion" ES 2 (February 1897): 39-40; George Gunton, "Discussion," ES 2 (February 1897): 42-43.

45. H.C. Adams, "Discussion," ES 2 (February 1897): 47.

46. David M. Grossman, "Professors and Public Service: A Chapter in the Professionalization of the Social Sciences" (Ph.D. dissertation, Washington University, 1973), pp. 32-33, 65.

47. L. Glenn Seretan, Daniel DeLeon: The Odyssey of an American Marxist (Cambridge, Mass.: Harvard University Press, 1979): 17, 16-19.

48. F.H. Giddings, "Address of Welcome," ES 2 (February 1898): 56.

49. A.T. Hadley, "The Relation between Economics and Politics," ES 4 (February 1899): 7.

50. DAB, s.v. "Hadley, Arthur Twining," by Robert D. French.

51. Hadley, "The Relation between Economics and Politics," pp. 16-24.

52. Ibid., p. 26.

53. Ibid., p. 27.

54. Ibid.

55. E.R.A. Seligman, "Discussion of the President's Address," _ES_ 4 (April 1899): 109-111.

56. John R. Commons, "Discussion of the President's Address," _ES_ 4 (April 1899): 111-113.

57. A.T. Hadley, "Discussion," _ES_ 4 (April 1899): 112-113.

6
Advocates of the Existing Order

By 1900 there was some consensus among AEA leaders about the expert role. They felt that the expert's task was a technical rationalization of industrial capitalism that enhanced the public's appreciation of the details of centralist ideology. Experts were policy scientists using their academic specialty to serve the common good and the national interest. Furthermore, they thought such service was a means of linking graduate certification and specialization in the public mind, and asserting a monopoly of social knowledge. Service, then, was critical to establishing social scientists' expertise.

But as social science leaders began to engage more frequently in public service, unanswered questions arose about whom the expert served when he acted for the state: did administrative service legitimate and consolidate the power of the established order, with all its economic inequities? In debating this issue at the turn of the century, AEA leaders reached a deeper consensus on the expert role and crystallized an ideology of expertise. They argued that scientific training inculcated objectivity. Specialized social scientists certified as experts in the graduate school were better able to apprehend and articulate the public good than those uninitiated in scientific method. Academic training enabled them to see the nation's general needs instead of viewing policy through the distorting lens of particular interests.

AEA leaders avoided questions about the part played by resource holders in shaping their expertise. Yet leaders' service, whether in public or private sector, revealed their alignment with the emerging economic center. In the main, they shared their expertise in common cause with owners and managers of large national corporations seeking to use the central government's expanding bureaucracy to shape federal policy. These corporate leaders saw that the state could be used to stabilize the political economy; they acknowledged and accepted the need for conservative reform to preserve capitalism. Whether in civil service reform organizations, good government associations or private policy forum groups, they lobbied for an administrative state. And the state apparatus was expanded by and responded to the steady pressure of reforming resource holders. Like social science leaders, these reformers saw their interest mirrored in a larger state that would be more responsive to the corporate center's technical and ideological demands.

Thus, when acting as experts for the state, social scientists also served the emerging economic center as advocates of the existing order, albeit augmented with ameliorative reforms. Private leverage was needed to influence public policy. Social scientists found it in corporate sponsors and the nonpartisan, middle-class reform groups they funded. With support from this constituency, experts rationalized and legitimated state policies designed to enhance and protect capitalism at home and abroad: federal regulatory commissions, the income tax, imperial expansion. In so doing, experts identified the public interest as that of liberal corporate leaders and the emerging middle strata who shared their concern for the conservative reform of capitalism. Service to the public thus offered a wide spectrum for varied and even conflicting expert activity. But it did not include producing expertise for those groups uncommitted to the conservative reform of the existing order: anti-imperialists, militant labor, socialists, agrarian radicals and the like.

In this chapter, we continue our analysis of presidential addresses and the debates surrounding them, looking at a deepening consensus on the expert role as social scientists entered state service. We first examine the AEA's Committee on Colonial Finance authorized by the association after the first Hadley speech. Here we see the part played by corporate sponsorship in influencing policy and gaining access for experts to state service. We then briefly review leaders' service stemming from this effort, looking at the deployment of expertise in the imperial arena. Next we inspect the AEA's 1900 debate and the development of greater consensus on the expert role, and its subsequent confirmation by later presidents. We continue contrasting the speakers' rhetoric with their careers as experts. And we continue to hear the voices of academics and intellectual actors contesting the AEA's definition of the expert role to remind ourselves that it was not inevitable.

The Role in Action: Service in the New American Empire

Between the first Hadley speech, where he outlined a strategy for social scientists in search of influence, and the second, where this was debated, the AEA's executive and nominating committees acted on his view of the expert by creating a special committee charged with organizing a volume on colonial finance.[1] This volume allowed AEA writers to show how the new social science could serve the interests of those who made imperialism a national policy by offering technical solutions to the immediate fiscal problems of colonies as well as providing ideological justifications for acquiring them. By putting their energies and resources behind Hadley's strategy, the association went a long way toward making academic further debate on the expert role.

The special committee's composition showed careful attention to the stronger adherents of imperialism and revealed policy-making know-how. Its five members were very active in corporate policy circles. Three were AEA leaders associated with the rough-riding Republican Roosevelt. Committee chairman J.W. Jenks of Cornell had worked with Governor Roosevelt on New York State's trust legislation beside corporation lawyers like James B. Dill, who drafted the New Jersey law allowing corporations based in that state to operate nationally without close oversight. Dill himself was later an AEA leader. Columbia Professor E.R.A. Seligman, son of an investment banker, advised Theodore Roosevelt and other statesmen on taxation.[2] Albert Shaw held a doctorate from Johns Hopkins, edited the Review of Reviews for British reformer W.T. Stead and offered Roosevelt (and others) both intimate policy advice and approving publicity rather than rash and radical muck-raking.

The two non-leaders on the special committee were also familiar faces in higher policy circles, circulating freely from business to state office and back. Charles S. Hamlin, wealthy lawyer, was especially active in domestic monetary matters and foreign metropolitan affairs. A former assistant treasury secretary, he helped settle disputes among the Japanese, Russian and British states. Edward H. Strobel was a lawyer turned diplomat and general advisor to colonial governments. A former assistant secretary of state, he helped the king of Siam deal with the French and "modernize" his political economy.

All five members of the AEA's special committee exhibited a willingness to advise established power holders and thus serve the ongoing social order. The AEA's selection of these men articulated their endorsement of American imperial policy, their own willingness to place their knowledge in its service, and an understanding of the part played by members of elite policy circles in shaping the state position on issues of the day. So did the volume the committee produced.

Essays offered the special committee's own recommendations, based on a comparative historical analysis of European colonial policy. In principle, the committee held against colonial exploitation and for aiding the conquered territories toward autonomous industrial development. In practice, the specific recommendations were aimed at creating an American version of comprehensive economic dominance.

Thus, the committee recommended that each colony be self-supporting with sources of revenue determined by the colony's function within the imperial scheme. If the colony were to be a hub of trade and transshipment, then import duties would pay colonial expenses. If the colony were totally underdeveloped, internal revenue taxes might be levied. All such arrangements were designed to relieve the metropole of paying direct colonial costs.

As conceived by AEA leaders, the colonial role of the imperial state was three-fold. First, it built and maintained economic infra-structure (railroads, canals, communication systems). Second, it administered fiscal systems so that "in the last resort the desires of the U.S. government, expressed by the proper authority, are to be paramount and its desires final." Third, the state offset inefficiencies in the local labor market by importing metropolitan labor. Blue-collar imports were foreseen in instances where "it is difficult to secure an adequate supply of efficient native labor," and white-collar imports when "inhabitants are not capable of managing important public works" or performing "absolutely essential" civil services, which must be "beyond question" in "ability and honesty." Such labor imports clearly imply that the colonies of the new American empire were to be stratified by race: skilled, imported white versus incompetent native non-whites.[3]

In sum, the recommendations made by the AEA special committee served the colonizer rather than the colonized, urging as it did an oppressive system of imperialism. The report also implied a role for the experts in the emerging American empire. The committee's fiscal recommendations strongly intimated that trained economists were necessary for a successful empire. It was they who must make a thorough study of local conditions to determine the correct fiscal system, gather data, create the appropriate administrative design and perhaps even implement it. In this way, the committee seconded Hadley's views in seeing imperialism as an opportunity for economists by identifying a large number of professional positions best filled by themselves.

The AEA sought sponsorship for the rapidly assembled volume, looking for a token of support for their effort to take advantage of the opportunity Hadley had so forcefully pointed out. Essays was their first concentrated, organizational attempt to develop pragmatic policy for immediate implementation. Since they undertook the project without any assurance that the expertise they mobilized would be used to inform federal policy or gain access to state service, support from authoritative figures in the business world was important: it served notice that their expertise was taken seriously by resource holders.

The five men found to act as financial patrons for Essays were wealthy businessmen, all leading members of the emerging economic center. They were well known for their interest in civic affairs, and some had an economic stake in overseas expansion. William E. Dodge was a partner in Phelps, Dodge and Company; he also had additional mining, railroad and banking interests. Theodore Marburg was an American Tobacco Company heir, independent investor, ardent advocate of imperialism and vice-president of the AEA when he contributed to the publication costs of the special issue. Isaac Seligman was head of a famous banking house with extensive overseas interests, many in Latin American countries. He was also the brother of AEA leader E.R.A. Seligman who, in turn, was a member of the Special Committee on Colonial Finance and had authored an essay in the volume. Stuart Wood had won Harvard's first doctorate in economics and served as an AEA vice-president in 1889. He did not pursue an academic career, instead overseeing his family's diverse manufacturing interests. But he continued his own studies in economics and reform, writing articles of the theory of wages, participating in AEA activities and providing leadership for the American Academy of Political and Social Science. Thomas Shearman was Jay Gould's attorney and then established his own firm which specialized in corporate reorganizations. He had a strong interest in economics, advancing a modified version of the single tax in whatever forums he could.

These five patrons put up two-fifths the cost of publishing Essays: $125.[4] More importantly, they symbolically endorsed the new social scientists' usefulness as advisors to fellow members of the emerging economic center seeking to use the expanding bureaucracy of the central government to shape federal policy, creating, in Kolko's phrase, a "political capitalism."[5] By accepting the sponsorship of such patrons, the AEA leaders acknowledged their willingness to serve the new corporate center and to implement policy in its interests.

However, corporate sponsorship did not place experts in the leadership role envisioned by Hadley, nor even in a position to provide influential advice. Instead, corporate sponsorship provided symbolic support and funds enough for academics to act as entrepreneurs for their profession by demonstrating their competence as managers of, in Weber's words, "state capitalistic" enterprises.[6]

And experts did demonstrate their competence as administrators in the new American empire. The national crisis provided access to state service for three early AEA leaders and six later social science leaders. The majority of those entering imperial service between 1899 and 1904 continued to supply American expertise in Third World countries throughout their careers. Hadley was correct when he predicted that the executive branch of the federal government would need experts to administer its colonial acquisitions.

Thus, J.W. Jenks of Cornell, an early leader and chairman of the special committee, was recruited by the War Department in 1901 as a special commissioner to visit English and Dutch colonies in the Far East and gather information relevant to Philippine legislation. This endeavor in foreign service led to others. For example, in 1903 he was named as the U.S. Commission of International Exchange's expert in charge of Chinese currency reform. Ever mindful of his profession's constant need for resources, he wrote to Roosevelt from China suggesting that the indemnity for the Boxer Rebellion be used to fund exchange professorships for a 30-year period. In the area of foreign policy, Jenks would go on to advise the Mexican government, serve under Wilson as a member of the Nicaraguan High Commission, and continue his long-run oriental interests by heading the Far Eastern Bureau.

The two other early leaders who served--W.F. Willcox, also of Cornell, and Roland P. Faulkner, chief of the Division of Documents of the Library of Congress--worked in Cuba and Puerto Rico. In 1900 Willcox conducted the first census on both islands, while Faulkner in 1903 was appointed commissioner of education in Puerto Rico. Willcox did not continue in foreign service, although he had an active expert career as a domestic statistician. Faulkner, however, went on to chair the U.S. Commission to the Republic of Liberia in 1909 and also served as a member of the U.S. and China's Joint Land Commission.

It was later leaders, or the "younger" social scientist charged by Hadley with taking advantage of imperialism's opportunity, who became involved in the day-to-day administration of the colonies. In the Pacific theater Carl C. Plehn of California was chief statistician of the Philippine Commission in 1900-1901. Like Willcox, he would become more involved with domestic statistics via the Census Bureau than with foreign affairs. But APSA leader Bernard Moses, another Californian, continued to be active in the imperial arena after his 1901-1903 membership on the second Philippine Commission. He went on to serve as an expert in Latin American affairs, participating in the series of Pan American Conferences held before the First World War. Another APSA leader, David Barrows, also served in the Philippines. He was superintendent of the Manila schools and director of education, staying in the islands from 1901 to 1909. While his later service was not primarily in foreign affairs, his Philippine experience stimulated a strong interest in the military, and in 1934, while a professor at Berkeley and a general in the California National Guard, he led the troops that helped break the San Francisco longshoremen's strike. His interest in military matters endured until the end of his career; during the Second World War he served the War Department and the Office of Strategic Services by participating in the forced relocation of Japanese citizens and aliens on the West Coast.

Other "younger experts" served in the Caribbean. In 1900 AEA leader J.H. Hollander of Johns Hopkins was appointed by Secretary of War Elihu Root as a special commissioner to revise Puerto Rico's tax laws. His service was so effective that McKinley named him treasurer of the island in 1901. Roosevelt called him back to service as special commissioner to Santo Domingo to report on the public debt. Married to the daughter of Abraham Hutzler, a prominent Baltimore merchant, Hollander was well acquainted with leaders of the international financial community, and used his connections to place Santo Domingan bonds with Kuhn, Loeb and Company. He rescued the island from financial panic but was investigated by a congressional committee for accepting $100,000 from the Santo Domingan government as a finder's fee while serving as an agent of the U.S. government. Although he was never prosecuted, Hollander's activities raised questions about expert ethics.[7]

T.S. Adams, another AEA leader, served as Hollander's assistant treasurer in Puerto Rico. Although he found his work "congenial, important enough to satisfy my self-respect, and very instructive," this Harvard professor's later service to the state was in the area of agricultural economics. Leo S. Rowe, an APSA leader from the University of Pennsylvania, was appointed by McKinley as a member of the Commission to Revise and Compile the Laws of Puerto Rico, and later as chairman of the Insular Code Commission. His expert service in Puerto Rico turned his academic interests from municipal reform to Latin American affairs. After extensive service with the state department and in private policy-making forums concerned with foreign affairs, he gave up his professorship on his appointment to the Pan American Union, an agency he headed from 1920 to 1946. Another APSA leader, W.F. Willoughby, took charge of Puerto Rico's treasury department after Hollander left. Willoughby would move between government service, academy and the private sector throughout his career. His interest in foreign affairs continued, and he served briefly as an expert in China in 1916. However, his major work was domestic--he headed the Institute for Government Research, later known as the Brookings Institution, from 1916 to 1932.

In developing the volume of _Essays_ as an attempt to influence policy and in their colonial service, AEA leaders took advantage of an opportunity presented by national crisis to secure corporate sponsorship in fielding their expertise. Here, we see a resource exchange between association leaders and the emerging economic center. The corporate sponsors' modest subsidy represented symbolic capital in the AEA leaders' efforts to gain routine access to state service. In return, these sponsors received both the AEA's confirmation of controversial imperial policy and its leaders' state service in their interest as experts technically rationalizing the administration of newly acquired territories for a state that was ill prepared to manage them. Essays and the leaders' subsequent service to empire points to the problem faced by specialists dependent on the university. In their addresses, AEA presidents constantly reiterated the importance of policy service in establishing a monopoly of expertise and building the social science career into the graduate school. Thus, imperialism, however regrettable, presented a main chance that could not be missed.

However, not all American social scientists supported the emerging center's expansionary adventure. Those with resources to sustain them outside the university did not feel compelled to act as experts for imperialism. Indeed, a number of ASSA leaders joined the widespread, very vocal, organized opposition to the war, assuming leadership positions in the Anti-Imperialist League even as AEA leaders were working on Essays. For example, A.P. Stokes was national president of the league, Gamaliel Bradford and F.B. Sanborn were Boston-based leaders. C.F. Adams was initially a supporter, while Henry Villard and Charles Elliot sometimes lent the league their names. For many of these now aging social scientists, the league was their last endeavor at influencing national policy and it was an exercise in virulent agitation. Not dependent on the university for livelihood, they used their own resources to bring their crusade against imperialism to the public, some even going so far as to join the 1900 campaign for "unsound" William Jennings Bryan. When these ASSA leaders saw capital centralized in powerful trusts as sustaining itself with politically corrupting imperialist expansion, their analysis sprang from New England intellectual and economic traditions grounded in abolitionism, free trade and sound money. Since their critique of imperialism was rooted in regional elite values and interests, they could not long sustain a political alliance with Western populists, workers and immigrants. With the second McKinley victory, imperialism became national policy and New York was acknowledged as the nations's emergent economic center. With their regional base declining and a lack of common occupational interest, the social scientists who had led the ASSA from Civil War's end to the turn of the century lost control of their organization. While still able to continue their own regional activities, they were gradually isolated from broader sustaining resource networks and left the formation of a national social science to the specialist associations' leadership.[8]

In summary, both ASSA and AEA leaders were guided by their perceived interests when taking a position on imperialism. ASSAers, speaking with the voice of New England's sound opinion, saw imperialism as the logical extension of a corporate centralization they considered socially destructive. Freed from the constraints of academic career, they were able to enter the political arena to mobilize the citizenry. AEAers, dependent on the university, looked to administrative service in a nonpartisan state bureaucracy to influence policy. Even had they wished to, they could not afford to enter the political arena in opposition to a cause favored by resource holders who supplied the modern university's funds. Instead, they acted on their own analysis of the career and resource potential provided by the Spanish-American War, ignoring the critique of the ASSA's anti-imperial leaders. By offering themselves as technicians of empire, academically based specialists sided with the emerging economic center against which ASSA leaders and other anti-war and anti-trust activists were fighting. The AEA leaders' historical analysis pointing to imperialism as an opportunity for experts proved accurate, and in choosing to serve empire they also aligned themselves with the winning side in struggles over the shape of political capitalism at home. The increasingly routine service of specialist association leaders after the Spanish-American War contrasts with the rapid decline of the ASSA, instructing us that expertise backed by power gets a hearing. But by permitting opportunity to guide their entry into public life, specialized social scientists became servants of power, not leaders of the body politic.

Role Consensus Deepened and Ideology Crystallized

Although the AEA's organization of the Colonial Finance Committee and the subsequent service of experts in the executive branch of government indicated the association's strong support for the role outlined by Hadley in 1899, Commons's criticism of that role signified the presence of some internal opposition. Thus, Hadley's 1900 address was specifically aimed at meeting objections raised by fellow social scientists. The debate served to win AEA consensus on Hadley's version of the role and did not treat the problems faced by institutionally dependent social scientists in expert service. While Commons was given opportunity to reply, the other participants in the debate by and large ignored the issues he raised and instead worked to build a professional ideology justifying expert service.

In this second address, Hadley granted that there were problems with the expert role and admitted that they centered on differences in economists' conception of what best served the common good, thus conceding there was no ready scientific answer to questions of social justice. However, he thought these differences need not pose insoluble problems for economics as a field. First, he made a distinction between objective and subjective economics. "Theory of distribution" described existing economic conditions as they are and was arguably objective. But the "theory of prosperity," which spoke of how distribution should be arranged, was exceedingly difficult to separate from normative assumptions and political prejudices. Thus, Marx and Ricardo agreed on theories of distribution but differed on almost every point on "theory of prosperity," or what was to be done.[9]

Hadley resolved this tension between an objective science and its subjective practitioner by arguing that the trained economist could stand "above the clouds of prejudice" where other men could not. Offering advice that would shape the future through legislation or administrative mandate might challenge the integrity of "the economist who strives to maintain a dispassionate and critical attitude," but since this is "where the possibility of influence is greatest" the discipline could not afford to forfeit these opportunities. Hadley held that the social scientist, disciplined by long years of training and informed by a universalistic methodology, could subdue his personal bias and represent the common good more accurately and dispassionately than the average citizen.[10]

Hadley then outlined his conception of the economists' role. Economic specialists were to overcome class and special interests by bringing together those leaders within class or faction who could agree to a constructive synthesis for the whole. Hard-and-fast formation of class lines in industrial society was as socially destructive as regional distortion of national economic development. Pluralistic competition between social groups created not consensus on the common good, but opportunity for the political machine. This type of corrupt political competition should and would be corrected by limiting the legislative sphere of action, making room for the strong executive and the expert. Thus, the economic expert was an objective scientist and custodian of the common good, standing above class and special interests as well as partisan politics. As private and political sectors were increasingly regulated in the name of the public to insure their social responsibility, the economic expert would have a greater role: his "high mission" was "to be the representative and champion of the permanent interests of the whole community."[11]

John R. Commons was the principal respondent in the debate following Hadley's address. He was severely critical of the analysis offered by Hadley and outlined an alternative public role for the economic expert. His central point of disagreement with Hadley was that, whether using theories of distribution or prosperity, experts were still resource dependent. Since they had no power base outside the university, they necessarily had to support one class or another if they were to have a voice in public affairs. Commons was sensitive to the problems faced by dependent intellectuals. After being fired from Syracuse, he found work in a political research group tied to the Democratic party only to be unemployed once again when his sponsor's political interests shifted elsewhere.[12]

In 1900 Commons elaborated the position he had taken at the last AEA meeting. Economists "must have the ear either of those who control legislation or those who are striving to get control" if they are to gain political power and influence. The economist is not called upon because he possesses disinterested knowledge, but because he is valuable to classes engaged in struggle for political power. Directly confronting Hadley, Commons argued the economist acts for a class by showing "to the nation as a whole that the interests of that class are for the permanent interests of the whole." In essence, Commons argued that the expert's central function is to advance the ideological hegemony of one class or another. The expert's only choice is which class he chooses to serve.[13]

Commons thought Hadley overlooked the economist's dependent position in the political economy of power. If the economist worked within institutions representing the existing order, he would inadvertently become "court preacher to the political bosses and irresponsible trustees" of corporate capital rather than an impartial expert serving the common good. The courtly expert might have influence; he might even accomplish great good. But "he will shut out from political influence all the economists who do not have the ear of the bosses and the trustees. He is the defender of the institutions by which these men have gained power." He could not escape serving the interests of the class controlling social institutions, and this same service discredited oppositional voices, thus contributing to the ideological hegemony of the dominant class.[14]

Commons proposed an alternative public role for the economist. Like other AEA leaders, he agreed that economists must seek public influence as experts and preserve independent scientific judgment. However, given the realities of the American power structure, the strategic issue for the economist as expert was which class best represented progress and the welfare of all. "When our conclusions lead us to champion the cause of a class . . . or expose another class, we should come squarely out and admit it is so; not because the class interest is foremost in our minds, but because the class is temporary means of bringing about the general welfare of all." As a social scientist, the economist should not be blind in his advocacy for a class, nor irrevocably committed to it. "But we should admit that we differ among ourselves, and that our fundamental differences coincide in general with class antagonisms in society. We are part of the social situation. History alone will decide between us."[15]

AEA leaders decided against Commons's class-conscious version of the expert role. In the subsequent debate, as elsewhere, they refused to entertain the notion that differences over economic theory might legitimately reflect class cleavage or that the policy expert could serve other interests than the public good. To do so would have revealed their alignment with the economic center and undermined their strategy for achieving influence by presenting social science as a value-neutral arbiter between class and special interests.

Seligman repudiated Commons's conception of class conflict over societal domination. Instead, he saw economic class struggle in a politically democratic society as producing a higher and more progressive harmony of interests. And while he recognized the continuing dangers of bias, he felt there was no alternative to striving for an objective economics. If "the economist can serve the public only through the class," it would "prove utterly fatal to the progress of economic science." In the final analysis, Seligman, like Hadley, thought the expert's long-term influence depended on an image of scholarly autonomy that denied class bias.[16]

E.W. Bemis, a rising young economist who had recently been fired from the University of Chicago for offending resource suppliers, politely refused to see great disagreement between Hadley and Commons, since in both views the economist acting on his convictions would either antagonize or favor dominant social interests according to his understanding of the interests of society as a whole. But, like Hadley and Seligman, Bemis assumed the economist could freely select issues as they presented themselves, siding first with one group and then with another. He did not deal with Commons's argument that the economist as a dependent intellectual might well have to make a long-term commitment to a particular class in order to be heard at all.[17] Bemis, whose long-run sympathies were with the vast bulk of Americans outside the nation's rising economic center, never held another academic or professional economic policy post. Instead, he served the city of Cleveland's popular reformers as superintendent of water supply while maintaining membership in the AEA.

Richmond Mayo-Smith, an AEA leader, well-known statistician and Columbia professor, along with Professor Powers, concurred wholeheartedly with Seligman and Hadley. They agreed that economists could not represent class interests in a public capacity, but only the common good. Indeed, both were personally affronted by Commons's implication that they could be thought to act as representatives of a class even though their particular behavior might inadvertently invite such an unfortunate interpretation.[18]

Hadley again had the final word. He refused to see class struggle as intrinsic to capitalistic industrialization or entertain the possibility that economists representing the public interest might perforce serve the existing order. He also argued, like Seligman, that support for a particular class would, in any event, undercut the economist's long-term quest for influence. Representing class interest might bring "petty successes" in the present, but if economists were "to be leaders of public opinion," they had to develop roles and support that would allow them to give advice independent of classes.[19]

The 1900 debate crystallized a professional ideology justifying expert service. According to Hadley and the debaters ranged against Commons, the expert, tempered by arduous training and dedication to a rational science, can transcend personal prejudice, class bias and party politics so that when serving, he represents the whole community's interests. This rhetoric served the profession in at least three ways. First, identifying specialized training as the means of bringing experts to the point where they can provide objective advice emphasized the importance of formal certification, thereby tightening the discipline's monopoly of knowledge. Second, claiming to be beyond class influence put them in a position to act as neutral arbitrators of social conflict, opening a wide area of service which they exploited fully in the Progressive era, working for example, in the Department of Labor, on federal industrial relations boards, and for the Bureau of Corporations. Third, if experts represented the public, then administrative decision making could be safely expanded without undercutting democratic values. Indeed, expert decisions on the ever-increasing number of issues defined as nonpartisan would remove them from the legislature, thus reducing party-based corruption. Thus, the expert role clarified around professional ambition, and objectivity was at least in part an artifact of career.

However, this ideology of expertise begged critical questions. Experts might claim to represent the public, but their society-wide phantom constituency was divided by class, region, ethnicity and gender. It had no means of making its diverse view known to these self-appointed spokesmen, let alone any way of holding them accountable. But the fiction of a unified public provided experts with a rationale for service convincing to their actual constituency—the Progressive wing of the corporate sector and the reform-minded middle strata who had a strong interest in maintaining social order by defusing industrial unrest through ameliorative reforms administered by the state. The expert's actual public lived in the ideological center defined by AEA presidents. Powerful and affluent, it was able to supply the resources to retain expertise. As Commons prophesied, when experts worked in established institutions, they served their actual constituency rather than the community-at-large.

Indeed, Commons's subsequent career illustrates the university-based expert's dependence on the predictable resources of the economic center and shows how his work inevitably serves its interests, despite the economist's intentions. Out of work and short of money, Commons became assistant secretary of the National Civic Federation (NCF), a forum for a core of the nations's largest businessmen during the Progressive era. He was particularly active in the NCF's settlement of labor disputes. He also assisted in the Carnegie Institute's economic history of American labor legislation, work that eventually led to a professorship at Wisconsin. While teaching, he worked on various state and municipal projects to rationalize capitalistic development. In 1912 he was named to the U.S. Industrial Relations Commission, an investigative body whose membership was designed to provide equal representation for capital, labor and the public. Although Commons was officially a public member, his appointment had been urged by the business-led NCF. Commons co-authored a minority report signed by the commission members representing capital, but not those representing labor.[20] As Commons himself said when looking back on his career, "I learned . . . that the place of the economist was that of advisor to the leaders, if they wanted him, and not that of propagandist to the masses."[21]

Ely and Seligman Affirm the Role

Like the participants in the 1900 debate, subsequent AEA presidents confirmed Hadley's conception of the expert's role. Richard T. Ely served as AEA president in 1900 and 1901. If anyone might have been expected to share Commons's early definition of the expert, it was Ely.

Like his Wisconsin colleague, Ely was sometimes described as so far left as to be outside the AEA center.[22] However, Ely's intellectual life was sifted and winnowed when his job was threatened by a member of the Board of Regents (see Chapter 4), and he abandoned labor advocacy and Christian socialism. By the time he addressed the AEA as president, Ely explicitly defined the expert's role as advocate of the existing order.

In his addresses, Ely, like those AEA presidents who had gone before him, saw competition as natural, permanent and beneficent. Yet competition called for ameliorative state intervention if the principle of social solidarity were to be preserved. A balance had to be struck between "the socialist extension of government activity . . . and that conservative demand" calling for unfettered competition.[23] In his second address, he elaborated on these themes, clarifying his conception of economic structure. Capitalist production provided the "material basis" for "industrial liberty," and cooperation was the key to social progress.[24]

Within this framework the role of the economic expert was to serve as capitalism's social engineer, adjusting the balance between popular demands for greater equality of opportunity and those "great institutions" of private enterprise that are "the very foundations of our civilization."[25] "In mutual adjustments of these two lines of evolution, namely, the equality of opportunity movement and the institutional movements, we have given to us one of the weightiest and at the same time most delicate tasks of the twentieth century."[26]

Like other AEA presidents, Ely saw the expert as arbitrating between competing socioeconomic groups, using state regulation of the economy as a means to achieve orderly progress. The expert built consensus, stressing cooperation rather than industrial conflict. He worked in an ideological center "midway between anarchism and socialism."[27] Although taking a position between these extremes sounded reasonable and equitable, corporate capitalism then became the economic center. The expert balancing claims between various groups short-weighted meaningful reform because the scales were already adjusted in favor of the existing order. Ely, then, confirmed the expert role outlined by leaders in the 1900 debate.

Ely's subsequent career gives an indication of the opportunity available for experts defending the economic center and confirmed

Commons's prediction that the expert who serves organizations controlled by the "dominant class" becomes "the defender of institutions by which these men have gained power."[28] After his trial by the Board of Regents, Ely gave up his scholarly work on the labor movement and turned to rural sociology and land economics. He sought expert service in accepted institutions, asking his colleagues to find him advisory posts in the federal bureaucracy. Eventually he accepted the directorship of the Institute for Research and Public Utilities. Funded by real estate boards, railroads and privately owned public utilities, the institute's conclusions seemed biased to Wisconsin's left-leaning Progressive era politicians. University managers asked Ely to choose between heading the institute and professing at Wisconsin. Ely chose his institute, moving it to Northwestern University where it continued to draw popular criticism and undaunted support from the economic center even in the teeth of a 1920s Federal Trade Commission investigation.[29]

E.R.A. Seligman, who served as AEA treasurer from 1886 to 1891, headed the association in 1903 and 1904. Like so many other presidents, he spoke to the expert's role in the maintenance of social order, in the formation of an ideology justifying capitalism to the public and in the development of techniques for intervention aimed at ameliorative reform. But rather than seeing experts as social engineers, he saw them as architects of the nation's future.

Like past presidents, Seligman presented economics as a policy science. In his opening statement he proclaimed: "Economic science is an outgrowth of economic conditions . . . of social unrest . . . of an attempt to unravel the tangled skein of actual conditions, and an effort to solve the difficulties of existing industrial society."[30]

This interpretation was used to point to the social utility of economics. Theory and service were not separate; indeed, economists of stature achieved their reputation by grappling with "the storm and stress of actual life" and discovering ways to reconcile the "inharmonious play of social forces." Only in his capacity as expert was the economist able to combine the discipline's historical interpretation and theoretical insights with active service aimed at "wise regulation" of an "ever enlarging" political economic life.[31]

Taken together, Seligman's two addresses illustrate the way theory and service are united in the expert role. In his first speech,

"Economics and Social Progress," he emphasized the epoch's need for expert regulation of the economy. The development of "industrial capital as distinct from agricultural or commercial capital . . . responsible for the landed and trading aristocracies of the past" signified the beginning of the modern era.[32]

"With the unification of the system and the supervening change in economic conditions, the content of our democracy is changing and the theory of extreme individualism is passing away."[33] This change in historical circumstances called for new economic theory. Seligman offered yet another rendition of an ideological center maintained by ameliorative state intervention, normatively bounded by laissez-faire on the one hand and socialism on the other. It varied only in minor detail and degree of sophistication from the position offered by other presidents.

He took as his premise the notion that "industrial capital . . . correctly analyzed and rightly controlled means not industrial aristocracy but industrial democracy." Like other presidents, he based this prognosis for the twentieth century on the "almost boundless" production of competitive industrial capital aided by modern science. As production increased, it would provide "an ever-broadening base for the benefits of trade and commerce." Any tendency toward "plutocracy" or a "new feudalism" would be checked by public opinion guided by economists. The result would be "effective social control of competition," or a "truer and more perfect competition based on the equality of contending forces." Seligman, then, justified reform capitalism, dismissing "the social unrest of today" as "but the labor-pains . . . of the new industrial order."[34]

In his second speech, "Social Aspects of Economic Law," he turned to his area of specialization, presenting a reconceptualization of public finance theory aimed at preparing the way for a federal income tax. He first analyzed current theories guiding taxation, demonstrating that taxes still fell most heavily on those least able to bear them. Next, he asked economists and statesmen to "frame a theory of taxation which will at once explain the objective conditions and respond to the sense of justice in the popular mind," thereby "showing the reconciliation of private wealth with public welfare."[35] Thus, theory informed plans for technical amelioration, and the resulting state intervention would serve the ideological function of protecting private wealth by arguing justice to popular unrest.

A large part of Seligman's career was devoted to developing the theory of taxation he called for in 1904. In 1911 he published a book explaining the economic conditions justifying federal income tax, thus preparing the ground for the 1913 constitutional amendment. Translating theory into practice, he advised Cordell Hull, then a powerful member of the House Ways and Means Committee, on income and general tax matters.[36] His interest in public finance extended to other areas. Along with AEA leaders and bankers Paul Warburg and Frank A. Vanderlip, he wrote and testified in the campaign for a central banking system that resulted in the Federal Reserve Act. Working through the NCF along with AEA and APSA leaders J.B. Clark, J.W. Jenks, and L.S. Rowe, he worked on the enabling legislation that led to the Federal Trade Commission.[37]

Through his service, Seligman demonstrated the expert role he delineated in his AEA presidential speeches. He asked the economist, as the "real philosopher of social life," to take a more notable part in future speculation and future legislation. As the proprietors of an "impartial science," they should represent "the general interest" in policy formation. When economics fully develops its predictive powers,

> it alone will be in a better position to apprehend and to explain the real content of existing conditions and the true method of making the actual conform to the ideal . . . to comprehend the living forces at work, and . . . to control them to ever higher uses. Economics . . . is the prop of ethical upbuilding, it is the basis of social progress.[38]

In Seligman's view, the expert was a modern prophet leading the nation out of a wilderness of social change. The activist social scientist provided technical advice for maintaining the social order and theory that contributed to its ideological hegemony, as well as the morality of economic expansion and increased consumption.

The expert role constructed by AEA leaders over two decades called for exchanges with resource holders. In the main, experts offered their political and economic sponsors a technical rationalization of industrial capitalism that reinforced public appreciation of the correctness of centralist ideology. In return, they got an opportunity to use their expertise. This exchange was not one-sided, for expert service had a number of implications for careers. First, social scientists were able to realize university managers' role expectations by illustrating the value of specialization, thereby advertising the possibilities of the industrial university to a wide range of potential resource suppliers. Second, experts were able to link specialization and university certification in the public mind, tightening their monopoly of legitimate social knowledge. Third, their stints in public and private sectors generated a demand for experts, creating careers for their students, heightening the value of the degree, and expanding the number of specialists necessary to teach a growing student body.

As degrees became part and parcel of professional life inside and outside the university, specialists' closer hold on legitimate knowledge did not go unnoticed and uncriticized. The same year that Seligman gave his first presidential address, philosopher William James of Harvard delivered a scathing denunciation of Ph.D. holders' growing monopoly of knowledge and challenged their claim to be the community's technical and ethical guardians. He saw certification of specialists as the product of university aggrandizement and professional ambition. Presidents and trustees regarded the degree "as a mere advertising resource, a manner of throwing dust in the Public's eyes," while students pursued it not for love of truth but for the "adventitious rewards" that came when "combination" was used to exclude competitors. Indeed, James thought reliance on the expertise of certified specialists so stifled natural talent and raw genius that "an enlightened public consciousness" ought to limit the Ph.D. octopus's eight-armed grasp on knowledge.[39]

However, by 1904 experts had established a firm hold on technical opportunities for social policy making by acting as advocates for the existing order. During their search for influence they had identified the emerging economic center--the Progressive wing of the corporate sector, and the professional and cultivated classes--as a constituency able to support their expertise. They tailored their centralist ideology to meet this constituency's needs, masking the naked power of wealth and privilege with the rhetoric of social justice; in return, they became the certified experts of reform capitalism.

Experts and Influence

While routine service as policy experts helped to make social science a viable career, leaders often voiced expectations that went beyond the successful institutionalization of their field in the modern university. AEA presidents spoke of social science experts influencing public policy, leading the body politic, acting as the social philosophers of industrial life. However, expert service did not often confer policy leadership on its practitioners. The careers of social science leaders considered thus far seem to indicate five levels of influence exercised by experts as they performed their tasks of technical rationalization and ideological legitimation. These were: technician, policy popularizer, policy manager, policy advisor and independent policy maker.

Technicians solved problems, especially data problems, set by others. Plehn and Willcox's work in running the imperial census provide examples of this level. Through such service, experts gained an opportunity to show their competence to those higher in the role system, and corporate leaders and statesmen had an opportunity to look over and socialize these "new boys."

Policy popularizers disseminated social science wisdom to the public, lending their reputations as nonpartisan, impartial specialists to particular policies or reforms. Academics' work on Essays illustrates expertise at this level of the role, as does Seligman's volume on behalf of the income tax. Policy popularizers usually devised or endorsed technical solutions to specific problems, and their efforts often opened the way for routine use of experts in administration.

Policy managers executed policies established by others, and often supervised technicians or mobilized policy popularizers. Henry Carter Adams's work as statistical head of the Interstate Commerce Commission shows the political economist as policy manager implementing agency directives with his own technical staff. John Bates Clark's service as director of the historical division of the Carnegie Endowment for International Peace provides an instance of a policy manager bringing together academic popularizers deliberating the appropriate balance of international power.

Policy advisors had the ear of decision makers in the corporate sector and government. They were usually well published, well placed in university circles and often socially well connected. These advisors gained prestige and some influence, while decision makers received academic advice they wanted to hear. Walker's work on international monetary standardization and Hadley's testimony before the Senate committee writing ICC legislation show the policy advisor in action.

Finally, a few social scientists achieved positions as independent policy makers after long years of expert service. Corporate leaders and statesmen gained levels of policy making congruent with their needs without attention to detail, while academics who reached these heights had some ability to influence the working out of national policy. Rowe's work as director general of the Pan American Union is a case in point, as is Willoughby's as director of the Brookings Institution.

Although these levels of role performance indicate a wide range of influence, most social scientists serving as experts acted as technicians, policy popularizers or policy managers. They held staff positions in the economic center, while a few advisors and independent policy makers served as line officers for corporate capitalism. Expert service became "an incident of the workings of government machinery," but their sponsors' role expectations usually confined experts to the lower influence ranges rather than providing them with a chance to lead the body politic.

In sum experts rarely gained significant influence, but their routine service demonstrated the utility of social science, building it firmly into the fourth faculty. And as their monopoly of knowledge was consolidated through their service to the economic center, other voices lost legitimacy. Populists and single taxers like Henry George were discredited, as were ASSA leaders opposed to imperial expansion and the development of trusts. The handful of radical and critical professors, like DeLeon or Bemis, were not heard in academic halls, let alone policy makers' councils. Warnings about the dangers of expertise issued by a few cultural leaders, such as William James, went unheeded. The AEA's constituency of conservative reformers, whether corporate capitalists or their middle-strata followers, controlled opportunities for state service and were hardly likely to seek out the opposition when they had at hand a willing corps of trained experts guided by an ideology they shared.

NOTES

1. "Report of the Secretary," Economic Studies 4 (April 1899): 50.

2. For a discussion of Jenks and Seligman's advice to Roosevelt, see G. Wallace Chessman, Governor Theodore Roosevelt: the Albany Apprenticeship, 1899-1900 (Cambridge, Mass.: Harvard University Press, 1965). Unless otherwise noted, all biographical information for persons mentioned in the text is taken from Dictionary of American Biography (New York, Scribner's: 1927-1973), Who Was Who (Chicago, Ill.: Marquis, 1943-1976), National Cyclopedia of American Biography (Ann Arbor, Mich.: University Microfilm, 1968), and The International Encylopedia of the Social Sciences (New York: Macmillan and The Free Press, 1968).

3. Essays in Colonial Finance by Members of the American Economic Association: Collected and Edited by a Special Committee in Publications of the American Economic Association, 3d series, 1 (August 1900) p. 19; see also whole number.

4. "Report of the Secretary," Publications of the American Economic Association (PAEA), 3d series, 2 (February 1901): 47.

5. Gabriel Kolko, The Triumph of Conservatism: A Reinterpretation of American History (Chicago: Quadrangle Paperbacks, 1967) p. 3.

6. Max Weber, "Science as a Vocation," in Max Weber: Essays in Sociology ed. H.H. Gerth and C. Wright Mills (New York: Oxford University Press, 1958), pp. 129-131.

7. David M. Grossman, "Professors and Public Service: A Chapter in the Professionalization of the Social Sciences" (Ph.D. dissertation, Washington University, 1973), pp. 91-92.

8. Daniel B. Schirmer, Republic or Empire: American Resistance to the Philippine War (Cambridge, Mass.: Schenkman, 1972), especially Chapter 7, "The New England Anti-Imperialist League," pp. 93-103.

9. Arthur T. Hadley, "Economic Theory and Political Morality," _PAEA_, 3d series, 1 (February 1900): 46-48.

10. Ibid., pp. 48-49.

11. Ibid., pp. 49-61.

12. John R. Commons, _Myself_ (Madison, Wisc.: University of Wisconsin Press, 1963).

13. John R. Commons, "Discussion of the President's Address," _PAEA_, 3d series, 1 (February 1900): 63.

14. Ibid., pp. 72-74.

15. Ibid., p. 79.

16. E.R.A. Seligman, "Discussion of the President's Address," _PAEA_, 3d series, 1 (February 1900): 80-84.

17. E.W. Bemis, "Discussion of the President's Address," _PAEA_, 3d series, 1 (February 1900): 84-85.

18. Professor Mayo-Smith, "Discussion," _PAEA_, 3d series, 1 (February 1900): 85-86; Professor Powers, "Discussion," _PAEA_, 3d series, 1 (February 1900): 86-87.

19. A.T. Hadley, "Discussion," pp. 87-88.

20. Marguerite Green, _The National Civic Federation and the American Labor Movement_ (Washington, D.C.: Catholic University Press, 1956), pp. 294-361.

21. Commons, _Myself_, p. 88

22. For a description of Ely as left-of-center, see Commons, "Discussion of the President's Address," _PAEA_, 3d series, 1

(February 1900): 69.

23. Richard T. Ely, "Competition: Its Nature, Its Permanency, and Its Beneficence," _PAEA_, 3d series, 2 (February 1901): 66.

24. Richard T. Ely, "Industrial Liberty," _PAEA_, 3d series, 3 (February 1902): 77.

25. Ely, "Competition," p. 68.

26. Ibid., p. 69.

27. Richard T. Ely, "Industrial Liberty," _PAEA_, 3d series, 3 (February 1902): 77.

28. John R. Commons, "Discussion of the President's Address," _PAEA_, 3d series, 1 (February 1900): 74.

29. Benjamin G. Rader, _The Academic Mind and Reform: The Influence of Richard T. Ely in American Life_ (Lexington, Ky.: University of Kentucky Press, 1966).

30. E.R.A. Seligman, "Economics and Social Progress," _PAEA_, 3d series, 4 (February 1903): 52.

31. Ibid., pp. 54, 69.

32. Ibid., pp. 60–64.

33. Ibid., p. 59.

34. Ibid., pp. 60–67.

35. E.R.A. Seligman, "Social Aspects of Economic Law," _PAEA_, 3d series, 5 (February 1904): 71, 73.

36. Dorfman, _The Economic Mind_, p. 351.

37. Kolko, The Triumph of Conservatism, pp. 274-279.

38. Seligman, "Economics and Social Progress," p. 70.

39. William James, "The Ph.D. Octopus," in Memories and Studies (New York: Longmans, Green and Company, 1971), pp. 333-337.

7
Organizational Differentiation and International Confirmation of the Expert Role, 1904

By 1903 AEA leaders had developed an expert role in complementarity with resource holders to guide their use of expertise outside the university. The men and women to whom experts turned for role resources were socially conscious corporate leaders from the emerging economic center, professional and middle-strata reformers, and graduate school managers. This constituency provided a wide range of fairly predictable resources: research funds, project subsidies, shared reform work, access to advisory positions. Thus, academic social scientists realized their initial expectations of using their skills to inform public policy, although not often as close advisors to statesmen and only within a context supporting the conservative reform of capitalism. However, experts were able to counter their dependence on resource holders by constructing an ideology of expertise. They advertised the expert as a value-neutral scientist whose role was to use objective knowledge in dispassionate service for the common good. Their constituency came to understand that advice offered by credentialed experts contributed to the technical rationalization of the economy and at the same time legitimated the existing order by demonstrating its capacity for limited reform. As the broad outline of exchange between experts and their constituency grew clearer, expertise became a routine part of the solution of social problems.

When political scientists and sociologists formed their own specialist associations, they were differentiated from economists by subject matter but not by role. A number of American Political Science Association (APSA) and American Sociological Society (ASS) leaders had shared in the formation of the expert role as AEA participants and did not question it. Instead, political scientists used their expertise to improve the state's capacity to administer the economy conservatively and to develop its procedures for defusing popular political unrest; sociologists used theirs to analyze uncritically the social structure of capitalism and treat problems not covered by students of the economy and the polity. Like AEA leaders, APSA and ASS officials were advocates of the existing order, continuing to exchange expertise for the resources needed to expand their specialities.

In this chapter, we look first at the organization of the APSA and ASS. Then the social characteristics of leaders from all associations are analyzed to see their contribution to the formation of an expert role rooted in the graduate university. Finally, the continuing use of the AEA's expert role in this wider variety of social science specialist associations is treated through leaders' participation in the St. Louis World's Fair. Leaders' presentation of their fields at the fair enables us to place the expert in an international context as well as within the consolidating American higher education system.

Political Scientists and Sociologists Organize

By the 1890s most graduate universities had social science or economics departments, although these were often ill defined and housed faculty with varied interests. Such departments seldom numbered more than three or four persons, but differentiation was encouraged by the elective system and the greater resource potential associated with specialization. Some professors within these departments began to define their interests more narrowly and refer to themselves as political scientists or sociologists rather than as political economists. Start-up money for journals was provided by university managers competing for an edge in new fields--for example, Political Science Quarterly at Columbia University in 1886 and the American Journal of Sociology at the University of Chicago in 1894.[1] At the same time the AEA became increasingly concerned with technical problems of economic regulation and less able to accommodate diverse topics. In organizing the APSA (1903) and the ASS (1905), new specialists sought forums better suited to their interests.

As the major specialist association for academically trained social scientists, the turn-of-the-century AEA contained within its ranks many of the academics who would found and lead the APSA and the ASS. For example, J.W.   Jenks and E.J.   James were top officers in both the economist and political scientist associations, while Simon N.   Patten, Franklin Giddings, E.A. Ross and Lester Ward were AEA leaders in the forefront of the sociologists' efforts to organize separately.   Such leaders and their associational followers fully shared the AEA's definition of social science and its view of the expert role.

Efforts to establish the APSA began with a circular letter soliciting opinion on the advisability of an "American Society of Comparative Legislation" to do "the work imperatively demanded in this field" and urged a session during the 1902 AEA and AHA concurrent meetings to crystallize such sentiment.   This session disclosed a "general belief" in a national association covering not merely comparative legislation, but the whole of political science.   A committee of 15 was established that sent out a second circular letter, chiefly to AEA and AHA members, asking their views on the need for a separate political science association.[2]   After reviewing favorable replies, the committee asked the AEA and AHA to schedule another meeting at the 1903 convention to explore the organizational forms such an association might take. In a third letter prior to the 1903 meeting, the committee outlined two alternative schemes. New sections could be created within the AHA, AEA and ASSA, or an entirely separate entity could be established.   However, the committee argued against new sections in the older associations. While such sections would offer opportunites to read and publish papers, they would not foster a newer corporate sensibility.

> Rather, what was needed was . . . some representative body that can take the scientific lead in all matters . . . encouraging research, aiding if possible in the collection and publication of valuable material and, in general advancing the scientific study of politics.

To this new body the committee wished to recruit not only academics but public administrators, "lawyers of broader culture," and all others "interested in the scientific study of the great and increasingly important questions of practical and theoretical politics." Finally, the letter urged the new political science association, in affiliation with the AEA and AHA, to "assume and maintain a leadership in these allied fields of thought that can be subject to no dispute."[3]

The December 1903 AEA and AHA concurrent meetings allowed time for the committee's session. The session organized itself as the APSA, drafting a constitution modeled on the shared AEA-AHS sense of social science and its expert. Accordingly, the APSA constitution limited the association's function and the political scientists' role to scientific studies and publication, without references to reform contained in the 1885 AEA Statement of Principles or the earlier James-Patten draft constitution.[4]

At the same Christmas holiday meetings that marked the organization of the APSA, sociologists began to speak of organizing their new field. Although some economists and historians discouraged the formation of yet another specialist association, especially one claiming to integrate the whole of social science, organizational efforts continued.[5] During the summer of 1905, George Washington University's C.W.A. Veditz began canvassing prominent sociologists on the need for a separate specialists' association. In the fall of 1905 a circular letter signed by Veditz, Chicago's Small, and AEA leaders Giddings, Patten, Ross and Ward, among others, sought wider opinions. At the winter 1905 concurrent meetings of the AEA, AHA and APSA, Veditz reported the results of these polling efforts. He told some fifty assembled social scientists that the "great majority" of respondents favored a new and separate association. After touching upon both the promise of new sections in older societies (including the ASSA) and the pitfalls of over-specialization, the session issued the American Sociological Society.[6] The ASS founding constitution followed the AHA-AEA-APSA model in supporting scientific production without mentioning reform or stating principles.

In sum, leaders of the new disciplines followed the pattern established by the AHA and AEA. As historians and then economists had organized under the ASSA's wide social science umbrella, so political scientists and sociologists came together under AEA auspices. However, APSA and ASS leaders, tutored by the AEA's early struggle over its Statement of Principles, made no mention of reform in their constitutions. Instead, the newer associations used the now time-tested formula to delineate their purpose: scientific study and publication in a specialized area. Like AEA leaders, the majority of political scientists and sociologists were institutionally dependent intellectuals who had specialized in advance of demand. They could hold their precarious place in the university only by finding clients for their expertise.

Leaders of the New Social Science Associations: A Collective Biography

At the turn of the century the ASSA had been weakened by internal dispute over the Spanish-American War, and the organization of political scientists and sociologists further contributed to its decline. By 1905 the ASSA found itself almost without its traditional function of defining social science expertise, well on its way toward becoming a status-production organization minting honorifics for an East Coast gentry genuinely out of touch with the social scientific edge of America's accelerating industrialization.[7] The decline of the ASSA helped the new academic associations operating at that leading edge "assume and maintain" leadership in their fields "subject to no dispute."

What was the overall character of that leadership? What sorts of "new men" were those heading up the social science associations? And what were the subject matters in the several fields they defined so authoritatively? A comparison of the collective biography of the ASSA officers with that of the emerging specialist associations will cast some light on the social correlates of the new captains of scholarly industry. And a later look at the 1904 International Congress of Arts and Science will illuminate the social processes and problems that each association claimed as its own specialty.

To discover something of the changing character of American social science leadership, we return to our sample of ASSA leaders. It contains 43 of the association's top officers from its founding until 1886, when the AEA emerged as its organizational competitor. The ASSA sample is a bench-mark, establishing for comparative purposes the biographical correlates of social science role definition in the two decades just after the Civil War and prior to widespread acknowledgment of the graduate university as the capstone of American higher education.

A second leadership sample contains those 34 persons who held the AEA's top posts--president, vice-president, secretary or treasurer--from 1885 to 1903, the years before the rise of the APSA and the ASS. These "early AEA leaders" represent a transitional group, one that can be contrasted with both the preceding ASSA leadership and succeeding sets of new social science leaders in the AEA, the APSA and the ASS. Between 1904 and the end of World War I (1920), the AEA had 47 "later leaders," while the APSA leadership numbered 43 and the ASS some 17.[8]

We have previously noted the ASSA leaders' deep New England roots (see Chapter 3). In contrast, the newer social science association leaders are somewhat more nationally representative. Many more of them were born to families settling later (Appendix, Table 2) and living outside New England, particularly in mid western and mid-Atlantic states (Appendix, Table 3), and the vast majority found their adult work lives spent outside New England in those two regions (Appendix, Table 4). However, this geographical shift in social science leadership was not from New England to the nation-at-large, for few were born or worked in the old Confederate South or the Far West. In effect, then, the newer turn-of-the-century American social science leadership shifted from New England to the rising, rapidly industrializing mid-Atlantic and midwestern regions.

Somewhat the same regional shift is seen in educational backgrounds. In the main, the ASSA's leaders attended New England's colleges and graduate schools, while the newer associations' leaders did not (Appendix, Tables 5 and 6). Here the early AEA leadership provides a clearly transitional case. A sizable number graduated from New England colleges, but in the absence of strong graduate programs in the United States the majority who attained doctorates earned them overseas. The early AEA leaders also earned the doctorate much more frequently than the ASSAers, establishing an attainment norm approached but unequaled by the later associational leaders (Appendix, Table 7). Similarly, early AEAers were more likely than any others to make their careers in higher education (Appendix, Table 9). Thus, early AEA leaders, who organized while the ASSA was still a vital association, present the sharpest contrast with it in terms of educational background and career.

Their strong commitment to the university may point to the more limited resources available before the value of the doctorate was confirmed by the routine use of expertise. During the decade after the AEA's 1885 organization, leaders had little opportunity for specialized work outside the university. Although AEAers came from families where fathers' occupations were similar to ASSAers (Appendix, Table 8), they were geographically diverse and could not rely on the resources of a regional elite for sustenance. So long as specialized intellectual labor was not widely appreciated, the developing graduate schools may have represented their only resource option. As opportunities for academic experts expanded and outside interest in the associations quickened at the turn of the century, the careers of later AEA and APSA leaders were not so exclusively academic (Appendix, Table 9).

Indeed, the training of later leaders reflects the successful growth of graduate education in the U.S. and increased opportunity for specialists. These later leaders more frequently earned their doctorates "at home," particularly in mid-Atlantic universities (Appendix, Table 6). The major regional shift in degree granting is from New England to the mid-Atlantic. The Midwest too began establishing viable social science graduate programs, but New England graduate degrees are as widely held as midwestern degrees among AEA and APSA leaders. In essence, midwestern institutions match but do not surpass New England's graduate educational contribution, while the South and Far West are grossly under-represented. The mid-Atlantic and midwestern graduate schools emerged with the economic growth of these regions and were incorporated with modernizing New England schools, creating the present day's higher educational system. This expansion beyond the ASSA's New England base resulted in a more nearly national system and multiplied specialist positions.

Although regional differences exist in birth, education and work place, the socioeconomic origins of the newer associational leaders were not strikingly dissimilar from those of the ASSA. In all five leader sets, the majority of the fathers for whom we have information were in better than middle-level occupations. Most were from the respectable business and professional strata. Indeed, this strata is strikingly over-represented. Farming and laboring fathers were notably few as were public officials (Appendix, Table 8). Thus, whatever the geographical shift, the social strata of recruitment was unchanged. It was solidly, even massively, better than middling.

Given our conventional sense of social science as a university-based vocation, a surprising amount of variation in higher educational involvement occurs among the samples. About a third of the ASSA leadership were "careerists," spending at least one-half of their work lives in higher educational posts (Appendix, Table 9). But over half the new social scientist leadership were higher educational careerists, with the early AEA and ASS sample figures being eight out of ten. These sizable proportions of higher educational careerists among the newer associations' leadership again reflect the rise of the modern university as an opportunity structure. These proportions imply an increasingly widespread and routine resource dependency upon university managers within each association's leadership, the import of which we have already noted (Chapter 4).

However, as the ASSA leadership was a combination of New England education, professions and capital, so too the newer associational officialdoms included other professionals and businessmen. This is particularly true of the APSA officials and the AEA later leaders. Of the political science association leaders 37 percent were not higher education careerists. Rather, they were the public officials, "lawyers of broader culture," businessmen and cultural professionals so eagerly sought by those founding the associations. Among the AEA later leaders the figure is even higher: 43 percent were non-higher educational careerists, mainly businessmen and lawyers. Only the ASS sample approaches the early AEA's overwhelming proportion of career academics.

While professors continued to dominate the specialist associations, the AEA and APSA's incorporation of nonacademics into leadership positions shows recognition of the soundness of the ASSA's use of experts and influentials to create social science. What were the contributions made by these eagerly sought nonacademics to the specialized social science associations? As we have seen, they could from time to time help finance urgent special projects, such as the AEA's volume on colonial finance. But such occasional efforts were simply part of their larger role in the assciations: they linked the new social science into the wider worlds and higher circles of business, finance and public affairs.

As public officials and businessmen active in reform, they were well positioned to draw on the associations' talents, providing access for experts in government, a wide variety of reform associations and private policy-making organizations. They, and their counter-parts among the memberships, made the new associations much like the ASSA, a union of academics, professionals and businessmen. These nonacademics linked the new social science into the everyday life of government and commerce, into the pragmatic world-views of well-situated participants in a rapidly industrializing capitalistic society. And while they no doubt transmitted academic views into these wider circles, so too they brought the conventional wisdom of those circles into their new social science associations' higher levels.

In brief, the newer disciplinary associations continued the older ASSA pattern uniting specialized knowledge and institutionalized power. Whatever else they were, these associations were not groups of impractical people from ivory towers, separate from the flow of everyday enterprises. Rather, they were not quite national unions of metropolitan-based, specializing academics, and interested professional and businessmen of the broader culture making clear to each other the uses of the new social science in North America. Only the ASS, last organized and least specialized, is an exception; it approximates the early AEA's heavy location of leaders in higher education.

Generally, then, the occupational pattern of the associations' leadership suggests (1) a very widespread and routine resource dependency upon university managers by the majority within each association who pursued academic careers, and (2) the linkage of each association's special social science into well-situated professional and business circles by the minority with nonacademic careers. These two biographical tendencies helped shape the new specialized social science into a mold supporting the continued expansion of American capitalism by technically rationalizing and ideologically legitimizing its rapid industrialization. The St. Louis Congress of Arts and Science provides some insight into the shape of the mold in two ways. First, it illuminates the relationship among resource suppliers in the society at large, university managers and resource-dependent professors, circa 1904. Second, the congress also supplies a ready inventory of the specific social problems and processes the AEA, APSA and ASS took within their special provinces.

ST. LOUIS, 1904

In September 1904 Max Weber went to the St. Louis World's Fair. So did 26 German, 18 French, 16 British and 20 Austrian scholars invited to read papers at the fair's intellectual festival--the International Congress of Arts and Science--a six-day celebration certifying the rise of the United States to first rank in the life of the industrializing West.[9]

The congress signaled the success of university modernizers and association leaders in constructing the resource base necessary both to upgrade the traditional professional schools and to provide the fourth faculty with the means of first-rate knowledge production. The congress's theme was the unity of human knowledge, but its organizational form actually exhibited the social dynamics subdividing the American academy into knowledge specialties directed by captains of erudition. And its content confirmed the substantive differences manifest in the organizational separation of the political scientists and the sociologists out of the AEA. By 1904 association leaders had fashioned the role of the modern social science expert and could stand as equals with representatives of the European universities where once they had trained.

The fair's Board of Directors was a cross section of St. Louis's political-economic elite using the hundredth anniversary of the Louisiana Purchase as an occasion to advertise both their city's and their nation's rising economic fortunes. After some initial consultation with Columbia University's President Nicholas Murray Butler and University of Chicago's President William Rainey Harper, the board underwrote the capital costs of the intellectual side of the fair, eventually spending another $140,000 in operating expenses. Then, the fair's business-based organizers delegated the actual running of the congress to an administrative board heavy with university managers. Columbia's Butler was in the chair. He was flanked by three other university presidents: Chicago's Harper, MIT's Harry S. Pritchett and the University of Missouri's Richard H. Jesse. Rounding out the administrative board were the director of the Field Columbian Museum, the Librarian of Congress, and a New York "lawyer of broader culture."[10]

This university president-dominated board turned to the professorate for the actual planning and staffing of the congress. It created a committee of plans and scope manned by five academics and a consulting engineer. Three of the professors--Albion Small (Chicago, ASS), Harvard's Hugo Munsterburg (psychology) and Hopkins's Simon Newcomb (mathematics)--authored competing plans for the congress. A version of Munsterburg's scheme won their superiors' approval. The three authors then became the congress's scientific organizing committee. Their tasks included writing well-placed magazine articles publicizing the event and defending its worth against scholarly and journalistic detractors, and recruiting participants both at home and overseas. In the U.S. they worked with the emerging specialist associations to select American speakers scheduled to fill the first two days of paper reading. They also spent the summer of 1903 crisscrossing Europe soliciting noted academics to round out the six-day event and shared in the $88,000 the congress spent on scholarly travel and honorariums.[11]

The organization of the International Congress of Arts and Science reveals the hierarchy of the maturing American university. Business leaders wanted scientific participation in proclaiming American progress to the world. They delegated this aspect of the fair to university managers, who in turn handed the details of planning to trusted academics. The professors competed against one another, proposing different plans for the congress. However, when the Munsterburg plan was approved, the three competitive planners then worked amicably together to further the fair, turning to colleagues in the specialist associations to recruit participants. While social science had come of age, the position of its leaders in the fair reflects their place in the academy's hierarchy; leaders reconciled differences to demonstrate expertise satisfying to university managers, who in turn depended on businessmen.

The addresses given at the congress allow us to see the substantive differences that existed within the period's academic division of labor among economists, political scientists and sociologists. Indeed, given the managerial majority of the congress' administrative board, the academic weight of its committee on scope and plans and the process by which its scientific organizing committee negotiated the American speakers' list with the several specialists' associations, there is no doubt that the congress's overall partitioning of intellect amounts to a broadly constructed consensus on the substantive subdivisions existing within university-based knowledge production, circa 1904. Accordingly, reading the congress's proceedings allows us to inventory the content of academic social science at the time the APSA and ASS were formed.

The Congress's Classification of Knowledge

As if to underline the process of organizational differentiation then in progress, the congress's knowledge classification scheme located each of the emerging specializations in a different "science." This placement reveals something of the particular social purpose university managers and academic leaders saw each of the new disciplines serving. Economics was put in the utilitarian sciences. It was no longer viewed as a speculative science more concerned with theories about the social justice of production and distribution than with concrete problems. Instead, economics was seen as a practical tool for stabilizing the economy. Politics won department affiliation among the sciences of social regulation, indicating a widespread understanding of its potential for social control through perfection of the administrative state. Sociology was one of two mental sciences, the other being psychology. This location of sociology suggests some uncertainty on the part of the congress's planners about the social purpose of the newest speciality, as we will see below.

Since the specialists' organizations had cooperated in selecting the speakers, it is not surprising that about half the addresses given in each of these areas were delivered by association leaders.[12] Of the 14 papers read in the economics department's seven sessions, 9 were by AEA leaders.[13] Taken as a whole, the intellectual content of the congress's economics department focused squarely on the industrializing economy, its orderly development under state regulation if necessary, reaffirming an understanding of the expert as a conservative reformer of the existing order.

What of the APSA leadership at the congress? For its part, the APSA held sway over the department of politics much as the AEA did over economics. Six of eleven addresses in the department were given by association leaders.[14] Overall, the congress's department of politics focused rather fully on state administration. This concentration on administration reflects their understanding of the expert role. While their constitution, like the other specialist associations, refers only to objective study, in practice leaders looked for outlets for their expertise in the pragmatic reform of the administrative state. Like the AEA, the APSA was committed to using expertise to improve the existing order.

Indeed, the APSA's concerns complemented the AEA's intellectual interests. The AEA increasingly concentrated attention on purely economic observations and interpretations, limiting its view to those institutions and organizations producing material goods and services to provision the industrializing nation. It argued for state regulation when and where its observations and interpretations showed objective conditions required such. Once state intervention occurred, then the political scientist stood ready to make public administration as effective and efficient as possible. The APSA essentially promoted knowledge production to perfect the state apparatus at all levels: federal, colonial, local and international. Such administrative perfection sought to make state intervention a better tool for furthering America's rapid industrial development by managing the political tensions attending capital and labor conflict, the imperial acquisition of the former Spanish colonies and the widely acknowledged "shame of the cities." In short, the political scientists helped the state manage the social tensions created in the wake of consolidating and centralizing corporate capitalism, while the wake itself was made broader, deeper and more powerful by the very economic interventions prescribed by the AEA-dominated discipline. But as the economists narrowed their focus to the essentially economic, so the political scientists constricted their vision to the purely political. These foreshortenings of scholarly perspectives had a major impact on what was to become sociology's subject matter. With the economy and the state firmly preempted by specialists centered in the AEA and APSA, sociologists had to find their focus elsewhere.

The St. Louis congress placed sociology with psychology in the division of mental sciences. Of the sociology department's seven papers, four were given by ASS leaders. Franklin H. Giddings and George E. Vincent sketched the field's general situation at a departmental session chaired by fellow leader Frank W. Blackmar. Lester Ward shared the social structure lectern with the Austrian army's Field Marshall Gustav Ratzenhofer and Germany's Ferdinand Toennies, while AEA leader Frederic W. Moore chaired. In sociology's only other section, E.A. Ross offered his observations on social psychology, while ASS co-leader E.C. Hayes acted as secretary.[15]

The sociologists were the only new social scientists to claim that the congress had misplaced their specialization. Blackmar, chairing the department's general session, delivered himself of the angry opinion that sociology was not a mental but a master science. Since it alone studied social structure--the basic recurring patterns among social actors seen in all social institutions--it could hardly be reduced to psychologisms. Because social structures made up all institutions--including political and economic ones--sociology was the scholarly sun under which all other social sciences would flourish.[16] And Ward argued much the same in his paper.

Of course, Blackmar's position was overdrawn. The claim of not being a mental science was weakened by the sociologists mounting a session on social psychology filled with exactly the sort of reductionism Blackmar protested. How could a science of social structure tolerate a section seriously using psychological metaphors, such as "the social mind." Furthermore, at ASS leader Charles Ellwood's estimation, three-fourths of work then being done in sociology was on social psychology, not on social structure.[17] Finally, while social structure might well be the key analytical unit in comprehending the sociology of political and economic institutions, knowledge production in these areas was already narrowly focused on practical problematics: the necessary conditions of state intervention and its administrative perfection. The ASS with sociology as "übersozial-wissenschaft" was too late, the crop had already been gathered.

In the main the ASS was left with those concerns other specialist associations had not appropriated from the ASSA. As the ASSA neared the end of its contribution to academic social science, sociology was its heir apparent. But of the ASSA's focal interests, the AEA and APSA had taken over economics and politics, medicine had assumed responsibility for public health, and university managers were concerned with education, especially public schools as university feeders.[18] In 1904, sociologists could only make claims on what was left over.

First there remained the ASSA's generalized concern with a unified and law-like social theory. This the sociologists appropriated and articulated in its most modern guise, the theory of social structure. It need be added that the ASS leaders--like the ASSA and indeed other new social science leaders--were quite selective in advancing notions of social structure. They were particularly sympathetic to English, French and German views supporting a reformed capitalism, precluding Marxian and other forms of critical analysis of social structure.[19] They were, in short, open to theories recognizing the economic center as a keystone of social structure and not to anti-capitalistic notions of social relations.

Second, there remained an odd lot of former ASSA concerns to focus the ASS around. What was available is suggested by the sessions held at the congress's department of social science, conceived as a specialty in a wider science of social regulation. Indeed, the department of social science's sessions forecast much of the content claimed by twentieth-century American sociology: "The family" (where ASS leader George Howard spoke), "the rural community" (at which Max Weber spoke), "the urban community," "the industrial group" (where Werner Sombart spoke), "the dependent group" and "the criminal group."[20] In time, these topics entered the university curriculum and the learned journals as principal subjects of the sociologists' specialized knowledge. While these subjects provided opportunities to put practical expertise to work integrating problematic groups into industrial society, sociologists were in the main less often called as experts than AEAers or APSAers. In many instances, the practical aspects of their subject matter were handled by professionalizing social workers or untrained reformers volunteering for charity work. Lacking routine outlets for their expertise, sociologists had difficulty in establishing reliable resource support. Indeed, the ASS remained the weakest of the specialist's associations until after the Second World War, with most of its members trained at Chicago where two leaders channeled resources to sociology: George Vincent was dean of the undergraduate school and later president of the Rockefeller Foundation, while Albion Small was dean of the graduate school. Together they worked to sustain sociology despite its practitioners' irregular access to expert service.

In 1904, then, sociology was beginning to establish its monopoly of knowledge from reformist European social theory and the ASSA's leftovers. While sometimes seeking superior standing as an over-arching social science, as a practical matter sociology gathered to itself those topics neglected by the earlier specialties formed out of the ASSA's concerns. If it was not an "over-science," it could try to monopolize theories of society as long as economists and political scientists ignored them.

The Organization of the New Social Sciences, 1904

The unrealized aspiration of sociology to be an "over-science" is ironic in view of the congress's thematic commitment to showing a unity of knowledge. However, other specialists' inattention to the possibility of an integrative or master science points to the function served by the differentiation of the disciplines in the U.S. The APSA breaking away from the AEA was an organizational embodiment of the disintegration of "political economy" as the elemental subject matter of American social science. This disintegration mirrored shifts in the social significance of the intellectual problems presented by rapid industrialization. During the AEA's first twenty years, 1885-1904, the pressing technical and ideological problem of the economy per se had found more or less adequate approaches, if not actually viable solutions, in the fragile knowledge base established largely at the aspiring graduate universities and husbanded by the specialists centered in the AEA. However, the very adequacy of these approaches and their expression in legislative action and regulatory schemes created newer administrative problems and political tensions requiring further academic attention. These problems and tensions the political scientists claimed as their particular occupational concern, continuing the economists' well-developed sense of exclusionary expertise. Where economists defined economic decisions as narrowly technical problems too detailed for everybody's evaluation, the political scientists saw popular issues best solved by administrative science in the service of a centralizing state rather than contested in the partisan arena.

Perhaps because they were heir to the most ill-defined and residual areas of expertise and hence self-interest, only the sociologists could grapple with the thorny question of who benefits from existing power arrangements and what society might be like if these were changed. While ASS leaders did not deal directly with the pragmatic problems of a nationalizing economy and a centralizing state, like their peers in the AEA and APSA, they were largely committed to American economic development firmly within a capitalistic framework. And like their fellow leaders, they wanted major social problems to be solved by academically based, "value-free" experts.

Evidence of the commitment of university-based social scientists to the expert role is nicely captured by their service to the expanding government sector (see Appendix, Table 10). Their efforts to improve the existing order through expertise shows the continuity of the ASSA's initial vision of social science as a policy science used for practical reform. Like the ASSA leadership, more than half of the discipline leaders held expert appointed posts at local, state and federal levels. The range of positions was considerable, including municipal charter, harbor, budget, revenue, parks, school and other commissions, state constitutional conventions as well as tax code, banking, insurance, "economy and efficiency" boards, federal bureaus dealing with labor, currency, railroads, immigration, the census and so on.

Although university-based specialists saw social science as a policy science shaping and implementing reform, the expert role was fashioned at least in part as a response to their dependence on the university. As a result, specialists, always careful not to alienate resource holders, did not enter the partisan political arena so often as did the ASSAers. Since Appendix Table 10 reports somewhat differing periods for each set of organizational leaders, the ratios of posts and persons within each set is the fairest measure of the university-based social scientists' reluctance to hold party posts and contest elections. Thus, the ASSA's leaders' service as appointed experts only slightly outweighs their political activity, the ratio of posts being one to two. In sharp contrast, the sociologists' ratio of appointive to elective posts is two to six, for political scientists, six to two, for "later" economists, five to seven, and for "early" economists, it is a remarkable 20 to none. And the ratios for "person" parallels that for "posts": one to four (ASSA); eight to none (ASS); five to four (APSA); five to eight (AEA-later); and ten to none (AEA-early). Again, the early AEA is a transitional group, differentiating itself most completely from the ASSA in the years when social science was being institutionalized in the modern university. However, the later AEA, as well as the APSA and ASS, continued to be resource dependent and their political activity did not begin to match the ASSA's.

Since specialists were wary of the political arena for fear of having their still tenuous knowledge monopolies challenged, they sought to move major social problems into the domain of "objective" university-based knowledge production. In this, they received support from their constituency—socially conscious corporate leaders, a host of middle-strata reformers and university managers--who were as much concerned with the political machine's mass base as a threat to their notions of social order as with halting graft and corruption. Thus, specialists and their constituency advocated solving major social problems through administrative decision making legitimated by "value-free" expertise as a necessary reform of government in a complex industrial age. However, as Henry George had warned, expansion of administrative decision making preempted popular discussion and debate on technical issues with moral and political implications for daily life and undermined the basis of democracy by making experts and not citizens policy makers. And while experts professed to be beyond party or class, they could not go against their constituency too often without jeopardizing their resource base.

Of course, the pattern of appointments reflects more than the declining popular control of state-employed expertise. The posts accepted by the discipline leaders also show somewhat substantive differences displayed at the St. Louis festival of the industrialized mind. For example, the AEA leaders, both early and later, found much work regulating domestic markets--labor, capital and infrastructure agencies were their expert bailiwick. For political scientists, the foreign scene and municipal matters were of special significance, while the sociologists seem as under-employed as their expertise was ill defined (see Appendix, Table 10).

Despite the considerable substantive differentiation apparent in 1904, the new social scientists reflected their common origins in the

AEA. They were agreed that social questions should be decided by experts like themselves, experts commanding monopolies of professionalized knowledge. According to the ideology of expertise developed in their associations, experts were entrusted with their monopolies because they were value-neutral scientists using objective knowledge for the common good. However, experts understood the wisdom of defining the common good as congruent with the existing order if they were to secure resources for their new fields. As experts, they reformed their system's most glaring defects while protecting its essential structure. Thus, the new specialist associations practiced the role learned by early AEA leaders in their dealings with university managers, nonpartisan reformers of the broader culture and leaders from the emerging economic center.

The Role in Action and Role Defence

In the next section of this book, we will look at academically based specialists practicing their role as experts in service outside the university. To do this, we will examine the part leaders played in the National Civic Federation (Chapter 8), in a variety of municipal reform movements as well as international agencies (Chapter 9) and in the foundations being started by the great philanthropists--Russell Sage, Carnegie and Rockefeller (Chapter 10). By seeing what experts offered their constituency through service, we will better understand the dimensions of the role.

Although association leaders first targeted state service as the arena for their expertise, they quickly realized that private-sector service was crucial for sponsorship to administrative positions as well as maintenance of contact with their constituency. Their understanding of the importance of private support for their work in public administration is captured by one of their earliest ventures in state service, the Committee on Colonial Finance, where private patrons were found to insure that their work received a hearing (see Chapter 6). Throughout the Progressive era, leaders continued this practice, working in private organizations that influenced state policy. The organizations with which they chose to work were almost invariably nonpartisan, funded by socially conscious corporate capitalists and often had memberships made up of middle-strata reformers. Their private service reinforced their state service, and vice versa, with the expert functioning as a link between the respectable classes and the bureaucracy.

Nonpartisan private-sector reform organizations were legion in the Progressive years and leaders participated in a wide spectrum: the National Civic Federation, the American Association for Labor Legislation, the national and international Chamber of Commerce, the National Tax Association, the National Consumers League, the National Municipal League, the Citizens Union, the League to Enforce Peace and so on. Indeed, leaders' biographies indicate that they could be found in almost any private reform organization that recognized the economic center as the keystone of the American social structure. The only associations they regularly eschewed were with groups who were popularly based and loud in their criticism of their constituency—industrial unionists, Socialists, Non-Partisan Leaguers and the like.

In the following chapters, we focus on only a few of the wide array of reform organizations and policy-making groups for which leaders provided expertise. Our choice of organizations was largely guided by their centrality to the subject matter that the disciplines claimed as their own. Thus, we concentrate on organizations that are regarded by scholars of the Progressive era as significant policy-making forums in areas of economic, political and social control. While leaders from all associations served in these organizations, the NCF was primarily concerned with economic policy; the National Municipal League and its ancillary municipal research bureaus with problems related to perfecting the state's administrative apparatus; foreign policy organizations with expanding administration internationally to smooth the workings of world capitalism. In the main, foundations reflected the policy concerns of these forums and worked to legitimate them with scholarly research.

Since these organizations were designed to influence public policy, when we look at the part leaders played in them, we see the interaction between private sector and the state in shaping public policy. We see too that as experts came to be routinely used in decision-making processes, questions about the legitimacy of their knowledge were raised by those to the right and left of the economic center. On the right, conservatives troubled by increased labor violence in the years immediately preceding the war began viewing reforming academics askance, and an outbreak of academic freedom cases resulted. On the left, criticism of workers and radical reformers before the U.S. Industrial Relations Commission caused the issuing of a scathing denunciation of foundation-funded research as producing knowledge that benefited sponsors rather than the common good. In Chapter 11, we look at social scientists' response to these attacks. Social science leaders organized the Association of University Professors Committee A and formally defined and defended the expert role. Their Declaration of Principles was based on their experience of the expert role in action of the Progressive era and is of critical importance, for it still forms the basis of the twentieth-century academic role. Thus, in our concluding chapter, we sketch the continuance of the role, now generalized to all academics, through the AAUP's Committee A.

NOTES

1. Albert Somit and Joseph Tanenhaus, *The Development of American Political Science: From Burgess to Behavioralism* (Boston: Allyn and Bacon, 1967), p. 36; for the funding of *AJS*, see Small to Harper, 18 December 1897, Albion Small Papers, University of Chicago Library.

2. "The Organization of the American Political Science Association," *Proceedings of the APSA*, 1 (1904): 5-6.

3. Ibid., pp. 7-12.

4. Ibid., pp. 12-17.

5. See for example Albion Small in discussion of F.H. Giddings, "A Theory of Social Causation," *Publications of the American Economic Association* (*PAEA*), 3d series, 5 (May 1904): 176; W.M. West in discussion of F.H. Giddings, "A Theory of Social Causation," *PAEA*, 3d series, 5 (May 1904): 194-198.

6. Official Report, "Organization of the American Sociological Society," *American Journal of Sociology*, 11, 4 (January 1906): 555-569.

7. Thomas A. Haskell, *The Emergence of Professional Social Science* (Urbana, Ill.: University of Illinois Press, 1977).

8. Our primary data sources are: *Dictionary of American Biography*, 25 vols. (New York: Charles Scribner's Sons, 1928-1977); *National Cyclopedia of American Biography*, 91 vols. (Clifton, N.J.: James T. White, 1892-1978); *Who Was Who in America*, 7 vols. (Chicago: Marquis, 1963-1976). Hereafter, these works are cited as *DAB*, *NC* and *WWW*. More details about the several samples are found in Chapter 2.

9. A.W. Coats, "American Scholarship Comes of Age: The Louisiana Purchase Exposition 1904," Journal of the History of Ideas 22 (July–September 1961): 404–412; George Haines, IV, and Frederick H. Jackson, "A Neglected Landmark in the History of Ideas," Mississippi Valley Historical Review 34 (September 1947): 201–220; Howard J. Rogers, ed., Congress of Arts and Science, Universal Exposition, St. Louis, 1904, 8 vols. (Boston and New York: Houghton, Mifflin, 1905-1907); Daniel Fox, The Discovery of Abundance: S.N. Patten and the Transformation of Economic Theory (Ithaca, N.Y.: Cornell University Press, 1967), p. 43.

10. Howard J. Rogers, "The History of the Congress," in Rogers, ed., Congress, 1: 1–44, and Haines and Jackson, "A Neglected Landmark," p. 207.

11. Rogers, "The History of the Congress," 1: 5-10, 17-18, 20, 44; Coates, "American Scholarship"; Haines and Jackson, "A Neglected Landmark," p. 208.

12. Rogers, ed., Congress, 1: 66-73.

13. Frank A. Fetter, "Fundamental Conceptions and Methods of Economics," in H. Rogers, ed., Congress, 7: 7–20; John Bates Clark, "Economic Theory in a New Character and Relation," in ibid., pp. 47-56; Jacob B. Hollander, "The Scope and Methods of Political Economy," in ibid., pp. 57-67; William Z. Ripley, "Problems of Transportation," in ibid., pp. 95-112; Carl Plehn, "Foreign Markets," in ibid., pp. 133-147; Horace White, "Our Monetary Equilibrium," in ibid., pp. 151-160; Henry Carter Adams, "Relation of the Science of Finance to Allied Sciences," in ibid., pp. 179-189; E.R.A. Seligman, "Pending Problems in Public Finance," in ibid., pp. 190-200; and B.H. Meyers, "Present Problems in Insurance," in ibid., pp. 236-252.

14. W.W. Willoughby, "Political Philosophy," in H. Rogers, ed., Congress, 7: pp. 309-325; George C. Wilson, "Problems of Political Theory," in ibid., pp. 326-338; James Bryce, "National

Administration," in ibid., pp. 339-352; Bernard Moses, "The Control of Dependencies Inhabited by the Less Developed Races," in ibid., pp. 399-416; Albert Shaw, "Relations of Municipal Administration," in ibid., pp. 419-433.

15. Franklin H. Giddings, "The Concepts and Methods of Sociology," in H. Rogers, ed., Congress, 5: 787-799; George E. Vincent, "The Development of Sociology," in ibid., pp. 800-812; Lester Ward, "Evolution of Social Structures," in ibid., pp. 842-855; Gustav Ratzenhofer, "The Problems of Sociology," in ibid., pp. 815-824; Ferdinand Toennies, "The Present Problems of Social Structure," in ibid., pp. 825-841; E.A. Ross, "The Present Problems of Social Psychology," in ibid., pp. 869-882.

16. Frank W. Blackmar, untitled remarks introducing the departmental addresses by Giddings and Vincent, note 27, in H. Rogers, ed., Congress, 5: 785-786.

17. For example, "The union of men concerns us . . . because their natures are correspondingly modified . . . the true community at once enlarges and imprisons minds. . . . The coincident ideas men have in their group become a spiritual structure, the group-individuality, which trenches upon, even overshadows and well-nigh supplants, their personal individuality," Ross, "The Present Problems," p. 871. Such ideas as "group-individuality" are also in W.I. Thomas's paper at the same session, even though Thomas begins by denying the "social mind" concept. See his "The Province of Social Psychology," in H. Rogers, ed., Congress, 5: 860-868. And according to ASS leader Charles Ellwood's remarks introducing the Ross-Thomas social psychology session, three-fourths of the work then being done in sociology was on social psychology not social structure. See his untitled remarks in ibid., pp. 858-859.

18. See, for example, Hugh Hawkins, Between Europe and America: The Educational Leadership of Charles W. Eliot (New York: Oxford University Press, 1972), particularly his work with the National

Education Association.

19. Herman and Julia Schwendinger, _The Sociologists of the Chair: A Radical Analysis of the Formative Years of North American Sociology, 1883-1922_ (New York: Basic Books, 1974), and Irving Zeitlin, _Ideology and the Development of Sociological Theory_, (Englewood Cliffs, N.J.: Prentice-Hall, 1968).

20. See Department 22, _Social Science_, in H. Rogers, ed., _Congress_, 7: 663-876.

8
"Both a Bathroom and a Piano:" The New Social Science Leaders in the National Civic Federation, 1903-1914

By 1904 the transformation of the ASSA's old social science was well under way. The new social scientists in the AEA, APSA and the ASS had divided up social studies into their particular occupational specialties. They shared a sense of role, accepting as their common aim the continuing technical perfection and constant ideological support of American capitalistic development. They willingly embraced their collective function as intellectuals in the service of the rising national corporate center. In this chapter, we trace their participation in the Progressive period's premier political economic policy forum, the National Civic Federation.

The National Civic Federation (NCF) as Opportunity Structure

From the new social scientists' perspective, political economic policy forums, like the NCF and the National Association of Manufacturers (NAM), were something of a "main chance" to advance their careers and their collective craft. Unlike classrooms and learned associations, these organizations did not meet under the direction and supervision of academics. Rather they were settings at which professors and their ideas were themselves examined and evaluated. Here social scientists could gain a hearing for technical schemes and ideological projects from socially aware industrialists, financiers and political leaders. Such well-off and sensitive audiences were receptive to social science's potential for increasing the overall efficiency of capitalistic enterprise and solving the many problems of rapid industrialization.

Academics who were invited to participate came eagerly to these forums to meet possible sponsors for their careers and crafts. The patronage opportunities were made abundantly clear by the very fact of the organizations themselves, since the bills were usually paid by the socially sensitive businessmen. Furthermore, the economic and political leaders controlling and contributing to these organizations often opened doors, sponsoring access to other powerful political-economic decision makers. In essence, these organizations were political-economic seminars where academic ideas could find appreciation and application, being corrected and confirmed as ameliorative blueprints before their deployment in city, state and nation. Such ideas--and their authors--were clearly candidates for sponsored access to the "right" person and research site. Academic careers and crafts were also candidates for immediate sponsorship by organizations like the NCF and its patrons, as when topical commissions and departments were established to survey politically sensitive economic or social issues.

By all accounts, the NCF was the most influential business-sponsored political-economic forum group operating during the Progressive period.[1] It sought wide influence in political-economic policy formation. It was dominated by bankers, financiers and officials from large corporations. It brought together business, labor and professional leaders to ponder the social consequences of rapid capitalistic industrialization. And it used willing academics to elaborate ideology within a capitalist developmental perspective and to blueprint technical solutions for problems therein defined.

The NCF's 1899 founding Statement of Purpose makes clear its desire

to organize the best brains of the nation in an educational movement towards the solution of some of the great problems related to industrial and social progress: to provide for the study and discussion of questions of national import, to aid thus in the crystallization of the most enlightened public opinion; and when desirable, to promote legislation therewith.[2]

The ideology guiding this "educational movement" stressed a self-conscious, practical conservatism, one claiming a business responsibility for the state of the nation. It assumed the desirability of a business system of capitalistic enterprise. It argued the essential harmony of all interests in society, denying any irreconcilable conflict between capital and labor. Finally, it sought a middle path between socialism on the left and the unpredictability of unregulated, competitive laissez-faire capitalism on the right. The NCF's ideology, then, was one of practical conservatism, stressing elite-guided, popular education as a mechanism of gradual social change planned to preserve and enhance the emerging corporate center.[3]

To serve its purposes, the NCF selectively recruited "the best brains," first from the worlds of business and labor, then from the academy. From business, the NCF successfully sought out the membership of the larger enterprises. Between 1900 and 1910, it had business members from almost a third of the nation's 434[4] largest firms, those with a capitalization of over $10 million. This, however, excluded from its conference tables representatives of smaller, regional firms. These firms were to find their interests articulated in alternative organizations, like the National Association of Manufacturers.[5] From the ranks of organized labor, the NCF gathered to itself anti-socialist leaders, drawing mainly from the AFL-affiliated trade unions. This excluded left-laborites of all stripes, including those organizing along industrial union lines, like the International Workers of the World (IWW).[6]

In theory the NCF was to concern itself with a broad cross section of social problems. But in its first five years, the NCF operated most notably at the frontline of capital-labor struggle, particularly in the larger industries from which it drew its dominant members. It actively mediated some 500 industrial disputes during these five years and was especially successful when both management and labor were NCF participants. In this work, employers were urged to recognize and cooperate with conservative union leaders, who in turn would encourage their membership to make demands consistent with the continued development of large-scale capitalist enterprise.[7] In effect, the NCF became the nub of a labor policy suited to one segment of the American economy: large-scale enterprise. Since this segment was rising to domination within the entire economy, the NCF became a vehicle for the emerging economic center's labor theory and practice.

Academic Participation

The use of the NCF as a labor relations organization for the
emerging corporate center was especially apparent to socialists of all
sorts and to businessmen whose small- and middle-scale enterprises were
vulnerable in an economy dominated by large-scale firms. Accordingly,
these leftists and economically threatened businessmen launched
independent ideological attack upon the NCF's labor theory and practice.
Leftists used forums everywhere. They even used the AFL's annual
conventions to question its leaderships participation in the NCF. The
middle business captured the National Association of Manufacturers and
created auxiliary organizations like the Citizen's Industrial
Association (CIA). They loudly denounced the NCF's labor schemes as
anti-capitalistic, mounting a militant anti-union "open shop" campaign
to break the NCF's successful combination of large-scale capital and
labor.[8] Thus, the NCF found itself in ideological battle with both the
left and the right on the details of its well-publicized labor
practices.

To defend itself as well as consolidate its position as a policy
enterprise, the NCF began a public relations counter-offensive and
dramatically enlarged its concerns beyond collective bargaining. It
turned to the nation's knowledge industry for the scholarship needed to
clarify further the fundamental capitalist concepts its labor policies
expressed and to devise additional mechanisms of technical amelioration.
It also began a journal of record, The NCF Review, to clarify its
policies and plans. Published irregularly, the Review was intended to
be sent

to the principal libraries and educational institutions of every
country; to the executive and departmental officials of every
nation; to the headquarters of all professional, literary and
scientific societies; to organizations, both national and local, of
employers and employees; and to thousands of editors, clergymen,
educators, and other leaders of thought in the professions,
commerce, finance and industry.[9]

Its first 40 issues from April 1903 through May 1914 are filled with the notices and reports of annual meetings, conferences, departments and commissions marking the NCF's massive efforts to influence public policy. They provide a useful if not exhaustive inventory of the decade's scholarship in the service of corporate power.

The Review reports some 142 educational managers, new social science association leaders and other academics participating in 20 NCF activities from 1903 to 1914. As shown in Table 3, some 57 were academic managers while offering themselves to the NCF. Some 45 were association leaders when found in the Review. Another 44 academics are named in the NCF's reported activities. Neither managers nor discipline leaders, these professors compose a fortuitous comparison group to measure the leaders' NCF work. These 44 professors involved themselves in 48 events, a little more than one each (1.1). The 57 managers participated in 74 activities, averaging about the same (1.3). In contrast, the 45 association leaders engaged in 139 projects, about three each (3.1). They are clearly "action intellectuals" when compared to either the academic managers or to their accidentally sampled peers.

Among the disciplines, of course, some variation occurs. The 12 political scientists are more active than the 33 economists, the averages being 4.6 and 3.3 respectively. The five sociologists are quite inactive when compared to the others, averaging about the same number of projects as the fortuitous comparison group (1.2). Such variation among discipline leaders reflects the content of their knowledge monopolies. In effect, the older political economy had been split into three related but different intellectual commodities. Both the economists and the political scientists had something sought after by those shaping the emerging center's positions on the issues of the day. The economists successfully claimed exclusive rights to define the academy's theory of business enterprise. The political scientists similarly seized the theory of the state and its administration. The sociologists had the rest: what was left over from the older political economy once the dynamics of firms and the state have been removed. In the NCF's patronage structure, then, the sociologists clearly have little special knowledge to exchange for resources. However, behind such shadowy quantitative results is a qualitative reality, one illuminated by a more direct inspection of the NCF's workings.

Table 3: Participation in Selected National Civic Federation Activities, 1903-1914

YEAR	NCF ACTIVITY	EDUCATIONAL MANAGERS	"OTHER ACADEMICS"	All*	DISCIPLINE LEADERS AEA	APSA	ASS
1904	Dept. of Industrial Economics	3	0	12	11	3	1
	Ownership of Public Utilities Comm.	2	5	13	10	5	0
1906	Dept. of Industrial Economics	2	0	5	4	5	0
	Conference & Dept. of Immigration	17	15	18	13	7	1
	Dept. of Conciliation & Arbitration	1	0	1	0	1	0
	National Conference on Election Laws	0	1	1	0	1	0
1907	National Child Labor Commission	0	0	1	1	1	0
	National Conference on Trusts	1	3	6	5	2	0
1908	Advisory Council	13	3	13	11	4	0
1910	Uniform Law Conference	5	4	6	5	3	0
	Conference on Social Insurance	0	2	1	1	0	0
	Compensation Department	0	1	1	1	0	0
1911	Commission on Railroads & Municipalities	0	1	6	3	3	0
1912	Dept. of Regulation of Corporations	1	0	6	5	3	0
1914	Dept. on Agricultural Conditions	2	1	1	1	0	0
	Dept. of Industrial Economy; Survey	23	12	23	17	7	3
1903-14	NFC Executive	4	0	6	5	3	0
	Drafts Legislation/Lobbies Congress	0	0	7	6	3	0
	Attends Annual Meeting	2	2	7	5	1	0
	Participates in Branches	5	2	5	5	1	0
	Sum of participations	74	48	139	109	55	6
	Number of participants	57	44	45	33	12	5
	Average participations	1.3	1.1	3.1	3.3	4.6	1.2

*Duplication occurs, since some leaders led more than one discipline.

Managers as Mediators

The 57 educational managers mentioned in the NCF's Review represent a broad cross section of those leading the American higher learning. Thirty-six were presidents. Another five served as trustees, chancellors or syndics. A final dozen were deans. But in the NCF, few of these educational executives were in a position to command. Only 4 of the 57 became members of the NCF's governing executive, even though each year there was room for many more. These four managers did sit with some of the nation's top capitalists and labor leaders and they no doubt made their contribution to the NCF's developing policies, but most educational managers did not reach that pinnacle of power in the business-dominated NCF.

Rather than sit on the executive and help govern the NCF most managers worked where the association leaders and other faculty did. All three participation distributions in Table 3 thicken and thin at roughly the same activities. On these projects, the managers helped define the social limits of the expert's role. As Veysey notes, turn-of-the-century university officials experienced a collective "drift away from inner conviction toward the role of promotional agent."[10] Such managers were as interested in resource procurement as were the discipline leaders on their staffs. The rhetoric used by educational management when setting expert limits is suggested in the diary of William Weyl, a promising Wharton instructor who opted in 1899 for a brilliant career as political journalist. Outside academia, he thought, "I am not obligated to consult anybody as to what I say. . . . I am not obligated to consider the effects of my words upon the revenues or prestige of the University."[11] In sum, then, the educational managers were big fish in their own ponds, but middle-level operatives at best in the NCF's many projects. As promotional agents for their several enterprises, they mediated as best they could the knowledge of their faculty and the power of the business leaders, setting expectational and behavioral limits on the words and deeds of their hired heads.

It should be added that few of the discipline leaders sat on the executive of the NCF. The proportion--6 of 45--is double that of the educational managers (13.3 percent versus 7.0 percent), although it is still low. More interestingly, only two of the six association leaders who saw the executive committee room were career academics. The four others were businessmen who linked the disciplines into worlds outside the university. Such businessmen, like the educational managers, no doubt mediated the relationship between knowledge and power on both the board and the projects of the NCF, underlining the expectational and behavioral limits of the expert social scientist serving the emerging corporate center.

Although the educational managers and associational leaders did not control the NCF's decision-making executive and hence its policy directions, they nonetheless came willingly to its projects. They did so because they were in fundamental harmony with its ideology. Indeed in the AEA's presidential addresses and debates, they had acted as its authors and spokesmen. Accordingly, they welcomed the NCF's invitations as opportunities to affirm and elaborate their vision of capitalist industrialization. Further, they found in such forums their own interests. Here were opportunities to apply and test their ideas perfecting the workings of the political economy. Here were chances to deploy schemes using their skills and training, thereby offering them the means of career and craft development. Little wonder that they made themselves available to the NCF, its sponsors and its patrons.

Creating Ideology

Some of the NCF's projects shown in Table 3 permitted the managers and leaders to exhibit their skills mainly as ideological spokesmen for the emerging order, while others allowed showing their talents principally as technologists and rationalizers making the system more efficient. Certainly, the Department of Industrial Economics (DIE) was intended to combat the counter-corporate propaganda generated by the NAM and its allied organizations.[12] Viewed as an effort in popular economic education, the DIE was to host meetings where prominent capitalists, labor leaders, public figures and economic experts would discuss policy issues, coming to solutions consistent with the NCF's ideological line. These foregone conclusions were then to be spread far and wide by the media. As the NCF's executive secretary put it, the DIE was to be the "hot air" department.[13]

The DIE from 1904 on held conferences examining industrial efficiency, the open shop, piece work, wages and working hour legislation--in fact much of the NCF's centralist labor policy. Espousing "the evolutionary rather than the revolutionary method" of capital-labor relations, the NCF pressed its conference results on opinion gatekeepers everywhere: the press, the bar, the church, the legislature and the university. These examinations and their conclusions were to be routinely presented as the results of citizens and experts meeting without ideological parameters.[14]

Sometimes, however, even the NCF's best-planned efforts at ideological production went awry. For example, Harvard's President Eliot proved a poor choice as the DIE's founding chairman. He took the DIE's well-publicized first meeting to expound his own evolving labor philosophy, one somewhat at odds with the NCF's policy. Giving clear comfort to the NAM's anti-unionists, he debated and devalued the NCF's endorsement of conservative, business unionism collectively bargaining its way to apolitical prosperity for its members. Eliot's emphasis was increasingly on one's right to work (or not), despite a union's collective agreement. Such individualism soon put Eliot well to the NCF's right on labor and disqualified him from continued leadership of the department. He shortly thereafter resigned from the NCF and a summary of his individualistic labor philosophy was routinely printed in the Square Deal, an NAM/CIA counter-corporate vehicle.[15]

Such failures only served to underscore the difficulties of creating an ideology sufficient to the emerging center's needs, enhancing the value of the skills brought to the NCF's forums by the associational leaders. The DIE continued its ideological production of "hot air." For example, it shared sponsorship of projects like the NCF's 1905 Commission on Public Utilities Ownership.[16] And educational managers and associational leaders continued giving themselves to such works as well as more generally endorsing the NCF's overall legitimacy by serving on its Advisory Council.[17]

"Both a Bathroom and a Piano"

Perhaps the high point of the academic managers' and association leaders' involvements in the NCF's ideological construction efforts was the 1913-1914 social survey project. Talcott Williams, head of Columbia's journalism school and NCF executive member, chaired the project's committee on plan and scope, where his labor was lightened by three AEA leaders: E.R.A. Seligman, J.W. Jenks (both of whom were on the NCF executive) and C.P. Neill.[18] Williams explained the purposes of the survey to the NCF's 1913 white-tie annual dinner meeting by noting both the growing electoral strength of the socialists and the increasing violence of the syndicalists. Such opposition from the left offered a new and significant ideological challenge to the NCF's efforts "to bring labor and capital into closer and more harmonious relations" within a community of interests. Since the socialists and syndicalists seemed to argue a shared ideological line, their challenge could be defeated by successfully debating that common position.

According to Williams, both socialists and syndicalists held that "the existing organization of society has worked injustice and social and economic exploitation of the many by the few." Therefore, he urged an NCF-sponsored inventory of social and industrial progress created by capitalist development in America. On the eve of its undertaking Williams offered more than the need for such a survey. He also proffered its overall conception and foregone conclusions.

First, the basis and plea of this social attack needs be met and answered. Second, the information already accessible in regard to the shortening of hours, the improvement of labor conditions, the increase in wages, the advance in the standard of living, the betterment in housing, the widening of education, the opening of opportunity, and the growth of the savings of the many, need to be made visible. . . . We have in America today that miracle the world has never seen before--the wage earner's house which has both a bathroom and a piano. To make that sort of thing visible is the object of this survey. What is needed is not simply to show what exists now, but to demonstrate that what exists now has come about by a steady, continuous improvement.[19]

To fund this Survey of Social, Civic and Industrial Progress, some $50,000 was raised. Significant contributors included W.K. Vanderbilt, Andrew Carnegie, AT&T's Theodore Vail and International Nickel's chairman Robert M. Thompson, who together put up one-third of the amount.[20] This money supported the deliberations of dozens of capitalists, corporate managers, educationists and academics who enlisted to work in the survey's 25 topical committees.

To direct the survey, the NCF turned to AEA leader Roland P. Faulkner, who had been employed as assistant director of their Immigration Department in 1907. Faulkner was aided by the survey's Executive Council, which included a number of fellow AEA leaders. Professor Jenks was chair of both the survey's executive committee and its immigration committee. Professor Irving Fisher, a physical fitness enthusiast, headed the public health committee. Banker E.R.L. Gould led the committee on industrial savings and loans and worked on the committee on the distribution of ownership in investments chaired by Professor E.R.A. Seligman, of the investment banking family. ASS leader and University of Minnesota President George Vincent headed the committee on educational opportunity.

Other associational leaders sat on the committees themselves. The APSA's W.F. Willoughby and AEAer Charles P. Neill served on the child labor committee. The AEA's Thomas N. Carver worked for the agricultural conditions committee, and he joined AEA and ASS leader Edward A. Ross on Jenks' immigration body. AEAers Frank Fetter and banker Paul M. Warburg worked on Seligman's committee of ownership in investments. Lawyer Frederic N. Judson served the free speech and public assembly committee, while fellow APSR leader and the U.S. president's son Harry A. Garfield sat on the municipal government committee. AEAer John B. Clark joined the committee on the theory of surplus value. Finally, most of these leaders also were members of the survey's advisory council, thereby further lending their legitimacy to the effort as did fellow leaders Henry W. Farnum (AEA), Ernst Freund and Leo S. Rowe (both APSA), Albion Small (ASS) and Albert Shaw (AEA and APSA).[21]

The social survey was to be an inventory of progress through capitalist development serving to defend the emerging corporate center against new ideological attacks from the left. But like the DIE's earlier adventure with Eliot's stewardship, it served to suggest the problems of ideology manufacture during the continuing chaos engendered by capitalist industrialization. As the survey moved toward completion,

NCF's labor members found themselves increasingly unwilling to support this whitewash of American capitalism, perhaps anticipating that a working class convinced that its evolutionary possession of bathrooms and pianos might well find union leaders unnecessary.

For example, in 1913 former United Mine Workers president John Mitchell had looked over the survey for the NCF executive. He told them the membership of the advisory council was open to criticism, since it was heavy with those who had good reason to be pleased with the status quo. However, he thought such criticism would be negated by the social science experts that the NCF would employ. In short, since "the actual work will be done by experts who will seek only for facts and as the conclusions will be drawn from facts," the question of pro-capitalist bias would be answered by the scientific legitimacy of academic experts.[22]

But Mitchell's hopes that the experts would draw unbiased conclusions "from facts" were illusionary. At least other labor leaders, like Warren Stone of the Locomotive Engineers, found the survey's report of evolutionary progress unsound and unsupportable on its face.[23] Where hopes in unbiased expertise floundered was the tacit assumption that social scientists had not already developed strong theoretical opinions in support of American capitalistic development. Given such expertise, the facts marshaled in the NCF's survey must reflect their origins in a fundamental acceptance and support of social progress though evolutionary capitalist development, including the emerging domination of the larger corporations.

And beyond some unionists' growing reluctance to see the report in print, there was the Second U.S. Industrial Relations Commission. Charged by Congress with uncovering the roots of the continuing industrial discord and labor unrest that underpin the socialists' and syndicalists' new ideological challenge to the NCF's centralism, it offered the nation well-publicized hearings into the political economy's shortcomings. Even more to the point, its hearings had spotlighted how capitalists routinely funded social science surveys in support of the emerging center.[24] With labor out of harmony with a whitewash and the public prepared to appreciate fully the meaning of the NCF's sponsorship of social science in the service of the emerging order, the survey was put on the shelf. In 1924 an updated version was published in another ideological context.[25] But in 1914 its central effect was educating both patrons and hired heads to the perils of sponsored research to affirm foregone ideological conclusions.

Technical Rationalization: Making the Economy More Efficient

Projects like the "hot air" Department of Industrial Economics and the social survey placed the discipline leaders at the frontlines of ideological combat. There they willingly defended the emerging corporate center from attacks upon its still-developing legitimacy. By fashioning arguments against ideological attackers on the center's right and left flanks, they worked to increase the rising political economic elite's capacity to command popular loyalty and energy for its own ends.

Such ideological construction was inherently abstract, being somewhat removed from the day-to-day processes of economic production. Unquestionably important in its own right, manufacturing ideas justifying the power of the emerging corporate center was only half of what the discipline leaders had to offer in exchange for a patron's support. The other half was the skill to rationalize production, to make the emerging order technically more efficient. Here social engineers drafted ameliorative blueprints within the framework of centralist development. The discipline-leaders-as-social-engineers were particularly welcomed at NCF departments, commissions and conferences involving economic and social regulation. On these projects, they offered a centralist interpretation of American industrialization and proposed schemes to encourage its more efficient evolution. They thus continued the AEA-based clarifying rhetoric of economic evolution while suggesting to the NCF some technical devices for scientifically regulating further corporate development.

The discipline leaders' role as social engineers is illuminated at two conferences on trusts. The first was in 1899 and gave rise to the NCF; the second, in 1907, deepened the regulatory schemes advanced by the AEA leaders operating in the NCF. Hundreds of influential political-economic leaders attended the conferences billed as bringing "light not heat" to the "general subject of trusts and trade combinations" which "occupied seemingly more than any other the public mind."[26] Sixteen AEA leaders were delegates to the 1899 four-day conference; seven spoke to the assembly. In 1907 six discipline leaders attended, and four addressed it.[27]

At these conferences, the discipline leaders first clarified fundamental concepts and then advanced ameliorative schemes which met their own resource needs as well as the technical needs of their potential sponsors in the corporate sector. Thus, Professor J.W. Jenks keynoted the 1899 conference by posing questions intended to clarify trusts.

> Are we to consider the new form of organization a means of saving energy comparable with a new invention like the steam engine or the railroad, so that we may be fairly sure that, although temporary suffering occurs, there will be enough savings to lower prices and to increase the demand for goods to so great an extent that the total demand for labor will in the long run be increased and the public benefited? Or, on the other hand, is the new form of organization a conspiracy of the few rich and powerful to oppress the many?[28]

Despite the seemingly open-endedness of such questions, the AEA leaders had long accepted large-scale corporate forms on evolutionary grounds. They had, in essence, consistently affirmed Jenks's first option and rejected the second. For them, the new centralized corporate form was a new and more socially efficient social invention, and not merely "a conspiracy" of the few over the many. Accordingly, temporary sufferings were but the teleological trauma of economic evolution to a more effective level of social production and consumption.[29]

Having thus illuminated the trust question, the leaders turned to technical schemes consistent with their analysis and interests. To ease the temporary problems of economic evolution, the state must act with the professional economist as its handservant. When discussing methods of intervention, the leaders stressed regulation by federal agencies akin to the Interstate Commerce Commission. As the ICC was intended to help rationalize the railroad industry, so some sort of "interstate trade commission" would make evolving large-scale business enterprise more economically efficient. As J.B. Clark put it, "massed capital does not have to bring with it a regime of true monopoly." Instead, state regulatory agencies would systematically gather corporate data and use publicity and administrative action to thwart the growth of socially inefficient monopolies whilst efficiently combining "the power of centralized capital" with "the power of the engine, the dynamos and the automatic machine."[30]

Regulation as suggested by the AEA leaders was consistent with their evolutionary views on "efficient" and "inefficient" masses of centralized capital. Such regulation was also consistent with their collective craft and career interests, since as specialists they were uniquely qualified to staff the expanding bureaucratic apparatus implicit in their schemes. Their rhetorical use of the ICC as model for an "interstate trade commission" suggested to their well-informed audiences the kinds of positions potentially available for them. And since their work with the ICC had clearly met the railroads' needs for order and stability, it also suggested to this audience the services they might offer the entire corporate sector.

For example, Hadley appeared as a favorable expert witness before the Cullom Committee framing the ICC legislation. Shortly thereafter he refused an offer to become first head of its statistical section. H.C. Adams accepted this post, hoping to obtain the funds necessary for a full fiscal analysis establishing an economically fair basis for railroad capital valuation and rate setting. Such funds never materialized, although money was found for other technical work including studies by W.Z. Ripley as special examiner and ASS leader Charles H. Cooley as statistician. Since the ICC lacked the funds for the full analytical determination of rail rates, political processes were used. Hadley and F.N. Judson sat on Taft's rail stocks and bonds commission recommending more profits and a new ICC Bureau of Valuation to help insure such profits. AEAers B.H. Meyer and W.M. Daniels were ICC commissioners when its "5% decision" gave effect to the recommended "just profit" and a Bureau of Valuation was established. The bureau also prevented intra-state commissions from nibbling away the investors' gains. John Gray became the bureau's chief analyst, working to guarantee the nation's railroads a profit higher than they could earn in a more competitive situation and freeing the lines' management from popular profit constraints at the intra-state level.[31] Finally, the AEA opened its organization to ICC personnel and railroad owners active in politically shaping ICC policies. Commissioners Martin Knapp and Charles Prouty as well as railway owner W.D. Hines used the AEA as a forum to publicize conservative federal (rather than intra-state) regulation.[32]

In essence, the AEA leaders at both conferences on trusts were offering potential corporate sponsors in their audiences a clarified ideology supporting centralized capital and technical schemes to make that massed capital more efficient. And they tacitly advanced themselves as specialists uniquely qualified to staff the expanding bureaucratic apparatus necessary to any form of state regulation, giving their ICC behavior as token of their sort of regulation-in-action. Here they joined interests with those capitalists and laborites in the emerging corporate center who accepted the inevitability of some form of state regulation. In exchange terms, the discipline leaders offered the corporate and labor leaders the ideological and technical skills necessary to create, support and legitimate governmental policy and programs favorable to the corporate center. In return, the corporate and labor leaders were to support an expanded state bureaucracy creating opportunities for social scientists skilled at data processing and interpretation, the stuff from which their collective craft and personal career were fashioned.

Although AEAers presented their centralist regulatory position to the 1899 conference on trusts, they did not find the consensus necessary to recommend any trust legislation. In fact, the AEAers were somewhat out of step with a large proportion of those who addressed the conference. A careful reading of their published addresses reveals that a large minority (39 percent) of the conference speakers rejected "trusts and combinations" as acceptable, let alone evolutionally correct modes of economic enterprise. Furthermore, only a bare majority (51 percent) shared the AEA's state regulatory position.[33]

Of course, the schemes of the center's intellectuals within the AEA were more fully expressed in other forums. For example, Congress in 1898 established the first U.S. Industrial Commission (U.S.I.C.) in response to public concern over the very visible increase in centralized capital. In 1900 the U.S.I.C., following the advice of Professor Jenks and other AEAers, recommended a federal licensing program for interstate enterprises. In this way, massed capital would be regulated in a correct evolutionary manner. In 1903 the Bureau of Corporations was created to begin regulation along such lines.[34]

The NCF 1907 conference on trusts drew its participants from a more narrowly centralist spectrum of opinion than did its 1899 counter-part,[35] since oppositional organizations refused invitations to attend. Accordingly, its committee on resolutions (with AEAers Albert Shaw in the chair and Professor John Gray as secretary) recommended further state intervention regulating economic evolution. Repeating the usual ameliorative line, the scope of both the ICC and the Bureau of Corporations was to be enlarged, providing greater possibilities for regulation and scholarly work. And a congressional commission was sought to ponder the legislative implications of recent anti-trust court decisions. Rather than establish such an anti-trust commission, congressional leaders asked the NCF to draft a bill representing the sentiment of its conference. This the NCF did. Aided by AEA leaders Jenks, Marburg, Shaw and Williams, it drafted and lobbied a bill offering interstate enterprises optional federal registration with the Bureau of Corporations. The bureau would gain access to corporate data sufficient for regulation, while the large-scale enterprise would obtain effective exemption from federal anti-trust legislation already on the books. Lobbied as the Hepburn-Warner bill, the proposal was defeated in Congress by representatives of middling and smaller capitalists opposing federal regulation for corporate ends.[36]

In the teeth of congressional defeat, the NCF redoubled its efforts to establish the evolutionary regulation of large business enterprise. It opened legislative offensives at both the interstate and intra-state levels and the discipline leaders reenlisted when asked. At the federal level after 1908, NCF committees continued drafting and lobbying regulatory proposals, and a new department of regulation of industrial corporations was formed, stressing now an "interstate trade commission" modeled on the ICC. These efforts enlisted the energies of discipline leaders John Bates Clark, J.W. Jenks, Frederick N. Judson, T. Marburg, Leo Rowe, and W.Z. Ripley. Their efforts were rewarded with a Federal Trade Act in 1914 reflecting the spirit, if not the letter, of their NCF labors.[37]

At the intra-state level, the NCF opened a campaign for uniformity in state legislation. Finding a bewildering variety of industrial and commercial law in the soon-to-be 48 states, the basic NCF strategy attempted to coordinate several ongoing organizations seeking uniformities, to draft model bills and to lobby them through a nation-wide network of state councils. These efforts aimed to create a standardized business environment, one with consistently predictable--and favorable--outcomes for centralist labor and corporate decision makers.[38]

The discipline leaders endorsed these efforts, since a standardized legal environment facilitated fairer competition among firms and contributed to the overall social efficiency of the nation's collective economic efforts. Such was the message delivered by the leaders who spoke at and helped organize the NCF'S 1910 Uniform Law Conference in Washington, D.C. E.R.A. Seligman outlined the need for uniformity in taxation, while Henry Farnum reported on the progress in uniform labor legislation--such as workmen's compensation--as seen from his post as president of the American Association for Labor Legislation, and Theodore Marburg stressed the elemental necessity of standard laws to ensure uniform state intervention in economic enterprise. Professors J.W. Jenks and Westel W. Willoughby along with F.N. Judson and T. Marburg helped plan the conference and its gala festivities in the nation's capital. These included a White House dinner for some of the NCF's leading figures, including Professor Seligman, since President Taft found both the NCF and its efforts at increasing efficiency via uniformity to his liking.[39]

The 1910 Uniform Law Conference and the 23 state councils organized to foster a standardized industrial and commercial law offered the discipline leaders great opportunity to display their craft and its uses to perspective patrons. So did the drafting of model bills, for a model bill implies an expert knowledge of both the law and the economic phenomena being standardized. The NCF sent several models to the state councils: one on workmen's compensation, another on minimum wages, a third on public utility regulation. The scale and scope of social science patronage--and the service to power--possible in model bill drafting is illustrated by the NCF's efforts in the public utility field from 1905 to 1911.

In 1905 the NCF's Commission on Public Ownership of Public Utilities began exploring the hotly contested issues surrounding public service corporations. After three years of study and some $50,000, the commission found reasons for strongly regulated municipal monopolies providing water, gas, electricity and transit. And although it stopped short of recommending exclusively private ownership of such urban infra-structure industries, it pointedly underlined the problems of mixing political opportunism with public service operations. Public ownership of municipal monopolies was pictured thereby as a risky political economic enterprise, at best. The commissions's report concluded, in essence, that "private operation was preferable to public if there was adequate regulation."[40]

For the discipline leaders involved in the commission, this conclusion could not have been surprising, since a broad academic consensus on the issue had long existed. It held regulated private control was indeed preferable to public ownership of "natural monopolies." The commission's three-year study simply reaffirmed these well-known views on municipal monopolies.[41]

Given these well-established views, it is easy to see the leaders enjoying the opportunities amply presented by their commission work. At an early planning meeting, for example, Professor Leo Rowe spoke to a table of resource-laden political-economic leaders, urging them to employ the technically necessary experts: accountants, engineers and statisticians. And at a later moment, Professor John Gray echoed Rowe's call for expertise, proving the plea with the observation that the "NCF is founded to bring the classes together." He then went to Europe on the commission's fact-finding summer junket, together with representatives of the capital and labor classes.[42]

In effect, the commission's 1908 report helped still public unrest over private ownership while providing a framework of conservative regulation.[43] This framework fostered banker and bondholder acceptance of state economic intervention. But did not go far enough; it did not offer detailed and uniform rules of regulation. In 1911, the NCF's department on the regulation of interstate and municipal utilities was established to draft a model state utilities bill. Headed by a banker, who as president and director of utilities in ten states was sensitive to the virtues of standardizing the legal structures regulating utilities, the department recruited six discipline leaders. Professor John Gray became director of the department's investigations and secretary of its controlling executive council[44] while Professor Leo Rowe headed the Committee on Accounts and Reports.

Not surprisingly, after three years of investigations, the department held that the public interest demanded the "initiative, zeal, enterprise and courage" of business methods rather than the corresponding ills of political control. Indeed, going the next step, it favored taking municipal utilities out of community politics altogether. Its model bill created a single state-wide agency regulating all public service corporations. This agency would have full authority to gather data, set rates and generally provide the stable, uniform and centralized industrial environment thought desirable.[45] Thus, on this second NCF public utility project, discipline leaders displayed their talents and deployed their legislative drafting skills in the service of power. They gained thereby the opportunity to trade their skills for the resources necessary to underwrite their further careers and the collective development of their discipline.

The Limits of Knowledge in the Service of Corporate Power

When the discipline leaders entered a resource exchange relationship with the nascent national corporate and labor leadership found in the NCF, they eschewed the available alternative analyses of laissez-faire and socialism. In choosing to work within the NCF, the discipline leaders differentiated themselves from other intellectuals, for example William Graham Sumner, who sharply criticized the ultimately political use of the ICC and other regulatory agencies, or William Z. Foster and Eugene Debs, who denounced the conservative unionists who led labor into collaborative alliances with capital, such as the NCF.[46]

Identifying the resource-rich corporate center as an appropriate support structure for building their careers and crafts, the discipline leaders entered into their own collaboration with the center's leadership. Together, in forums like the NCF, they constructed the expert advisor's role, a set of shared expectations and behaviors that guided the exchanges between social scientist and political-economic patron. And from the long record of knowledge meeting power in the NCF, we can also see that there were several limits to the uses of the NCF as a site for constructing the expert role. Most importantly, NCF projects were limited by the quality of organizational leadership and the emerging principles of labor-capital collaboration. Thus, as Green and Weinstein hold, the exact content of NCF projects varies somewhat with its official leadership. Mark Hanna headed the organization into industrial conciliation and arbitration work, reflecting his own social origins in owning and managing extractive and manufacturing enterprises. August Belmont as a finance capitalist with interests in urban transit saw the public service corporation as worthy of the NCF's attention. Seth Low's career combined urban wealth with educational management, and he broadened the NCF's concerns to include even the declining rural sector with a Department on Agricultural Conditions (1910). And Ralph M. Easely offered all three NCF presidents his vast energies, organizational skills and sense of the middle way as executive secretary over the entire period.[47]

The reason that leadership made such differences was the volunteeristic nature of the NCF. Although its bills were always paid by capitalists, their contributions could not be coerced. Accordingly, NCF projects were self-sustaining where possible and usually impossible when not. In this situation, whoever headed the organization also headed its funding attempts, seeking resources for those projects he could sell the best--those closest to his experience and interests, and those most clearly needed by the press of social unrest.[48]

The emerging principles of labor-capital collaboration meant that either party could limit the NCF's agenda of concerns. Laborites allowed the NCF to mount departments specifically devoted to welfare capitalism, since such projects offered some benefits to workers. Labor leaders permitted the NCF's very extensive immigration conference and department (1906) to be born and engage the participation of some 18 discipline leaders. But since labor's immigration interests were strongly opposed to those of its business collaborationists, the project could not long live within the NCF's confines. When Congress established its own Immigration Commission (1908), the NCF gladly gave its files to the governmental body.[49]

Discipline leaders participating in NCF projects were offered some instruction in the limits of knowledge in the service of corporate power by observing the organization's funding procedures and the necessities of collaboration between capital and labor. But their most direct learning was in acting out the role of the expert advisor to power.   Of course, not every social scientist entering the NCF's portals nor every corporate leader sitting on a departmental executive played out all of the role's potential. And as always is the case, some role players were more competent or less lack-luster than others. But such performance variations aside, by working together on a wide range of projects, the discipline leaders and their business and labor counter-parts in the NCF did fashion the expert advisor role from one part power and one part knowledge.

For the discipline leaders, the limits operating on this exercise in role construction were not so much intellectual as organizational. The thesis of corporate economic control was not problematic for the disciplinarians participating in the NCF. As the AEA's presidential addresses and debates make clear, they accepted such middle-way development well before the NCF was launched. Furthermore, they accepted the social authority of the center's capitalists themselves, willingly submitting to organizational domination within corporate-led forums like the NCF, to say nothing of their submission to managers of erudition in colleges and universities. As factory workers in the then emerging mass-production plants increasingly understood themselves to be hired hands, so too the discipline leaders knew themselves to be hired heads.

In this context of organizational dominance, the discipline leaders creating the expert advisor role should be seen as working to establish some discretionary role range, some autonomous territory to realize their personal aspirations for craftly control and academic accomplishment. Nonetheless, such recalcitrant autonomy came only after the fact of submission to centralist authority. For example, disciplinarians accepted their usual non-participation in the NCF's decision-making executive without recorded protest. In like manner, they accepted exclusion from certain NCF exercises, notably projects involving managerial prerogatives.

Perhaps the most striking case was their non-participation in the several large welfare departments operating within the NCF. In these departments, employers met without unionists to explain to each other their schemes designed to ameliorate some of the personal costs of capitalist industrialization while bringing the workers ever more tightly under corporate control.[50] Discipline leaders saw social science skills as useful in these tasks. Yet, they were not invited to show their obvious skills and talents within the NCF departments specializing in rationalizing welfare capitalism. In addition, they were invited in only small numbers to NCF projects touching very directly on labor-capital relations. Thus only one discipline leader is reported in the Review as participating in the Departments of Conciliation and Arbitration (1906) and Compensation (1910); the Child Labor Commission (1907); and the International Conference on Social Insurance (1910).

Such minimal NCF participation does not mean that the discipline leaders did not lend their heads to rationalizing efforts in these areas. The American Association for Labor Legislation (AALL) made good use of them on workmen's compensation as did the National Child Labor Committee.[51] It does mean that social scientists bargaining for resources in volunteeristic policy forums like the NCF learned to take (or refuse) what resources were offered. They thus learned that their knowledge could not be employed and enriched without sustained sponsorship, and their expert's role could not be developed without reliable resources. Such lessons could not but reinforce their sense that the state with its power to coerce resources offered a potentially solid base for the development of their craft and careers.

NOTES

1. William Domhoff, The Higher Circles (New York: Random House, 1970), pp. 156-250; Marguerite Green, The National Civic Federation and the American Labor Movement, 1900-1925 (Westport, Conn.: Greenwood Press, 1973); James Weinstein, The Corporate Ideal in the Liberal State: 1900-1918 (Boston: Beacon, 1968); Gordon Jensen, "The National Civic Federation: American Business in an Age of Social Change and Social Reform, 1900-1910" (Ph.D. dissertation, Princeton University, 1956); Philip S. Foner, History of the Labor Movement in the United States, vols. 2 and 3 (New York: International, 1955 and 1964), pp. 384-387 and 61-110.

2. Jensen, "The National Civic Federation," p. 65.

3. Ibid., pp. 81-96 and 330 ff.; Weinstein, The Corporate Ideal pp. ix-xv; Green, The National Civic Federation, pp. 90-189.

4. Jensen, "The National Civic Federation," chapter 4.

5. On the membership of the NAM, see Albert K. Steigerwalt, The National Association of Manufacturers, 1895-1914 (Ann Arbor, Mich.: Bureau of Business Research, 1964).

6. Green, The National Civic Federation, pp. 133-189; and Foner, History of the Labor Movement, 3: 61-70 et passim.

7. Green, The National Civic Federation.

8. Steigerwalt, The National Association of Manufacturers; and Foner, History of the Labor Movement, 3: 106-110.

9. Green, The National Civic Federation, p. 85, quoting Ralph Easely. The Review was published in two runs, the first from April 1903 to May 1914 with a second from 1918 to 1920.

10. Laurence R. Veysey, _The Emergence of the American University_ (Chicago: University of Chicago Press, 1965), pp. 364, 408-413.

11. Charles Forcey, _The Cross-Roads of Liberalism: Croly, Weyl, Lippmann, and the Progressive Period, 1900-1925_ (New York: Oxford University Press, 1961), p. 64.

12. Green, _The National Civic Federation_, pp. 90-132, esp. 111 ff.

13. _National Civic Federation_ (NCF) _Review_ 1, 9 (November 1904): 8 and 10; Green, _The National Civic Federation_, pp. 87-88, quoting Ralph M. Easely to John Mitchell, 24 February 1905 (at page 88).

14. Ibid., as quoted in _NCF Review_, 1 (November 1904): 8.

15. Green, _The National Civic Federation_, pp. 111-113, 175-176, 327, 488; _NCF Review_ 1, 5-10 (July through December 1904).

16. _NCF Review_ 2, 6 (November 1905): 8.

17. The Advisory Council was to cooperate with and assist the NCF executive between annual meetings, acting not as a deliberative or decision-making body so much as a sounding board--if at all. _NCF Review_ 3, 5 (September 1908): 10.

18. Weinstein, _The Corporate Ideal_, p. 124.

19. _NCF Review_ 6, 3 (March 1914): 1-4.

20. Weinstein, _The Corporate Ideal_, pp. 126-127. Dependence on capitalist funding was routine in the NCF. See Sidney Sass, "The NCF, 1900-1914," (M.A. thesis, Columbia University, 1948).

21. _NCF Review_ 6, 3 (March 1914): 1-4.

22. Green, _The National Civic Federation_, p. 185.

23. Weinstein, The Corporate Ideal, p. 130; Green, The National Civic Federation, p. 188.

24. U.S. Commission on Industrial Relations, Final Report and Testimony, U.S. Senate, Doc. 415, 64th Congress, 1st. Session (Washington, D.C.: U.S. Government Printing Office, 1916), esp. vol. 1, section V: The Concentration of Wealth and Influence.

25. Green, The National Civic Federation, pp. 395, 460-461.

26. Franklin H. Head, "Preface," Chicago Conference on Trusts (Chicago: Chicago Civic Federation, 1900), p. 5.

27. Chicago Conference on Trusts: Proceedings of the National Conference on Trusts and Combinations (New York: National Civic Federation, 1908).

28. J.W. Jenks, Untitled Remarks, Chicago Conference on Trusts, p. 33.

29. See Chapters 5 and 6 above for analysis of the AEA position on large-scale capital as it developed within that organization from 1885 until 1904. For additional detail, see H.C. Adams, H.W. Farnum, B.H. Meyer, E.W. Bemis and J.H. Hollander, "Trusts," PAEA 5 (May 1904): 91-197. All but Bemis were AEA leaders. Finally, all the AEA leaders speaking at both conferences indicated acceptance of the "new social invention."

30. J.B. Clark, Untitled Remarks, Chicago Conference on Trusts, p. 404.

31. David M. Grossman, "Professor and Public Service, 1885-1925: A Chapter in the Professionalization of the Social Sciences," (Ph.D. dissertation, Washington University, 1973), pp. 32-33, 65. For a fuller account of the AEA leaders involvement in the ICC, see Gabriel Kolko, Railroads and Regulation, 1877-1916 (New York: W.W. Norton, 1970).

32. Martin A. Knapp, "The Regulation of Railway Rates," _PAEA_ 6 (May 1905): 20-30; Charles A. Prouty, "National Regulation of Railways," _PAEA_ 4 (February 1903): 71-83; W.D. Hines, "Legislative Regulation of Railway Rates," _PAEA_ 4 (February 1903): 84-103.

33. Computed from David M. Grossman, "Chicago Conference on Trusts" (M.A. thesis, Johns Hopkins University, 1965), pp. 41-43.

34. Weinstein, _The Corporate Ideal_, p. 69.

35. Green, _The National Civic Federation_, p. 200.

36. Ibid., pp. 199-209; Weinstein, _The Corporate Ideal_, pp. 74-87; _NCF Review_ 3, 3 (February 1908): 18 and 3, 4 (March 1908): 14.

37. _NCF Review_ 3, 6 (March 1909): 12; 4, 11 (July 1911): 16; and 4, 12 (February 1912): 3; Weinstein, _The Corporate Ideal_, pp. 87-91; Green, _The National Civic Federation_, pp. 209-221.

38. Weinstein, _The Corporate Ideal_, pp. 32-35; Green, _The National Civic Federation_, pp. 76-78.

39. "A Movement for State and National Unity," _NCF Review_ 3, 7 (July 1909): 1 ff.; "A Great Conference on Vital Problems," _NCF Review_ 3, 9 (March 1910): 1 ff.; "States Declare for National Unity," _NCF Review_ 3, 10 (September 1910): 1 ff.

40. Green, _The National Civic Federation_, pp. 221 and 128-130; Weinstein, _The Corporate Ideal_, pp. 24-26.

41. Carroll D. Wright et al., "Discussion--The Investigation of Municipal and Private Distribution of Water, Gas, Heat and Electricity," _Handbook of the AEA_, supplement to _Economic Studies_ 3 (February 1898): 57-76.

42. _NCF Review_ 2, 6 (November 1905): 1, 7-9 (Gray quote at p. 9), 12-13, 17; 2, 9 (March-April 1906): 8, 14; 2, 10 (July-August

1906): 1; 2, 10 (December 1906): 8; and 3, 1 (September 1907): 4-5, 19-20.

43. Green, The National Civic Federation, pp. 222-223; Weinstein, The Corporate Ideal, p. 26.

44. NCF Review 3, 12 (February 1912): 6; Weinstein, The Corporate Ideal, pp. 33-35.

45. NCF Review 4, 3 (March 1914): 22.

46. William Graham Sumner, The Conquest of the United States by Spain and Other Essays, ed. Murray Polner (Chicago: Regenery, 1965); William Z. Foster, From Bryan to Stalin (New York: International, 1937), p. 51; Ray Ginger, The Bending Cross: A Biography of Eugene V. Debs (New Brunswick, N.J.: Rutgers University Press, 1947).

47. Green, The National Civic Federation, pp. 483-496; Weinstein, The Corporate Ideal, pp. 37-39.

48. Green, The National Civic Federation, pp. 313-327.

49. Bruno Ramirez, When Workers Fight: The Politics of Industrial Relations in the Progressive Period, 1898-1916 (Westport, Conn.: Greenwood Press, 1978), chapters 7 and 8; Green, The National Civic Federation, pp. 299-300; Weinstein, The Corporate Ideal, pp. 26-27.

50. Ramirez, When Workers Fight, pp. 147-159; Green, The National Civic Federation, pp. 245-293; Weinstein, The Corporate Ideal, pp. 18-20.

51. On the AALL and the NCF, see Domhoff, The Higher Circles; Walter I. Trattner, Crusade for the Children: A History of the National Child Labor Committee and Child Labor Reform in America (Chicago: Quadrangle, 1970).

9
Economy and Efficiency at Home and Abroad

In Chapter 8 we saw how the contest for control of an industrializing economy provided association leaders with an opportunity to demonstrate the uses of their expertise. In this chapter we look at the ways in which urbanization and American overseas expansion enabled them to display their skill at rebuilding the machinery of government for the twentieth century. Of particular interest is social scientists' deployment of expertise in the struggle to control public bureaucracy at home and abroad.

According to association leaders, both industrial cities and American empire would be made safe through expertise. Indeed, Harvard's President A. Lawrence Lowell, an APSA leader, saw the rise of the metropole and the expansion of empire as integrally linked, and amateurs had no place in the administration of either. Making his point by historical analogy, he argued that Rome fell not so much from lack of moral fiber as "the lack of experts in public service":

> When instead of governing a small town and an agricultural district, the people were called upon to rule a huge metropolis, to administer vast provinces, to regulate the commercial affairs and control the destinies of the western world, the system broke down. . . . Surely it is abundantly clear that government by a succession of amateurs, without expert assistance, had proved itself hopelessly incapable of maintaining an orderly administration. . . . The state had outgrown its machinery.[1]

So, too, municipal governments, meagerly staffed with untrained political appointees, as well as the American state department, run by a handful of self-taught civil servants on the eve of the Spanish-American War, had to be transformed into modern bureaucracies.

Social science leaders built bureaucracy in at least two ways. They worked with private organizations at the local, state and national level intent on influencing the development of public administration, and they served as experts holding appointive positions in budding government bureaucracies. Concurrent private-sector and government service enabled experts to bridge the gap between the responsible classes and emerging bureaucracies, increasing the routine use of academics as adjuncts in policy making. We will look, then, at leaders' work in the National Municipal League and local and federal bureaucracies as well as their service to private organizations concerned with shaping foreign policy and their work for the Department of State.

Although leaders from each of the disciplines worked to build state bureaucracy, political scientists, organized expressly to deal with the polity, perhaps labored more diligently than others. As Frank Goodnow—first president of the APSA, father of the academic study of public administration and future president of Johns Hopkins—told the assembled political scientists at their premiere gathering, the concern of the new field was "perfecting the various operations necessary to the realization of the State will."^{2} Thus political scientists are the principal but by no means the only social science actors in this chapter.

Economy and Efficiency at Home: The National Municipal League

Association leaders first brought their expertise to problems of public administration at the municipal level. At the turn of the century, America's burgeoning cities housed factories spawned by the industrial revolution and the increasingly immigrant working class who labored there. These urban centers were as chaotic and volatile as the economy, the stage set on which were played the dramas of strikes and protest, brazen boodling and petty graft, street crime and organized vice. Since the industrial city was a problem that confronted every urban dweller who walked out the door, it presented political scientists unbounded opportunity to use expertise when they made common cause with business-led reformers.[3]

Business leaders first began to treat urban problems through their city clubs. When local clubs serving as centers of conviviality as well as civic purpose proved inadequate to treat what was beginning to be viewed as a national urban crisis, a country-wide, single-focus organization, the National Municipal League (NML), was launched. In 1894 the call for the league was put out by the City Club of New York and the Municipal League of Philadelphia and answered by delegates from clubs and associations local and national, widely known and obscure, but all characterized by the civic sensibility commonly displayed by solid citizens.[4]

Although the league was partially financed by membership dues from taxpayers who wanted their money's worth from city government in small towns, approximately half of its budget came from contributions made by corporate leaders often quartered in large urban centers. Among the more generous supporters were department store giants like Marshall Field, Edward Filene, and V. Everett Macy. Also contributing were financier R. Fulton Cutting located in New York City as were the Vanderbilts, Rochester's George Eastman of camera fame, and the McCormicks of Chicago. Gifts were also made by the C.F. Taylor Trust, the Julius Rosenwald Fund, the Economic and General Foundations, the Davidson Fund, the New York Foundation and the Allied Store Corporation.[5] These organizations and the men who led them were committed to shaping the industrial city to accommodate their corporate needs as inexpensively as possible.

Like so many American forum groups concerned with social problems, the NML engaged in agitation and education while seeking reform through administration. Although its mode of operation mirrored that of earlier organizations, such as the ASSA, like the associations of learned disciplines, it adapted to industrial conditions through specialization. The NML was not concerned with a broad range of social problems; instead it concentrated exclusively on the organization of city government. As given in its constitution, the league's purpose was to bring together "good citizens" to solve municipal problems through substituting trained men of integrity for the incompetent and corrupt, especially in the area of "civic administration." This would be accomplished through investigation and discussion of public administration, with particular attention directed to mechanisms of selection and appointment. The results of the NML's investigations and deliberations would be widely disseminated, educating all good citizens in "the cause of Good Government."[6]

As with the ASSA, the "educated and responsible" middle strata were the focus of mobilization. However, by the turn of the century, such organizations, now national in character, could not be sustained simply by individual efforts on the part of the comfortable classes; corporate sponsorship was also necessary. Nor were citizen and expert so frequently combined in one person as had been the case with the ASSA. Instead, career social scientists, especially political scientists, offered themselves and their students as trained specialists whose integrity was guaranteed by the doctorate.

To understand leaders' work with the NML, its principal journals were examined and their participation as officers, board, council and committee members as well as speakers recorded. From 1894 to 1911, the official organ of the NML was the Proceedings of the National Conference for Good Government, issued annually. In 1912 this was replaced by the National Municipal Review, a quarterly which continued long past 1921. Each journal in turn reported the NML's yearly meeting and listed officers, appointments and committee work.

Table 4 shows the emerging differentiation of expert service by discipline. While leaders from all the social science specialist associations participated, political scientists played the greatest role in the era's central organization for the reform of civic administration. Twenty-six or 60 percent of the APSA's leadership participated in the NML while only 19 percent of the AEA's and 13 percent of the ASS's did so. The APSA leaders in the NML also had a much higher level of activity than leaders from other associations; 6.5 was the average number of participations for the APSA, compared to 1.8 for the AEA and 1 for the ASS. Some APSA leaders penetrated the highest reaches of the league's leadership, with eight (19 percent) serving as vice-presidents. But only one, Bon Ami heir and corporate executive Richard S. Childs, achieved the presidency. More contributed to the secondary level of the league's executive organization; 11 (25 percent) held positions on the council, advisory or executive committees. But their greatest contribution was content and its management: they

TABLE 4 Participation in Selected National
Municipal League Activities, 1894-1921

YEAR	NML ACTIVITY	Discipline Leaders			
		ALL*	AEA	APSA	ASS
1894-1921	Leadership Roles				
	Officers	9	1	9	0
	Advisory, Council or Executive Committee	13	3	11	0
	Editorial & Association Bus.	17	0	17	1
	Presentors at Meetings	80	14	69	1
1894-1921	Committee Services				
	Municipal Program	3	0	3	0
	Instruction in Government	4	0	4	0
	Collegiate Instruction in Govt	11	0	11	0
	Municipal Taxation	3	3	1	0
	Uniform Municipal Accounting	5	3	3	0
1908	City Finance and Budget	2	0	2	0
1910	Improvement in Statistical Methods of Municipal In-struction	4	0	4	0
1912	Operation of Commission Govt	3	0	3	0
1915	Municipal Program	4	0	4	0
1918	City Manager as a Profession	3	0	3	0
	Federal Relations to Municipalities	2	0	2	0
	County Government	3	0	3	0
	State Government	4	0	4	0
	Reconstruction	2	0	2	0
	Uniform City Reports	2	0	2	0
1920	Model Municipal Indebtedness	2	1	1	0
	Other	11**	2	10	0
	Sum of Participations	187	27	168	2
	Number of Participants	43	15	26	2
	Average Participations	4.3	1.8	6.5	1

*Duplication occurs, since some leaders led more than one discipline.

**Other refers to those committees on which only one disciplinary
association leader served: Committee or Municipal Accounting Book (1907);
Municipal Health and Sanitation (1907); Application of Municipal Program
Principles (1907); Electoral Reform (1909); Municipal Reference Bureaus
(1909) Taxation and Benefits City Growth and Excess Condemnation (1910);
City Finance and Efficiency (1912); Police (1912); Liquor (1912); Joint
Committee on Public Training (1915); Intercollegiate Work (1918).

addressed meetings and filled and managed the journal as well as the routine business of the association. Thus 19 (44 percent) of the APSA leaders presented 69 articles or speeches, while 10 (23 percent) filled 17 slots on the editorial board and business committees.

The association between social scientists and league leaders was mutually beneficial. As this chapter will demonstrate, academics supplied endless content, both technical and ideological, that gave substance to the league's corporate sponsors' conception of a public administration tuned to business needs and economic development. In return, social scientists found an outlet for their expertise that reached an audience beyond the academy. The league provided a forum for experts' continued influence on policy making after their stints in public administration and also launched experts' careers as government consultants. Finally, as indicated by the extensive service of APSA leaders on the committee on collegiate instruction in government, initiated the year the political scientists organized, the NML gave the association a lobby for its new field.

The importance of the league to the APSA is suggested by the reputations of the seven most active leaders, each of whom was engaged in 11 or more NML endeavors. They were among the discipline's theoretical and practical leaders, and the league was a forum where they could test their ideas while engaging in reform. Thus, Charles Beard, famous for his economic interpretation of the Constitution, was head of Columbia's politics laboratory and, from 1915 to 1917, also director of the training school at the New York Bureau of Municipal Research, a local municipal reform bureau closely tied to the NML. After he left Columbia in protest over the firing of anti-war professors, he was bureau director from 1918 to 1921. Richard S. Childs, in the early phases of his long career as a corporate manager, still had time to found and lead the Short Ballot Association (1910), write a volume on the subject, and help create the city manager plan. Frederick A. Cleveland was an authority on municipal budgetary systems, a professor at New York University, director of the New York Bureau of Municipal Research and chair of Taft's committee on economy and efficiency. Frank J. Goodnow, Columbia professor, was called the father of the field of public administration and is remembered for strongly formulating the need for a strict separation of public administration and partisan politics. He was active in the formation of the New York bureau, served on Taft's committee on economy and efficiency, as a political advisor to the Chinese government, a trustee of the Institute for Government Research, and president of Johns Hopkins. Augustus R. Hatton was an authority on city charters and first incumbent of the chair in political science provided by the Marcus A. Hanna Foundation at Western Reserve. Harvard's William Bennett Munro was a contributor to the theory of public administration who also influenced reform efforts as an editorial writer for the Boston Herald and through his service on many local-level governmental commissions. Leo Stanton Rowe of the University of Pennsylvania had a long-standing interest in municipal reform, and he remained active in the NML even after his success with the Pan American Conferences turned his intellectual energies to foreign policy. The league, then, sustained leaders' reform efforts by providing them with an ongoing forum in which to forge ideas for the policy process.

Like the associations, the league claimed to be nonpartisan, concerned with good government, not the championship of a particular party. However, social scientists observed the letter rather than the spirit of their "nonpartisan" clauses in work with the league. Its purpose was clearly political, and if the Republican party did not embrace its platform, a fusion ticket served. As H.W. Foulkes, officer and organizer of the newly formed NML bluntly told the AEA in 1895, the most valuable voluntary organizations were "quasi-political," and their most important function was "forming a nucleus of public opinion prior to preliminary legislation."[7]

The central problem faced by business reformers who led the league was how to create a political culture able to contain the radical potential of popular democracy while preserving a Republican government that represented their interests. Business reformers were profoundly disturbed by the unpropertied urban masses and feared that the mob would use the privilege of franchise to erode capitalism, thus undermining national prosperity. Or, as the APSA's Goodnow put the problem, "It has been felt that city government must, to be efficient, be emancipated from the tyranny of the national and state parties, and from that of the legislature--the tool of the party. . . . [But] to avoid tyranny and preserve control is not easy."[8] Thus, business-led reformers and social science experts in the NML sought means to wrest control of urban government from political machines and prevent popular reform parties--Socialists, Populists, Single Taxers--from gaining control of the cities.

The NML addressed these problems through its model municipal programs. Serving on the 1898 committee that drew up the 1900 model city charter were the APSA's Goodnow of Columbia, Rowe of the University of Pennsylvania, and Albert Shaw, Johns Hopkins Ph.D. and editor of the Review of Reviews and confidant of Theodore Roosevelt. The solution offered for controlling modern industrial cities was strengthening the administrative branch of government at the expense of the legislature. Such changes were justified on grounds of the greater economy and efficiency an expertly staffed and scientifically managed bureaucracy would provide.

In practice, however, the specific program recommended by the NML meant that the vast majority were increasingly unable to make their voices heard through their legislators or to serve government themselves. The NML mechanisms for realizing economy and efficiency were: home rule, the short ballot, at-large elections, a city council reduced in size, a strong mayor, executive budget and merit system. Home rule freed city politics from rural- and party-dominated state legislatures. The short ballot required that many elective positions become appointive, drastically reducing the number of persons that city voters chose to represent them. At-large elections did away with party labels, making it difficult for candidates not widely known to be identified with a particular platform. Moreover, the reduced number of city councilors were required to serve without pay, making politics the prerogative of the well-to-do. The mayor's policy-making powers were greatly increased when he, rather than the legislature, was assigned the development of what came to be called the executive budget. This power was consolidated by giving the mayor increased control over the meritocratic appointment of experts, who executed his expanded responsibilities.

However, the reforms advocated in the first municipal program proved inadequate; they could not assure public decision making predictably favorable to business interests. The people had a strong sense of their own self-interest and quickly saw that the NML program seldom benefited the uneducated and unwashed. Reform tickets carried the day only to be swept away in the next election. The strong mayoralty was easily captured by party politicians backed by a machine that commanded voters' loyalty through bribery, political appointments and extension of welfare services.[9]

In 1912 when it became apparent that business-led reformers would be unable to make permanent political gains without accommodating popular demands that compromised academic and corporate leaders' concept of economy and efficiency, NML and APSA leaders flirted briefly with the idea of commission government. This form of municipal government called for election of a very small commission that combined executive and legislative functions and managed the city like the board of a corporation conducting business. But businessmen were not always elected to commissions, and as the APSA's A. Lawrence Lowell pointed out, "Now election by popular vote is a very poor way of selecting expert administrators."[10] Moreover, commission government blurred the distinction between legislative and executive authority, decreasing opportunities for administrative decision making.[11]

In the second municipal program, first offered in 1915, the NML tried to devise a more comprehensive and enduring plan for guaranteeing economy and efficiency in city government. Working on this program were APSA leaders R.S. Childs, A.R. Hatton, A.L. Lowell and W.B. Munro. The second municipal program moved from piecemeal reform of public administration to city systems management. This program built on the work of the committees on municipal taxation, uniform municipal accounting, and city finance and budgeting. Between the first and second municipal programs these committees had worked at redesigning city financial procedures to make a budget drawn by the administration the major mechanism for shaping urban policy.

The key was executive centralization through the office of the city manager. The manager was the "chief executive officer" chosen by a small council for an indefinite term "solely on the basis of his executive and administrative qualifications." He was in charge of six administrative departments: law, health, works and utilities, safety and welfare, education, and finance, organized in functional groupings with department heads accountable for their staff. All were governed by detailed civil service rules that standardized and classified positions according to duties and responsibilities. The budget process reflected new systems development which called for work programs, lump sum allotments that increased administrative discretion, multi-year planning by a board composed of one administrator and two citizens appointed "because of their knowledge of city planning." The ballot remained short and elections nonpartisan. Provisions made for proportional representation, initiative, referendum and recall were hedged with restrictions and complicated by elaborate rules, forms and waiting periods.[12]

In short, the second municipal program called for an administrative system as closed as possible in a democracy, with experts making decisions formerly made at the polls. The importance of a powerful executive chosen by a handful of councilors rather than popular election was underlined by the NML's 1918 committee on the city manager as a profession, which outlined the credentials and skills necessary for the new position. As APSA leader W.B. Munro proudly noted when commenting on the program, "Legislation is entrusted to a body which is large enough to be adequately representative; [but] the concentration of administrative functions is made complete. The councilors are laymen, without expert knowledge or special interest. The city manager is a professional administrator."[13]

Indeed, the new model charter had so centralized and concentrated executive authority that popular access to public administration became very difficult. Only those skilled at bureaucratic manipulation--such as social science experts and the businessmen who funded them--could make the new machinery of government work. As Charles Beard, one of the APSA's few critics of the NML version of economy and efficiency complained, "municipal government . . . is tied hand and foot with red tape and complex charter limitations."[14] The league itself indicated a certain degree of uneasiness over the program's excessive concentration of power in the executive. A cautionary note was attached to the charter, insisting that it be adopted in its entirety, since the safeguards built into it were essential to success. While the manager plan "was probably the most advanced and scientific form of municipal organization yet suggested . . . owing to its own concentration of executive and administrative authority in the manager, [it] might prove to be susceptible to perversion in the interest of a boss in cities with an undeveloped and inactive public opinion."[15]

The league's administrative ideology was shared by other private groups concerned with shaping the development of local and national bureaucracy. For example, the New York Bureau of Municipal Research maintained close ties with the NML, sharing sponsors, office space and expert social scientists. The same was true of Chicago's Bureau of Public Efficiency. These groups were also influential in shaping public policy at the federal level. The New York bureau and the league played a part in the establishment of Taft's Commission on Economy and Efficiency in Government (1910), a blue-ribbon presidential commission of whom half the members were also joint APSA and NML leaders. When the commission failed to strengthen greatly the president's administrative powers, league, bureau and social science leaders created the Institute for Government Research (later the Brookings Institution). Like the NML and the New York bureau, the Institute for Government Research sought to make the executive budget the primary mechanism for setting government policy. Persistence and experience paid off. In 1921 the Budget and Accounting Act, commonly regarded as the cornerstone of the executive presidency, was signed into law.[16]

Although the Institute for Government Research provides a suggestive and dramatic case, overall it is not easy to assess the league and the APSA's impact on city government. Other agencies and reform groups with similar programs were also active at the local, state and national levels. In some instances the league's model charters clearly influenced reform. For example, the Chicago charter commission of 1906, sponsored by a reform administration and staffed by APSA leaders and University of Chicago professors Ernest Freund, A.R. Hatton and Charles Merriam, reprinted the text of the NML's 1900 model charter and incorporated a number of its features in the final recommendations.[17] But the NML reforms most commonly adopted in large urban areas during the Progressive era did not include the city manager so important to the 1915 program. Instead cities implemented executive budgets, the use of experts, and the departmental organization of public administration. Very often the worst features of machine and reform were combined, with graft and corruption sheltered by an inaccessible administration.

Another way of looking at NML and APSA leaders' influence on Progressive reform of public administration is to contrast their program with available alternatives. Certainly the Good Government and business leaders with whom social scientists worked were not the only proponents of administrative reform. Populists, socialists and reform factions within the dominant political parties all had platforms aimed at building efficient and economical bureaucracies.

Agrarian radicals and farmer labor parties proposed municipal and national centralization of administrative units easily and popularly shaped and policed through devices like initiative, referendum and recall. Socialists, who elected officers in over 300 cities between 1900 and 1910, saw the city's inhabitants as equal shareholders in a social corporation, called for public ownership of city infra-structure, and advocated the extension of welfare services, including day nurseries, free medical assistance and health education for mothers. While Socialists highly valued efficiency, they cautioned that "democracy . . . is even more vital than efficiency." Like the Socialists, ward bosses and party leaders sought to extend welfare services, realizing that such programs were a way of tightening their hold on immigrant and working-class populations. Like business-led reformers, machine politicians turned to limited use of experts when they understood the strength of popular support for administrative reform.[18]

In the main, social science leaders opposed these alternative modes of administrative reform. They were concerned with placing urban problems in a national context, not with regional self-sufficiency. Although they were briefly enamored of direct legislation, seeing it as a way of by-passing the machine, many came to regard with alarm extreme forms that allowed uncomplicated popular access to government decision making. Social science leaders usually opposed public ownership of potentially profit-generating city infra-structure and also looked askance at making welfare programs a public right. Programs put forward by big city machines were usually ignored because academics were so used to seeing the major parties as the object rather than the vehicle for reform.[19]

Finally, social science leaders' work in the field of administrative reform can be approached in terms of whom they served. Populists, Socialists and machine leaders concerned with shaping emerging bureaucracies all had at least one organization or administrative niche capable of sustaining experts working on problems of public administration. However, social science leaders chose to offer expertise primarily to business-led reformers. According to a 1913 NML survey, there were at least 21 bureaus of municipal research, 14 privately endowed and 7 publicly funded. Only one leader worked extensively with a public agency.[20] He was John R. Commons who helped Victor Berger reorganize Milwaukee "on an efficiency basis" for the two brief years the Socialists held power.[21] In general, private bureaus backed by wealthy businessmen were the preferred site of service, offering a more stable resource base, albeit a very different sort of reform.

In sum, social science leaders' work with the NML and other private agencies indicates that science and training alone could not command public attention. Social science leaders needed support for long-term lobbying efforts to create bureaucracy that consumed their expertise. They chose to align themselves with that group best able to supply resources predictably, the business-led reformers, with whom they also shared occupational interests, civic values, sometimes class position and almost always class ambition. But in negotiating such supports, they accepted forms of public administration that served business needs. Thus, they manufactured ideology able to preempt alternatives, designed technical mechanisms to still the unpredictable voice of the people and avoided the issue of how the benefits of bureaucracy are distributed.

However, political science was able to claim public administration as a strong subspecialty. In 1896 only three or four of the largest universities offered instruction in public administration as an independent course, while 46 did so in 1908 and 95 in 1916.[22] The harvest reaped from APSA leaders' alliance with business-led reform movements was a new and verdant field. The struggle over the bureaucracy was by no means won, but continued battle only provided APSA leaders with greater opportunity to engage in expert service and to demand more funds from corporate sponsors.

Economy and Efficiency in Empire

As social science leaders made the machinery of government at home, so too they built bureaucracy abroad. Eager to carve out new territory, they took the opportunity offered by American expansion. Turning away from "the developed states of Europe and North America," leaders looked toward what today we call Third World countries. By approaching world politics through imperialism, they saw a greater chance to demonstrate what their science could do for statecraft. As APSA leader Henry Jones Ford said:

> Doubtless it will take the labor of generations of scholars to bring political science to a position of authority as regards practical politics, but certainly no undertaking could be more inspiring of effort, since success means the power to give rational attainment to the destinies of nations.[23]

As was the case with reform of municipal and federal administration, private forums were necessary to sustain social science leaders' efforts to shape foreign policy. Before World War I, the key private-sector forums concerned with foreign policy were peace societies and international law organizations: the Lake Mohonk Conference on International Arbitration, the American Society of International Law, the American Peace Society, the American Society for Judicial Settlement of International Disputes, and the New York Peace Society. All these groups were interconnected and concerned with international administration, and funded from corporate coffers as well as foundations. Although some social science leaders were associated with each of the organizations, they were most heavily concentrated in the law societies.

The American Society for International Law, organized in 1903, was led by academic lawyers and relied heavily on the Carnegie Endowment for International Peace for funding. APSA leaders, over half of whom held law degrees, were well represented in its leadership. Simeon Baldwin, A.B. Hart, J.B. Moore, P.S. Reinsch, L.S. Rowe, G.G. Wilson, and Theodore Woolsey were all active. The society stood for international arbitration where the rule of law, not force or unpredictable diplomacy, would create a global order that fostered the stability necessary for expansion of American commerce. The American Society for Judicial Settlement of International Disputes, organized and funded by AEA leader and American Tobacco heir Theodore Marburg, was a special-purpose organization working within the broad outlines established by the international lawyers, but particularly concerned with establishing an international judiciary. Both associations promised American businessmen efficient and economical administrative machinery that would do for world bureaucracy what expertise had done for the executive branch of municipal and federal government.[24]

Work with these private policy-making organizations led to social science leaders' appointment to foreign service positions, and outstanding foreign service led to influence in these privately funded forums. Thus, leaders held posts in law and peace societies, with federal departments that managed foreign affairs and as international agents attached to foreign states. Although leaders from all associations worked overseas, political scientists, whose legal training and area of specialization best fitted them for the job, served most heavily (See Appendix, Table 10).

Their service can be grouped into four rough categories. First, as E.R.A. Seligman had predicted in 1899, leaders were sent in during crises--in Panama, Nicaragua, Mexico--where their technical expertise was used to negotiate claims between nations, run governments in the aftermath of failed revolutions, and shore up the shaky currencies of debtor nations in a policy framework that accepted U.S. world hegemony. Second, they participated in the Inter-Americas Conferences, which established U.S. policy in Latin America. Third, they were experts employed by foreign states, particularly China. Fourth, some few were briefly attached to U.S. embassies in Europe in a technical capacity or represented the U.S. at European scientific congresses. Neither their fragmentary work as experts in emergencies nor their brief sorties in European service resulted in sustained provision of expertise. We will concentrate, then, on their efforts to hold open the door for American enterprise in Latin America and China.

Expertise in South America

At the end of the nineteenth century, Latin American countries displayed a political instability as disturbing to American investors as were the inroads being made by European capital south of the border. The Inter-Americas Conferences were a series of U.S.-dominated talks called to work out the nuts and bolts of predictable, efficient commercial relations. As was the case with administrative reform movements at home, the conferences focused on the organization of government--codification and uniformity of laws, accounting systems and bureaucratic procedures--that would make the world safe for American capital.[25] At the Third Conference, held in Rio de Janeiro in 1906, these gatherings took permanent organizational shape with the formation of the International Bureau of the American Republics.[26]

At this time, social science leaders who were active in the American Society of International Law began to serve. One AEA and seven APSA leaders were U.S. delegates to the Inter-Americas Conferences between 1906 and 1921. Their work was facilitated by the Carnegie Endowment for International Peace. Together with the American Society for International Law, the Carnegie Endowment established a program for disseminating American legal concepts in Latin America by setting up international law societies modeled on the parent American society. The organization of these groups in each of the Latin American republics prepared the ground for the meshing of U.S. and Latin American commercial law sought by the Inter-Americas Conferences.[27]

As it became clear that the International Bureau of the Americas, reorganized in 1910 as the Pan American Union (PAU, later the Organization of American States, OAS) provided a suitable outlet for political scientists' expertise, the APSA strengthened ties with it. Particularly active in bringing the discipline into a closer relationship with the PAU was Leo S. Rowe, APSA leader, American Society of International Law official and University of Pennsylvania professor. In 1910 he brought a resolution that the APSA petition the U.S. Congress to hold the upcoming Pan American Scientific Congress in Washington, D.C., where political scientists could participate. In 1913 with APSA leader Wilson in the White House and Moore at the Department of State, the resolution was accepted, and the congress, jointly sponsored by the APSA and PAU, was scheduled in 1915.[28]

As the congress was being planned, the outbreak of the European conflict presented opportunities U.S. capital could not overlook, and the PAU called a financial conference made up of representatives of business and government. The conference, of which Rowe was secretary-general, confirmed as policy business leaders' demand that the U.S. take advantage of the struggle across the Atlantic by supplanting European investment in Latin America with U.S. capital.[29] As conference participant Charles Hamlin, a financier who had sat on the AEA's 1898 committee on colonial finance and now served alongside AEA leader Paul Warburg on the federal board, said, it was now possible for the U.S. to become the banker of the Western Hemisphere.[30]

On the advice of the only delegate representing Latin America, the Dominican Republic's Dr. F.J. Peyando, the financial conference decided that a strong propaganda effort was crucial. If the massive investment program were to be a success, the anti-American sentiment so prevalent in South America had to be stilled. The scientific congress, sponsored jointly by the APSA and PAU, was identified as the agency for this "educational campaign."[31]

Wilson used the congress to unveil his proposal for the "Pan-Americanization" of the Monroe Doctrine. Although speaking about co-equal development of policy among nations forming a "continental family," he distinguished between Pan-Americanism, the international policy of the Americas, and the Monroe Doctrine, the national policy of the U.S. Beneath the rhetoric, the U.S. still claimed the right to unilateral military intervention, and behind the scenes, corporate capital pushed for economic hegemony as well.[32] Thus, the APSA served empire by providing a forum that legitimated public policy designed to serve American business interests. In the ensuing years, the PAU worked to create the administrative apparatus and ideological climate for expansion of American commerce in Latin America.

Rowe, like the handful of other social science leaders who were able to make foreign service a significant part of their careers, was well rewarded for his expertise. He went on to serve as Wilson's secretary of treasury in charge of Latin American affairs, then headed the Latin America desk in the state department, and became director general of the Pan American Union in 1920, a position he would hold until 1945. Even after his death, he graced the halls of the PAU, his ashes in an urn, his bust opposite that of Carnegie, who built the PAU's palatial Washington home in 1910.

Administrators and Ambassadors in China

Before the Revolution of 1910, China had been inhospitable to foreign experts. Scientific knowledge threatened the Confucian-based examination system controlling access to state rewards and power. But in republican China, European nations organized in the Five-Power Consortium carved out spheres of influence in the Middle Kingdom's interior, and their experts moved beyond the old bailiwick of customs house and treaty port to work for the Chinese government on all manner of development projects.[33]   Only the U.S., committed to opening the door to China through competitive commercial imperialism, failed to supply the Chinese government with experts.

In 1913 Chinese officials, hungry for foreign funds and concerned that lack of American experts indicated a lack of American interest, asked Harvard's President Eliot to look into the matter. Eliot, who had recently refused Wilson's offer of an ambassadorship to Peking and was instead touring China for the Carnegie Endowment for International Peace (CEIP), said the U.S. was unprepared to appoint officials to serve another government. However, he agreed to petition the CEIP for a list of prominent American experts from whom the Chinese could choose.[34]

As a result, APSA leader F.J. Goodnow sailed to Peking to become constitutional advisor to the Chinese government, and AEA leader H.C. Adams to serve the Ministry of Communications as an expert in railway accounting. When Goodnow returned in 1916, the Willoughby twins, W.F. and W.W., replaced him.[35] The association leaders' numbers in China were further strengthened by Wilson's appointment of APSA leader Paul Reinsch as ambassador from 1913 to 1919 and AEA leader Charles Crane in 1920.

Although the roads to China were many, they seem to have been traveled by academics experienced in public administration and outfitted by business leaders with international interests. For most, China was the culmination of a long apprenticeship to power, in which government service, corporation and foundation had smoothed the way to positions of personal and academic influence. The possible exception was Wisconsin's Reinsch, who spent years maneuvering for his diplomatic post. He wanted sufficient funds to fill his life with paintings and music as well as a position from which he could influence world affairs. Yet he found the poorly paid academy more congenial than the courtroom where he briefly worked. A diplomatic appointment seemed a way to resolve the dilemma of wealth and scholarship. He carefully cultivated relations with LaFollette, Attorney Joseph E. Davies, who had managed Wilson's campaign in Wisconsin, and the AEA leader Charles R. Crane, the plumbing fixtures millionaire who was Wilson's largest campaign contributor and who advised him on patronage in the Midwest.[36] Although Reinsch was not Crane's first choice, as he was Davies's, Crane was not averse to him. When Crane was persuaded that his favorite, ASS leader E.A. Ross, had unsound social views, Reinsch was offered the ambassadorship Crane would briefly hold after him.

Although the China posts were extremely lucrative, association leaders sought more than their own fortunes. Echoing political scientists' domestic concerns, association leaders, as Goodnow put it, wanted to bestow upon China "the great triumphs of European efficiency and . . . management of the material things of human life" so China could develop its industries and natural resources "under foreign controls."[37] But China followed its ancient policy of using the "barbarians to control the barbarians" and exploited its advisors as adroitly as they tried to exploit China.[38]

The Goodnow Memorandum provides a striking instance of Chinese manipulation of American experts. Asked by President Yuan Shai-Kai to prepare a memorandum as to which was most suited for Chinese conditions, the republican or monarchical form of government, Goodnow replied with all the unconscious arrogance of the Western academic, stressing that while China must recognize the "superiority of Europe to Asia" in matters of government, she was not yet ready to handle sophisticated forms. Instead, she must prepare for democracy slowly, recapitulating European development, especially in cautious extension of the franchise. Like the king and the estates of feudal Europe, China should create a strong central administration with representatives from the merchant, land-owning and literary classes appointed by the executive. As in Europe, "popular democracy" would slowly filter downward. In this way, the poltical instability so characteristic of developing countries and so damaging to foreign investors would be avoided.[39]

Far from being offended, President Yuan Shai-Kai boldly used the memorandum as an American endorsement for his ambition to reconstitute the monarchy with himself as emperor. Reinsch excused Goodnow on the grounds that "advisors had been so generally treated as academic ornaments that Dr. Goodnow did not suspect that in this case his memorandum would be made the starting point and basis of positive action."[40] Although Goodnow defended his memorandum as an essay in real-politic, the Wilson administration, committed to making the world safe for democracy, was embarrassed.

Altogether, the advisors found the Chinese difficult to deal with; graft and corruption were rampant in the new republic. Officials seemed more interested in using emergency foreign loans to buy support for their shaky regime than in building industrial infra-structure that would meet the long-term needs of foreign investors. Adams complained to Reinsch that progress in unifying railroad accounting seemed impossible. "Accountability, honesty and efficiency" were beyond the means of government officials who depended on graft to make ends meet. And Reinsch's own grandiose economic development schemes were often frustrated by the Chinese tendency to sell concessions twice and thrice.[41]

The expert's response was the same one they gave to corruption, graft and popular democracy at home. They called for administrative economy and efficiency. As Reinsch said:

> The real importance of the present effort for efficiency standardization [in China] lies in the fact that it represents that American organizational faculty addressing itself to details with a view to once for all subordinating them to certain rules of action so that in the future they may all be perfectly controlled without a constant wearing attention to each of them. . . . It is pioneer work which requires . . . the experience of men accustomed to handle large affairs according to the most severe tests of modern efficiency.[42]

And they comforted themselves in the chaos that was China by reproducing the organizational forms they had built at home. The Chinese Social and Political Science Association was organized by Adams, Goodnow, Reinsch and the Willoughby twins, complete with quarterly journal, to distill nonpartisan ideology and expertise in the Middle Kingdom. The NML's municipal charter, which had already guided city reorganization in Manila, Havanna and San Juan, was introduced to Peking, and Goodnow organized a municipal research bureau.[43]

By and large their schemes to reorganize China for American capital came to naught. Reinsch was more ardent for expansion than corporate leaders at home. He was impatient with the American Group, headed by Morgan interests, for their tardiness in making use of options. To speed up American investment in China, he personally developed finance schemes and worked with AEA leader Frank Vanderlip of National City Bank to put together the American International Corporation. He corresponded heavily with corporate contacts like Crane and Willard Straight, trying to tempt them to bring his plans to fruition. And he constantly tried to commit the state department to some show of concern for the protection of American investment in China.

American investors, however, were chary of the political situation in China and would not act without ironclad guarantees of loans. Throughout the period, American investment averaged roughly $50 million, representing only 3.1 percent of the total foreign investment in China, a figure which drove Reinsch to frenzy. Generally, U.S. capitalists preferred Latin America.[44]

Reinsch resigned in 1919 when Wilson betrayed his six years' work with the Lansing-Ishi notes. In this exchange, the U.S. recognized Japan's special economic interest in China and began to close the door Reinsch thought Wilson wanted him to open wider. Like W.W. Willoughby, Reinsch did not return to academics but served as the Chinese representative in Washington, D.C., for $20,000 per year, a substantial sum in the 1920s. However, Willoughby, who retained close contacts with the state department and was on the staff of the Institute for Government Research directed by his twin, became China's trusted advisor while Reinsch had trouble collecting his salary.[45]

Although APSA leaders had hoped to influence "the destinies of nations," the expansion of the State Department and the establishment of the Foreign Service School after World War I made foreign service a full-time career. This prevented academic experts from moving easily between classrooms and embassies. Foreign affairs retained an important place in political science, since it was a prerequisite for placing well in state department examinations, but area specialities followed by on-the-job training became the preferred method for preparing diplomats. The international arena had enough glamour to attract high-caliber careerists, and students not statecraft became the main opportunity for political scientists interested in foreign affairs. Although unable to keep control of the rude administrative apparatus they had jerry-built in the emergency of a suddenly acquired empire and rapid overseas economic expansion, association leaders' service to imperialism strengthened their claims on students' preliminary training and allowed them to maintain foreign affairs in the university as part of their field.

Conclusion

With that curious blend of "altruism and exploitation"[46] perhaps characteristic of men of ideas in a materialist society, social science leaders tried to build bureaucracies where they could use their specialized knowledge to shape national policy decisions. Yet their ardent and sincere desire for economical and efficient public administration was compromised by their alliance with business-led reformers, as such an alignment vitiated the popular appeal of economy and efficiency.

However, as resource-poor intellectuals, their choice showed rational appreciation of the long-term interests of their discipline. They turned to that sector of the reform movement farthest from the vagaries of the political process, closest to their own understanding of administration of a national industrial society and best able to provide enduring financial support. The relatively stable reform groups of the era--the NML, the New York bureau, peace and foreign policy organizations--were able to sustain leaders' work as adjuncts to the policy-making process. Thus, leaders moved back and forth between federal commission, state department, municipal government and league, bureau and institute, all the while building demand for expertise.

With a few exceptions, like Rowe, Moore and Willoughby, leaders acted more as lobbyists for their corporate sponsors' concept of bureaucracy than as independent policy makers. Most functioned as technicians and policy popularizers in private policy forums, although some, like the directors of the New York bureau, served as policy managers, and others, like the China hands, as policy advisors. But in the main they manufactured an ideology of economy, efficiency and expertise that justified expansion of public administration and constructed technical mechanisms to insure it could best be operated by those familiar with bureaucratic organization--businessmen, government officials and experts. Experts became the link between corporate leaders and the state and were granted a degree of independence because of the importance of their function but were unable to take issue with their sponsors in the long run. As a result, the business community received a disproportionate share of the benefits of public bureaucracy.

However, exchanges between leaders and their corporate and government sponsors were hardly to social scientists' disadvantage. In return for expert service, political scientists received the content of their curriculum, together with a built-in clientele. Municipal government, public administration and foreign relations, especially area studies for developing countries, became viable specialties within the graduate university. Thus, APSA leaders built bureaucracies that called for expert staff, ensuring that students would fill their classrooms and bringing about the continued expansion of the discipline.

NOTES

1. A. Lawrence Lowell, "Expert Administrators in Popular Government," American Political Science Review (APSR) 7 (February 1913): 481.

2. Frank J. Goodnow, "The Work of the American Political Science Association," Proceedings of the American Political Science Association (PAPSA), 1905, p. 37.

3. For a vivid account of industrial cities at the turn of the century, see Lincoln Steffens, The Shame of the Cities (McClure, Phillips and Co., 1904, reprint ed., New York: Hill and Wang, 1957).

4. "Call for the Conference and Endorsement," Proceedings of the National Conference for Good City Government (Philadelphia: The Municipal League, 1894). The relationship between the patrician reformers, often Mugwumps, who peopled the Good Government groups, and the plutocrats or corporate leaders who dominated organizations like NML, has been a point of some controversy. Richard Hofstadter in The Age of Reform (New York: Vintage, 1955) perhaps best represents the position that argues for competition over status in the arena of politics between GooGoos, as the Good Government types were sometimes called, and newly rich industrialists. Robert Weibe, in his The Search for Order (New York: Hill and Wang, 1967) suggests that the dynamics of professionalizing occupations and the drive for business efficiency, not status anxiety, stimulated reform in the Progressive era, while Gerald McFarland, Mugwumps, Morals and Politics (Amherst, Mass.: University of Massachusetts Press, 1975) and Martin J. Scheisl, The Politics of Efficiency: Municipal Administration and Reform in America, 1800-1920 (Berkeley, Calif.: University of California Press, 1977), point to the gradual merging of Mugwump and plutocrat in the common quest for economy and efficiency after the turn of the century. The leadership of the organizations studied in this chapter seem to bear out this last interpretation.

5. Frank Mann Stewart, A Half Century of Municipal Reform: The History of the National Municipal League (Berkeley, Calif.: University of California Press), p. 187.

6. Ibid., p. 21.

7. H.W. Foulkes, "A Symposium--the Sphere of Voluntary Organization in Social Movements," Handbook of the AEA, supplement to Economic Studies 1 (April 1896): 147-157.

8. F.J. Goodnow, as quoted in Stewart, A Half Century of Reform, p. 39.

9. Schiesl, The Politics of Efficiency, p. 131.

10. A. Lawrence Lowell, "Expert Administrators in Popular Government," APSR 7 (February 1913): p. 61.

11. Schiesl, The Politics of Efficiency, especially chapter 7, "The Businessman as Administrator," pp. 133-148.

12. Stewart, A Half Century of Municipal Reform, pp. 55-60.

13. W.B. Munro, as quoted in Stewart, A Half Century of Municipal Reform.

14. Charles A. Beard, "The Bolshevik Session of the Annual Municipal League Annual Conference," National Municipal Reform (NMR) 7 (September 1918): 450.

15. Stewart, A Half Century of Municipal Reform, p. 56.

16. For the New York bureau, see Jane S. Dahlberg, The New York Bureau of Municipal Research (New York: New York University Press, 1966); for the Institute for Government Research, see W.F. Willoughby, "The Institute for Government Research," APSR 12 (February 1918): 50-62; for the foundations of the executive presidency, see David

Eakins, "The Class Consciousness of Some Social Justice Progressives, 1905-1921," unpublished MS, AHA panel "Administrative Liberalism," December 29, 1973, San Francisco; and Larry Berman, The Office of Management and Budget and the Presidency, 1921-1979 (Princeton, N.J.: Princeton University Press, 1979).

17. Barry D. Karl, Charles E. Merriam and the Study of Politics (Chicago: University of Chicago Press, 1974), pp. 50-55.

18. For agrarian radicals and farmer labor parties, see, for example, Grant McConnell, The Decline of Agrarian Democracy (Berkeley, Calif.: University of California Press, 1953); and Robert L. Marlow, Political Prairie Fire: The Nonpartisan League, 1915-1922 (Minneapolis, Minn.: University of Minnesota Press, 1955); for the Socialists, see James Weinstein, The Decline of Socialism in America, 1912-1925 (New York: Vintage, 1969); for party reformers, see Schiesl, The Politics of Efficiency.

19. Exceptions to social scientists' position on direct legislation were Charles Beard, Jesse Macey and Charles E. Merriam. For social scientists' attitude to public ownership, see chapter 8 on the NCF Public Utilities Commission; for their position on social welfare, see chapter 10 on the Russell Sage Foundation.

20. Edward M. Sait, "Research and Reference Bureaus," National Municipal Review 2 (January 1913): 55-56.

21. John R. Commons, Myself (Madison, Wisc.: University of Wisconsin Press, 1964). Commons and his career also raise the question of administrative reform at the state level and the place of the "Wisconsin Idea" in the various administrative reform movements of the day. Generally, the largely urban-based association leaders were not concerned with the state as an administrative unit until late in the period under consideration. However, for those midwestern academics in rural areas, especially those at land grant universities, the state was the only politically meaningful unit. Yet service to the state was public and subject to all the

unpredictability and instability that association leaders feared. Merle Curti and Vernon Carstensen give a good account of the political strife and constant pressure faced by academic experts in state service in The University of Wisconsin, (Madison, Wisc.: University of Wisconsin Press, 1949), 2: 267-294.

22. W.B. Munro, "Instruction in Municipal Government in the Universities and Colleges of the U.S.," NMR 5 (January 1916): 570-573.

23. Henry Ford Jones, "The Scope of Political Science," PAPSA (1906), p. 206.

24. C. Roland Marchand, The American Peace Movement and Social Reform, 1898-1918 (Princeton, N.J.: Princeton University Press, 1972), especially chapter 2, "Courts, Judges and the Rule of Law," pp. 39-73; chapter 3, "Businessmen and Practicality," which treats funding, pp. 75-100.

25. See J. Lloyd Mecham, The United States and Inter-American Security (Austin, Tex.: University of Texas Press, 1971).

26. Leo S. Rowe, The Pan American Union and the Pan American Conferences, (Washington, D.C.: Pan American Union, 1940), pp. 9-10.

27. Marchand, The American Peace Movement, p. 65.

28. "Report of the Secretary," PAPSA (1910): 37; "Report of the Secretary," PAPSA (1913): 45.

29. Marchand, The American Peace Movement, pp. 173-174.

30. Sidney Bell, Righteous Conquest: Woodrow Wilson and the Evolution of a New Diplomacy (Port Washington, N.Y.: Kennikat Press, 1972), p. 122.

31. Ibid.

32. Ibid.; see also Mecham, The U.S. and Inter-American Security, p. 79.

33. Jonathan Spence, To Change China: Western Advisers in China 1920-1960 (Boston: Little, Brown and Company, 1969), p. 129.

34. Paul S. Reinsch, An American Diplomat in China (Garden City, N.Y.: Doubleday Page and Co., 1922), p. 68.

35. For a discussion on Henry Carter Adams's career, see chapter 4; for the Willoughby's, see chapter 6.

36. Noel Harvey Pugach, "Progress, Prosperity and the Open Door: The Ideas and Career of Paul S. Reinsch," (Ph.D. dissertation, University of Wisconsin, 1967), pp. 86-97.

37. F.J. Goodnow, "Reform in China," APSR 9 (May 1915): 216, 219.

38. Spence, To Change China.

39. F.J. Goodnow, "The Parliament of the Republic of China: A Memorandum Submitted to the President of China," APSR 8 (November 1914): 541-562.

40. Reinsch, An American Diplomat, p. 173; Goodnow, "Reform in China," pp. 209-223.

41. Reinsch, An American Diplomat, p. 31; Pugach, "Progress, Prosperity and the Open Door."

42. As quoted in Pugach, "Progress, Prosperity and the Open Door," p. 290.

43. Reinsch, _An American Diplomat_, pp. 153-155; Clinton Rogers Woodruff, "The National Municipal League," _PAPSA_ (1909): 146; see also the "News and Notes" section in the _APSR_, 1912-1921.

44. Pugach, "Progress, Prosperity and the Open Door," pp. 271-272. See also Jerry Israel, _Progressivism and the Open Door: America and China, 1905-1921_ (Madison, Wisc.: University of Wisconsin Press, 1971).

45. Pugach, "Progress, Prosperity and the Open Door," pp. 526-544.

46. Spence, _To Change China_, introduction, unpaginated.

10
Tainted Wealth, Tainted Knowledge: Professors and Philanthropists Define Their Inter-Relationship

Social science leaders realized that the philanthropic foundations being invented by wealthy capitalists at the turn of the twentieth century were treasure troves of enormous potential. They were well aware of the uses to which such massed capital might be put in industrializing their inquiries. The university-based disciplinarians knew particularly that such financial patronage frequently figured in their own past schooling and present salaries. In fact, their daily occupations--teaching, reading, writing, research--often occurred within walls named for this or that donor.

Yet the resource-thin leaders did not greedily grasp the philanthropists' hand when extended. Nor did they quickly push themselves on the funders' payrolls, becoming so many hired heads energetically elaborating ideology and technical amelioration for, in effect, the highest bidder. Indeed, lean and hungry though they might have been, the associational leaders as specialists in knowledge engaged philanthropists as potentates of power in a several-decade-long courtship. During these years, they avoided a marriage of convenience, one inevitably de-legitimizing their emerging monopoly of professionalizing knowledge. Instead, both parties sought to discover and formalize role expectations and procedures to guide and regularize their mutually beneficial dealings. In effect, they explored complementary terms of trade, exchanging the professors' social science knowledge for the potential power damned up in the philanthropic foundations.

To this search for complementary terms of trade, the professors brought a social science formulated within the AEA, one selecting a corporate capitalist road to industrialization as the most fitting for American political economic development. This path was drawn by the AEA's presidents half-way between populist socialism and anarchistic laissez-faire. And it was followed by deeds supporting the emerging corporate center, service rendered in public and private agencies like the ICC and city charter commissions as well as the NCF and NML. Such words and deeds clearly announced social science's essential centralist intentions. Their object of barter was thus made more attractive to the economic center.

For their part, philanthropists like Andrew Carnegie, Mrs. Russell Sage and the Rockefellers brought to the bargain the corporate wealth of the economic center. They also brought a sense of issue stemming from the center's recent growth. Since 1870 an economy rooted in thousands of smaller farms and businesses had become based in larger corporations characterized by centralized capital and administered by ever-larger armies of managerial and clerical staffs. As smaller-scale, decentralized enterprises were replaced by large-scale, concentrated ones, enormous wealth and power were consolidated. Such consolidation in oil, rail, steel, sugar, and so on made philanthropy possible.

Consolidation also made philanthropy necessary, for these larger enterprises required an expanded white-collar labor force to keep track of the papers coordinating the bureaucratically controlled firms: papers replacing spoken orders; papers recording previously rule-of-thumb calculations of price, profit and loss; papers noting work flow and inventory formerly visually appraised and reckoned. This growth in paper handling is suggested by the rapid expansion of schooling to train a new white-collar strata in the techniques required.

The emergence of this white-collar strata greatly intensified the always highly complicated problems of ideological production and distribution. On the one hand, efficient coordination of concentrated capital required labor that was considerably literate, relatively spontaneous, capable of delegated autonomy, and schooled in collaborative effort and social cooperation. But such new levels of literacy situated within an increasingly clear interdependent social division of labor created a new audience for popularly organized anti-corporate capitalist groups advancing alternative ideological interpretations of power arrangements. In their role explorations with the social science leaders, foundation trustees and managers were continuously concerned with gaining access to this new audience in what amounted to a cut-throat competition among ideologies, a battle for the hearts and minds of the new white-collar workers.

The Tainted Money Debate

Philanthropy based on centralized enterprise was itself subject to ideological combat. For example, Andrew Carnegie in 1889 authored a series of magazine articles on giving away wealth, celebrating a decade of his own innovative endowments. Thus, he cheered his paying for buildings in communities willing to fill them with books and supply operating expenses to service the print-hungry new white-collar strata. Generally, his articles argued that dying rich was a social disgrace. Better that private wealth should be actively administered as a public trust during one's lifetime than irresponsibly husbanded for one's heirs.

But Carnegie sought a public trust without corresponding popular accountability, one expressing in its paternalistic administration the will of its accumulator rather than any more general aspiration. Thus, libraries were set up for the literate rather than higher wages won by workers or industrial democracy struggled for by populists. Indeed, Carnegie's philanthropy was less the mother of radical reform than its surrogate. Wisely administered, "surplus wealth" became a means of reconciling the rich and the poor. Corporate-based philanthropy was thereby a flexible and powerful alternative to more radical schemes redistributing privatized property and control.[1]

Carnegie's self-centered poems for philanthropy were contested by those with alternative schemes, for example, partisans of the "social gospel." Men of the cloth and other reform activists were not long in condemning what they scornfully termed Carnegie's "gospel of wealth." In a sustained attack from the pulpits, in old established forums like the National Conference of Charities and Corrections (NCCC) and in magazine articles, they questioned the philanthropy of "robber barons," "pirates of industry" and "spoilers of the state." They asked if churches and universities could accept as gifts "tainted money" made in morally reprehensible ways without condoning the methods used, tacitly accepting the donor's moral standards.[2] And energetic muck-rakers relentlessly informed the reading public on the methods used to centralize corporate capital. Thus, Ida Tarbell told millions how Rockefeller's Standard Oil Corporation had violated the Protestant ethic and spirit of capitalist accumulation by using raw power rather than theoretical efficiencies of scale and technology to gather together almost all the nation's petroleum refining facilities into a virtual monopoly. Because, as Tarbell showed, he ruthlessly used railroad rebates and drawbacks (rebates on other's shipments) to centralize refining capacity (95 percent in 1880), Rockefeller's fortune was "tainted money" in the era's widely accepted terms.[3]

From time to time, disciplinary leaders were called upon to comment on or assist philanthropic ventures rooted in such "tainted money." Their responses to the Russell Sage Foundation are informative. In 1906 the noted robber baron left $65 million to his wife. She granted some $71 million to various charities over the next dozen years. Aided by long-time educational manager Daniel Coit Gilman and NCCC activists, she gave $15 million to the Russell Sage Foundation created in 1907 for "the improvement of social and living conditions in the USA [by] any means . . . including research, publication, [and] education."[4]

When the reforming voice of Charities and the Commons asked "what university men think of the Russell Sage Foundation," nine AEA leaders were among the 15 whose answers were published. All nine discipline leaders urged the new foundation to centralize and deepen the data base of the charities movement. This, they agreed, would facilitate discovering and preventing the causes of poverty. Unlike the muck-raking journalists, these university men did not think Sage's money "tainted." Nor was such "surplus wealth" the result of the exploitative appropriation of "surplus value," as Marxists and other anti-capitalists held. Accepting capitalist industrialization, the AEA saw poverty, not philanthropy, as the social problem.[5] Other leaders in the discipline expressed similar satisfaction with Sage's potential in other periodicals and offered their thoughts on the best uses for Sage's funds.[6] In 1908 the AEA elected the Russell Sage Foundation's head to its third vice-presidency. By such positive responses, the AEA leadership placed itself squarely in the continuing tainted-money debate, strongly supporting corporate-based private wealth used for publicly unaccountable philanthropy.

For its part, the Sage Foundation did not directly return the favor. It did not devote funding to the learned societies nor the college and universities, per se. As a matter of first principles, it ruled out meeting individual, church or higher educational needs.[7] Rather, Sage aimed to coordinate and centralize the locally based charity organization movement. It sought to give national coherence to that movement, rationalizing the emergent public and private social service sectors while encouraging social workers to create their own occupational monopoly of knowledge and practice.[8]

Given the Sage's focus, the disciplines (and their leaders) were rarely beneficiaries of the foundation's largess. Its money funded an applied science based outside the university, gathering data and applying systematic theory to a social service sector increasingly essential to centralizing corporate capital. Indeed, Sage's crucial contribution to the period's university-based disciplines was freeing them from a possible focus on precisely such charitable and social service concerns. Sociology in particular was separated from such possible practice, and hence knowledge creation.

All in all, then, the discipline leaders entered the "tainted-money" ideological lists on the side of the foundations. They thereby supported philanthropic efforts rooted in corporate capitalism to make the nation safe for continued capitalist development via the amelioration of its ills and the indoctrination of its emerging white-collar ranks. Of course, this general support was matched by more specific scholarly efforts and more exacting exchanges of resources for knowledge.

Management Expectations

When the AEA's leadership went beyond generalized support for the philanthropic ventures of corporate capitalism in the Progressive period, they entered a relatively uncharted domain of social relations. So did the foundation managers. Working willy-nilly within an over-arching, shared ethos facilitating capitalistic industrialization's accelerating advance across the North American continent, they developed the roles that now guide and channel the energies and expectations of contemporary social science funders and grant recipients.

AEA economists, when employed in universities, were subject to a resource-distributing management that was quite sensitive to the promise and pitfalls typical of academic intellectual production. When making internal resource allocations, the administrators had some sense of professors' propensities to propose projects polished bright with promise only to have such works tarnished by the routine imperfections inherent in massive industrialized data collection and organization and buffeted by emergent issues of analysis and interpretation. Furthermore, university managers had learned that the pressing demands of researchers' classroom work and departmental politics, of their university life and professional obligations, of personal desires and household needs all competed with optimistically scheduled knowledge production timetables. Indeed, educational administrators, especially those whose present positions had academic roots, both realistically discounted and entrepreneurially encouraged the emerging professorate's often over-blown research proposals.

Others, however, were less learned in the folkways of university-based knowledge production. Foundation managers with fullsome experiences organizing centralized capitalist production and distribution were often less intimately acquainted with the accepted uncertainties of academic work. Industrialists and financiers whose prosperity depended on negotiated contractual obligations, bargained for relatively well-defined products and services, and expected to hold suppliers to agreed-upon exchanges. Extending these expectations to proposals funded by philanthropy incorrectly assumed that idea-workers could predictably create their commodities in much the same way that other skilled crafts could. Correcting such expectations meant making clear to these resource controllers that knowledge production was not organizable in quite the same way that railroads, steel mills or textile factories were. Rather, it required a somewhat specialized structure of management before its manufacture might be successfully supported by their funding.

Of course, the many political leaders and cultural elites sitting on foundation boards had had many opportunities to notice the normal duplicities of campaign promises, bureaucratic rhetoric and traditional bohemian dare-do and, thereby, sensed something of the usual uncertainties of academic knowledge production. But even their more educated expectations were tried by those academics whose career aspirations and research proposals exceeded their grasping ability to seize and deliver the knowledge promised to gain the grant. As both foundation managers and disciplinarian social scientists came to realize, they had to find new means of appraising and increasing the probabilities that professors could and would complete their negotiated research enterprises. After directly confronting the uncertainties of social science knowledge production in projects like the Carnegie Institution in Washington's Department of Economics and Sociology, foundation managers and their social science counter-parts developed mediating research management organizations like the Social Science Research Council to establish and monitor more reasonable and reliable research expectations between funders and grantees.

The AEA and the Carnegie Institute of Washington

In 1900 Carnegie desired to create a centralizing research unit in American higher eduction. Knowledge specialists there would operate on the very frontiers of the disciplines, setting the analytical pace, tone and aesthetic, defining the fields' metaphors and paradigms for co-workers scattered throughout the decentralized colleges and universities. He explored establishing a national university at Washington, D.C. But on the advice of Andrew D. White and Daniel Coit Gilman, founding presidents at Cornell and Johns Hopkins, he set up instead the Carnegie Institute of Washington (CIW). Founded in 1901, the institute was to "conduct, endow and assist investigation" in all learned fields securing for the United States "leadership in the domain of discovery and the utilization of new forces for the benefit of mankind."[9]

To supervise the deployment of the institute's multi-millions, its board was filled with a cross section of the period's power elite. These initial trustees brought to the CIW's board their own far-flung industrial, political and cultural interests.[10] Led by these elite trustees, the institute articulated Carnegie's desire to discipline new forces of production. Thus, it housed departments of experimental evolution, marine biology, terrestial magnetism, geophysics, botany, nutrition, meridian astronomy and embryology. It also provided, perhaps for the first time in the U.S., sustained resource support for a specific group of academics and public service professionals engaged in producing ideas that addressed clearly defined social issues: its Department of Economics and Sociology.

Since the genius of many of the trustees lay in corporate centralization, the institute's basic method was "the substitution of organized for unorganized effort" in the domain of intellectual production.[11] In essence, the CIW--like the Sage and other foundations--used its resources to organize and rationalize existing knowledge-production groups already approaching the issues of the day from an ideological position favorable to their shared elite interests. So it was for the Department of Economics and Sociology's funding of established AEA political economists working piecemeal on uncoordinated research but sharing wholehearted acceptance of the newly emerging forms of concentrated industrial capital.

To define the department's problematic, the board turned to a three-man economics advisory committee. Trustee Carroll D. Wright, internationally known labor statistician and soon to become president of Clark College, was its chairman. For decades, he had specialized in transforming potentially raucous cabinet-level state and federal agencies into calm labor statistics bureaus thus stilling skilled worker unrest and white-collar unease. And on occasion, such as the Pullman strike of 1894, he headed ad hoc governmental commissions whose findings soothed the body politic.[12] The other two advisory committee members were AEA leaders Henry W. Farnum of Yale and Columbia's John Bates Clark. Both AEA economists had worked with many of the CIW's trustees in business-led associations like the NCF and both would later act as foundation managers themselves.[13]

The advisory committee recommended a comprehensive political economic history to document "the economic and legislative experience of our state," especially (1) social legislation and its results, (2) the labor movement, (3) the industrial development of each state, (4) their taxation and fiscal arrangements, and (5) their regulation of corporations.[14] This definition of departmental scope neatly combined Wright's long-cherished desire to chart the industrial evolution of the United States,[15] with the AEA's ability to locate and recruit trained intellectual workers willing to work on bits and pieces of the larger puzzle.

When the CIW's board of trustees approved the department's focus, its advisory committee turned to the AEA's council to staff the scheme. With AEA President E.R.A. Seligman facilitating negotiations, the department's work was subdivided by the council into eleven sections. The AEA's council nominated seven of the department's initial eleven section heads from its own number.[16] The CIW trustees accepted the AEA council's self-nominiations as section heads and provided $30,000 in start-up funds. In return, it expected each section's results to be packaged in books within five years, which when placed end-to-end would account for the political economic evolution of the United States. As it turned out, the total grant amounted to a quarter of a million dollars over a dozen years (1904-1916), and the project never found its way to the library shelves.[17]

In its negotiated form, the arrangment between professors and trustees was mutually beneficial. Economists of the Progressive period defined themselves as able to understand scientifically and intervene amelioratively in the course of history if they could but secure the opportunities necessary for full development of the discipline. Trustees accepted professors with an ideologically safe, even kindred, sense of problem to investigate the politically critical issues of the day and provided them with the resources and the autonomy to arrange their own work. In return for such support, the institute expected production of a data base that would permit "a forecast of American social and economic development." As the institute's second president Robert Woodward put it in 1905, the Department of Economics and Sociology shared "the goal of science," namely, "a capacity of prediction." Accordingly, he foresaw that "economic and social science are . . . plainly destined to play an increasingly important role in the progress of mankind."[18]

Social scientists, then, were seen by foundation managers as developing predictive capacity while organizing historical data in ways that pointed to "safe" solutions for current social problems. Furthermore, as the Department of Economics and Sociology gathered data, it would, in trustee Carroll Wright's words, "put the matter before the people in a way so much needed at the present time."[19] Thus, the

ideological function of CIW's social science research was to show (1)
that U.S. capitalistic development was understandable, controllable,
reformable, and even inevitable, and (2) that public welfare could be
served and private wealth preserved within the power parameters of
corporate capitalism.

In sum, the research undertaken by the Department of Economics and
Sociology was expected by foundation managers and academic
disciplinarians to serve several purposes: (1) to produce the tools for
prediction; (2) to use the tools in stabilizing an economy that was
based on highly concentrated, privately controlled industrial capital;
(3) to present information to the public that defined and legitimated a
political economic order as open to the evolutionary process of
incremental reform.

The project, however, was more easily negotiated than delivered. In
the first several years, the economists began to appreciate the
immensity of the task they had defined. In essence, they contracted to
deliver an exhaustive historical accounting of the U.S. political
economy at both the state and federal levels. This would have been a
most difficult task under the best of circumstances. But their
situations were far from ideal. For example, no provision had been made
for leaves of absence or indeed even a permanent staff. Under the press
of academic and civic duties, the eminent professors who functioned as
moon-lighting section heads were frequently forced to subcontract topics
to graduate students in need of research support.[20] The graduate
students in turn renegotiated areas and timetables of research to meet
personal needs and degree requirements, fragmenting any hope of a
unified treatment of problem areas. In this way, more professors and
more graduate students were funded, with hundreds of scholars receiving
small subsidies.[21] Yet by 1909, the date initially scheduled for
project completion, very few of the department's works had reached
publication.[22]

Such poor productive performance did not sit well with a
high-powered board of trustees, one wanting to fund projects with
predictably "sure results."[23] When Trustee Wright, who headed the
department and managed its labor movement section, died in 1909, the
board audited the project. The economists had to convince a somewhat
skeptical board to continue the operation at all, since the department

had not produced the promised volumes, let alone predicted the nation's industrial future and calmed its population's ideological uncertainties. To meet the possibility of the department disbanding, another of the original advisors, Yale's Henry Farnum, agreed to assume its chairmanship, pledging to manage it for greater and more efficient production.[24] He negotiated the transfer of Wright's labor movement section to a competitive--and separately funded--knowledge production center: Richard Ely's University of Wisconsin-linked American Bureau of Economic Research.[25] Furthermore, he put the other sections on more realistic timetables for their work's completion, even though the force of events still intervened as when a Mississippi researcher was forced to lose a year's scholarly production defending his plantation's crop from boll weavils.[26]

Farnum also attempted a managerial tour de force: reorganizing the department on a more permanent footing, a scheme developed with the approval of the department's governing Board of Collaborators, which was heavy with the AEA leaders.[27] They proposed that the CIW fund a newer version of the department, one with a full-time, resident staff. Its mission would be to set up "a clearing house for economic thought . . . with the necessary bibliographic apparatus." It would advise and assist state and university-based researchers working on the economic issues of the day. Its own staff would take particular interest in the leading public questions, such as prices and cost of living, wages, population, taxation, economic pathology, industrial cycles, public utilities and the trust question ("the effects of large-scale production on prices, wages and efficiency").

In his annual department reports to the trustees, Farnum stressed improved productivity, rationalized scholarship, increasing publication and the need to make the now well-functioning knowledge creation unit a permanent, full-time operation of the CIW.[29] He noted some sure results. "Our studies in economic history . . . have an important bearing upon practical questions. In these days of rapidly increasing government regulation of business and labor, the one safe guide is the experience of the past."[30] And beyond such practical and technical guides, Farnum offered the expectation that the department could serve ideological ends. It could be a scientific bulwark against socialism. Looking backward, he noted: "Since we began our work, not a few books in

American economic history have been published by writers under the influence of the Marxian doctrine of class conflict." Belaboring such authors for undue emphasis on "material and egoistic motives" and generally biased scholarship, Farnum claimed for a permanent CIW department "the scientific spirit . . . that will have an authority that cannot be possessed by the work of those who write a theory to prove."[31] Here Farnum refused to see that a Marxian economics aiming at democratic revolution made the same claim to scientific status as did a centralist AEA version committed to incremental, non-revolutionary change. He ignored also the patent contradiction of a scientific social science, such as his department claimed, unscientifically dismissing out-of-hand Marxist analysis and its socialist answers to current public questions. In effect, Farnum renewed the department's undaunted commitment to manufacture ideology justifying American capitalistic development while providing for the technical amelioration of the social questions raised during industrialization.

The CIW board responded to the departmental collaborators' proposal for permanent status with repeated encouragement between 1912 and 1916. For example, in 1913 President Woodward reported "no dissent" to Farnum's proposal, nor any doubt that the department's "effective pioneer work" was needed "indefinitely into the future."[32] Yet in 1916 the board "discontinued" the department, awarding the remaining funds--some $16,000--to its collaborators to wind up operations.[33] The trustees thereby denied the department even temporary casual connection, let alone permanent staff and status. It also refused to reward the collaborators' substantial increment in scholarly productivity and even denied to itself the "sure results" of publishing the monographs completed during Farnum's rationalized management.

In backing away from its encouragements of the Department of Economics and Sociology's aspirations for permanent status and from its own desire for "sure results" by sponsoring publications ready for the presses, the CIW trustees revealed their collective sensitivity to the second U.S. Industrial Relations Commission (IRC). It its Final Report, the commission capped months of well-publicized inquiry into the linkage between tainted philanthropic money and tainted knowledge produced by foundation-supported researchers.[34] Unwilling to meet the ideological challenge of the Final Report, the CIW trustees completely cut off funds to the period's best-known, best-funded and, under Farnum, best-organized social science collaborative research effort. For insight into the ideological skills necessary for foundation-sponsored, social science research, we now turn to the activities of the Rockefeller enterprises that invited the IRC's attention.

Corporate Philanthropy and Ideological Management

The problems of ideological management associated with philanthropic support of social science research pivot on the widely held expectation of value neutrality. A populace schooled in American egalitarianism understood that the grantor must not directly influence the recipient's results. Nor may the researcher wittingly support the grantor's specific interests. In the Progressive period this management problem was acute. The tainted-money debate and other raucous anti-corporate capitalist campaigns had prepared the public to anticipate that corporate funding would violate value neutrality. Thus, tainted money would sponsor tainted knowledge.

These widespread anticipations were, as we have seen, largely correct. The AEA leadership was prepared to produce sponsored studies in support of the rising corporate center coming to dominate capitalism in America. But the discipline leaders were not usually available to manufacture findings in support of this or that capitalist's interests, unless it was congruent with the larger hegemonic interest. Rather than serve specific capitalist's interest, they saw themselves as articulators of more general ones. They defined their work in terms of the wider community and its knowledge needs: in the name of the national public interest.

Serving the public national interest meant recording social and industrial progress for the NCF in its ideological struggles against socialists. It meant joining the NML and rationalizing the local, state and federal governing apparatus by removing policy matters from public debate and accountability. It meant endorsing Russell Sage's funding of centralized social services treating some of the structural consequences of industrialization--impoverished households, abused and abandoned children, loan sharks--while ignoring others--socially irresponsible wealth, industrial concentration, political corruption. It meant trying to organize a historical data base for the CIW to justify America's political-economic past and even predict and control its present and future.

Such work was done in exchange for the social and material resources necessary for discipline development. It also occurred within a framework of national interest that accepted as appropriate the inevitability of emerging corporate capitalism's domination within the political economy, a domination legitimated and technically perfected by knowledge producers such as the AEA leaders. For those industrialists, financiers, politicians and scholars who shared this sense of national interest, value neutrality meant affirming the general interests of the emerging center.

Those who opposed this framework of national public interest raised the issue of violated value neutrality, arguing that tainted money produced tainted knowledge. However, they raised the issue most dramatically by unmasking the fictive value neutrality of sponsored knowledge production created in the clear interests of specific capitalists. Such unmasking was indeed effective in helping to shut down the NCF's social survey and the CIW's Department of Economics and Sociology. But raising the tainted-knowledge issue at this level of specific interests left unexamined the wider, more general interests at play. These interests were nonetheless sufficiently imperiled to urge foundation and discipline leaders to create organizations fostering the necessary fiction of a manifest value neutrality in the eyes of those requiring such a vision. This fiction met the public's expectations for equal and common decency in knowledge production: value neutrality between sponsor and researcher. Such organizations also clarified and solidified expectations on exactly what was fundable. In principle, knowledge in support of the economic center's interests was always expected and supportable. However, knowledge furthering particular interests was fundable only when those interests were congruent with the economic center's concerns.

Tainted Knowledge

The period's clearest unmasking of tainted knowledge involved the Rockefeller Foundation (RF). The RF operated differently than other major foundations. Sage and Carnegie were gifts offered to the public by persons no longer actively involved in industrial production or finance; their trustees and managers did not profit directly from disposition of funds. Sage and Carnegie could and did claim they represented the public rather than any private interest when deploying resources. The Rockefeller Foundation, too, was legally separated from the Rockefeller corporate enterprises. However, the foundation shared offices and key decision makers with the business group. While legally separated, the two were in fact interlocked at the top where all crucial resource decisions were made.[35] Thus, although the Rockefeller Foundation also argued that its resources were spent for the public good the case could always be made that Rockefeller's good, and not the nation's was being served.

As the RF's organization was at odds with other foundations, so too the Rockefeller labor policy was at variance with that held by its peers in the emerging economic center, the nation's largest corporations. The Rockefeller position was more akin to the National Association of Manufacturers. It opposed union recognition in principle and vigorously upheld the right of robber barons to control their industrial fiefdoms absolutely. This was a markedly more laissez-faire policy than that taken by many "enlightened" corporate leaders, such as the Morgan group and many financial and industrial leaders in the National Civic Federation. The more liberal corporate leaders held that recognition of class collaborative unions was not objectionable, since it permitted organized labor and large-scale industry to negotiate a division of efficiently produced wealth within a framework of mutually accepted capitalism.[36]

Such differences in labor policy did not isolate the Rockefeller interests from their economic peers, particularly when industrial conflict and social upheaval intensified. Then Rockefeller philanthropists were invited to, in the words of the RF's executive secretary, "a conference . . . held between representatives of some of the largest financial interests of this country, in order to see whether something might be done to relieve the general unrest through some well-organized agency of investigation and publicity."[37] Meeting in J.P. Morgan's Office, the idea of creating a publicity bureau to give business's side of economic arguments to disquieted citizens was discussed by John D. Rockefeller, Jr., his father-in-law, U.S. Senator Nelson Aldrich, banker and Morgan partner Henry P. Davidson, and Theodore M. Vail President of American Telephone and Telegraph) among others. Davidson and Vail each promised an annual quarter of a million dollars for five years for such a project. Capitalist W.K. Vanderbilt and B & O Railroad president Walters each pledged a yearly $50,000. The Rockefellers were asked to guarantee a further $250,000 a year toward the project's annual $1 million budget.[38]

As discussion proceeded on what $1 million might buy, two competing views emerged. One urged that popular unrest be stilled by a flood of propaganda. Accordingly, "what was needed was a constant stream of correct information, put before the public" to reach "the middle and lower classes upon whom the demagogues chiefly preyed." This "publicity bureau" would supply prompt and detailed information on current topics of controversy: labor disputes, rail rates, tariffs and the like.[39] However, the Rockefeller representatives at the conference proposed a more sophisticated strategy. In addition to a propaganda bureau, they wanted a permanent research organization to manufacture knowledge on these subjects. While a publicity organization might well "correct popular misinformation," the research institution would study the "causes of social and economic evils," using its reputation for disinterestedness and scientific detachment to "obtain public confidence and respect" for its findings. And, of course, the research findings could be disseminated through a publicity bureau as well as other outlets. Given these differences, the conference "came to naught."[40]

The RF decided to build its own social science knowledge factory: an Institute for Economic Research "for the study of important social and economic questions vitally effecting the welfare of society at the present time."[41] Meeting with the RF's executive committee, AEA leaders J.B. Clark and W.C. Mitchell along with Yale's Henry C. Emery, Chicago's J.L. Laughlin and Harvard Business School's Edwin Gay opined that economics did indeed have topics that could be supported by such an institute. The RF executive committee then turned to a second committee for advice on the general direction and specific topics such an institute might take. Thus, Gay and Laughlin were joined by University of Virginia economist Thomas Page, Chicago banker Harry A. Wheeler, and New York corporate lawyer Victor Morawetz: they, in turn, urged the institute to establish a reputation for "scientific, impartial and unprejudiced" work on income distribution, prices and perhaps profit sharing, while possibly starting a publicity bureau as well.[42] However, events threatening the Rockefeller business interests removed the Institute for Economic Research from the RF's grants list on the eve of its creation.

The Colorado Coal War of 1913-1914 provided the stimulus for the RF dropping the institute scheme and picking up another sort of social science, one more immediately useful in defending their business interests. In this war, union recognition was the key issue, and a Rockefeller firm led capital's resistence to it in Colorado. On April 20, 1914, the militia, acting in capital's interests, attacked an enclave of miners at Ludlow, looting and firing tents, wounding and killing scores. Union leaders called upon the state's workers to take up armed struggle against the state and company armies. To a shocked nation, President Woodrow Wilson declared a state of insurrection, sending in federal troops.[43]

With the Ludlow Massacre, the Rockefeller group became a target for both those repelled by the violence as well as those who preferred union recognition to insurrection. To meet this crisis, the Rockefeller management group hired corporate public relations specialist Ivy Lee and Canadian social science expert William Lyon Mackenzie King. Schooled in Canada, the U.S., and Britain, King had refused an economics position at Eliot's Harvard, becoming instead Canadian labor minister. In Ottawa he became famous for compulsory investigation, a scheme that defused labor's strike weapon. And like the Rockefeller group, he did not find union recognition a necessary pre-condition for social peace and justice. Through the summer of 1914, King counseled the Rockefeller interests on how to resolve the Colorado conflict without union recognition. He also coached John D. Rockefeller, Jr., on how to field embarrassing political-economic questions, helping to draft briefs defending the Rockefeller position before several investigating commissions.[44]

In this expert role, King was clearly a "hired head" creating technical and ideological schemes to protect the specific interests of Rockefeller business enterprises under attack by strikers and the public. In August 1914 the RF selected King to concretize their aspirations in social science research. On October 1, the RF announced publicly that King was to conduct an impartial "Investigation of the Industrial Relations" for the foundation.[45] A nation schooled by the tainted-money debate and shocked by the Ludlow Massacre correctly suspected that tainted knowledge was being commissioned. King's study would yield a whitewash of Rockefeller's responsibility for leading the capitalist army in the Colorado Coal Wars.

The second U.S. Industrial Relations Commission (IRC) became a significant vehicle for such popular suspicions. The IRC was the period's largest, longest and most widely followed political-economic road show and value forum. It was conceived by a group of social reformers and university-based intellectuals centered around the Charities and the Commons reborn as the Sage-subsidized Survey. It was their response to the ideological shock waves generated by the 1910 dynamiting of the militantly anti-union Los Angeles Times. After intense negotiations with the White House, the group devoted a Survey issue to the dynamiting. It lobbied the 28 learned societies meeting in Washington at years end to petition a predisposed President Taft to propose an IRC to Congress. Congress obligingly funded the IRC to explore the causes of labor unrest. But the Survey group was shocked when Taft's nine nominations for IRC commissioners excluded economists, women and industrial workers. They publicly protested, gaining from the incoming President Wilson a new--and more acceptable--set, among them AEAer John R. Commons.[46]

The AEA leadership was deeply involved in the Survey group's efforts. Three wrote for the Survey dynamite issue. And the discipline leaders supplied 11 of 40 signatures to the Survey's editorial confidently petitioning Taft for a second IRC. Many also signed the petition protesting Taft's nominees, a document drafted at a rump meeting immediately following a joint AEA-American Association for Labor Legislation session at the 1912 Boston learned societies meetings.[47]

The depth of discipline leader involvement reflects their centralist ideological commitments. The Survey group focused its demand for an IRC by stressing the period's increasing labor violence. They framed the issue in terms of union recognition. They argued the social justice and economic necessity of trade unions collectively representing worker's interests against concentrated capital. They rejected "the open shop," since it threatened union viability. They made a distinction between "good" and "bad" unions, bad ones being socialistic. In this qualified endorsement of unions, the Survey group supported the emerging center's labor policy as practiced in such organizations as the NCF and articulated to the IRC by the AEA leader Jacob Hollander as the common sense of most academic economists.[48]

This solid ideological congruence between the Survey group, the emerging center and the discipline leaders was fully understood by the oppositional groups. The NAM, for example, lobbied Congress for salary ceilings to prevent distinguished social scientists from being IRC commissioners, noting "we have more to fear from erratic college professors than any other source" for they "hang on the ragged edge of socialism and lack experience, poise and practical contact with industrial affairs." And as the NAM rejoiced with Taft's slate on nominees, chortling that the "college element is utterly without recognition," so it was dismayed when Wilson appointed John R. Commons from among nine IRC commissioners more sympathetic to the emerging center's pro-union recognition and labor collaborationist practices.[49]

After touring the nation for three years and interpreting worker unrest as a problem solvable by the center's collaborationist trade unions, the IRC turned to the tainted-knowledge question. In May 1915 the nation's capital hosted four days of testimony by Rockefeller operatives. While fully exploring Rockefeller's anti-unionism, its head Frank Walsh zeroed in on the relationship between the Rockefeller Foundation and the Rockefeller business empire. In his examination of John D. Rockefeller, Jr., and Mackenzie King, Walsh used his experience as a prosecuting attorney to point out to the public the potential of the Rockefeller Foundation to produce ideology that defended the Rockefeller enterprises. Under questioning, John D. Rockefeller, Jr., maintained that the foundation was separate from the corporation, that it was established for the common good rather than Rockefeller's private interest and that King was an impartial investigator. Walsh then produced subpoenaed correspondence from the summer of 1914 between King, now director of the Rockefeller Foundation Industrial Peace Study, and Rockefeller, owner and director of the corporation, that spelled out King's suggestions for containing militant labor in Colorado without union recognition. Walsh hammered home the interlocking relationship between foundation and corporation again and again, pointing to the impossibility of the foundation's impartiality and labeling the King industrial peace project as an exercise in ideology rather than science.[50]

When King testified, he took the position that he had functioned as a technical expert advising Rockefeller on modern means of industrial peace in Colorado while conducting a more general study of the same phenomena world wide. He argued that his work for Rockefeller was technical and did not affect his impartiality. However, when Walsh--echoing Henry George four decades before--asked if the technical expert in a democracy should place the facts as he sees them before the public, King indicated his preference for serving power: "More will come about" more quickly by advising those with power and influence "than . . . years spent . . . trying to focus [popular] opinion [on] industrial conditions." King here betrayed the propensity of the period's disciplinarians to serve power rather than public. He confirmed Walsh's point that social scientists working for foundations might well have a proclivity for gathering facts most useful to foundations' managers.[51]

In essence, the Walsh-Rockefeller-King testimony addressed the issue of the potential service of foundations to knowledge production. As developed by Walsh, it denounced foundation support for social science research. It questioned the researcher's ability to maintain scientific integrity while investigating social problems, when their work was being paid for by those who had interests in the conclusions reached. It asked if foundations set up by corporate capitalists should fund research on socially controversial issues, issues that in a democracy should be decided by a public unswayed by interpretations manufactured by social scientists on foundation payrolls.

In its Final Report, the commission offered a lengthy and detailed summation of its analysis of "The Concentration of Wealth and Influence." After noting that six financial groups with a total capitalization of $20 billion employed 28 percent of the labor force, the report urged a more enlightened labor policy upon these capitalists. It linked foundations into this concentrated capital, seeing them as the results of "exploitation"--workers' low wages and consumers' high prices. Foundations used these ill-gotten gains beyond public accountability and influenced policy at colleges, universities and research bureaus. And since much of the foundations' assets were in corporate securities, the elemental interests energizing the foundations' influence attempts were clearly the same as the corporate sector. Foundation funding then increased corporate capital's already sizable control over educational institutions and the press in directions supportive of concentrated wealth. Thus was tainted money linked to tainted knowledge. Finally, the IRC recommended that foundations be treated much as the AEA leadership suggested that trusts be controlled: by information disclosure, publicity and federal regulation. In brief, the IRC asked if foundations magnificently endowed by great capitalists produced objective research or ideology. It answered that ideology was more likely than objectivity.[52]

In response, direct social science sponsorship from the emerging corporate center ceased. The NCF, anticipating the IRC's position, suppressed its clearly ideological Social Survey of industrial progress. The CIW abandoned its adventure in social science: the Department of Economic and Sociology. The RF put on the shelf its plans to establish an institute for economic research. King completed a highly personal campaign document, rather than the promised "investigation."[53] After a decent pause, the RF hired ASS leader George Vincent, University of Minnesota president, to head its increasingly centralist operations and assert the necessary fiction of value neutrality. And more fundamentally, in the 1920s academic holding companies rooted in the discipline associations--for example, the American Council of Learned Societies (ACLS) and the Social Science Research Council (SSRC)--emerged to mediate the direct contact between wealth and knowledge exposed and denounced by the IRC.[54]

Clearly, the dialogue on role expectations between social science association leaders and philanthropists in the Progressive period had its own dynamics. Academics and capitalists, while sharing a general commitment to rapid industrialization, found their conversation halting, filled with ambiguity, uncertainty, differences, and misunderstanding, and thereby somewhat frustrating. Nonetheless, they continued, since the social scientists needed the resources and the givers needed the technical and ideological skills.

What the Leaders Learned

When Mrs. Sage declared higher education beyond her purse, discipline leaders used the occasion to wish her foundation well. The wish was returned by Sage's funding of social work into a more coherent professional enterprise than even the social scientists own. In so doing, Sage unintentionally removed practical application from academic sociology's structuralism, while relieving economics from the need to directly confront the human cost of rapid industrialization.

The main chance for disciplinarian social science came with the CIW's Department of Economics and Sociology. AEA leaders rushed on board and filled the ship, only to have the project become hopelessly becalmed in the anarchy usual to the day's academic practice. Farnum's managerial skills saved the department, since he disciplined the collaborators' expectations to industrial levels sufficient to manufacture the knowledge, as expected by the CIW's trustees. Here academic opportunism typical of de-centralized production and the trustee's sense of material domination were tested, found wanting, and recast.

The IRC as a widely observed traveling value forum was an even more critical expectation-setting experience. In the midst of raucous labor unrest and rampant white-collar unease, it dramatically shaped expectations. Using King's expert efforts on behalf of specific Rockefeller business interests, the IRC directly linked tainted money to tainted knowledge. And it did so forcefully enough for sponsors at the CIW--and the NCF--to shut down ongoing social science projects. The IRC's dramatic unmasking of King's unwarranted claims to value neutrality undermined these sponsors' ability to maintain a similar claim for their own projects.

Later, indirect conduits for funders would help create the necessary fiction of value neutrality for a social science in the service of power. And if the IRC's school for scandal taught researchers and patrons the public's expectations for a value-neutral social science, it also contained a special instruction for the disciplinarians. By virtue of their subject matter, they were at the professorate's leading edge of public controversy and hence the most vulnerable to such unmaskings as King's. Accordingly, association leaders moved to focus and speed the emerging definition by the American Association of University Professors (AAUP) of the American professor's duties and rights vis-à-vis students, colleagues, educational management and the community-at-large.   By so doing, in 1915 they laid firm foundations structuring North American concepts of academic freedom and tenure for the entire professorate over the rest of the century.   And they crystallized as well a theory of exchange between professions and community that has been elevated into an ideology protecting the occupational interests and rewards of all mental workers.

NOTES

1. Joseph F. Wall, Andrew Carnegie (New York: Oxford, 1970); Robert H. Bremner, American Philanthropy (Chicago: University of Chicago Press, 1960); Andrew Carnegie, "Wealth," North American Review 148 (1889): 653–664 and "Best Fields of Philanthropy," North American Review 149 (1889): 682–698. Both these essays were reprinted in 1901: see Andrew Carnegie, The Gospel of Wealth and Other Timely Essays, ed. Edward G. Kirkland (Cambridge, Mass.: Belknap Press, 1962).

2. Bremner, American Philanthropy, pp. 112–113, Washington Gladden, "Tainted Money," Outlook 52 (1895): 886–887, contains the quoted phrases.

3. Peter Collier and David Horowitz, The Rockefellers: An American Dynasty (New York: Holt, Rinehart and Winston, 1976), pp. 15–47 et passim.

4. Matthew Josephson, The Robber Barons (New York: Harcourt, Brace and World, 1962), pp. 209–211, inter alia; John M. Glenn, Lilian Brandt and F. Emerson Andrews, Russell Sage Foundation, 1907–1946 (New York: Russell Sage Foundation, 1947), pp. 3–40, quote at p. 11.

5. Charities and the Commons 18, 6 (May 11, 1907): 186–191.

6. Glenn, Brandt and Andrews, Russell Sage Foundation, pp. 15–17, 21–22.

7. Ibid., p. 26.

8. Sheila A. Slaughter and Edward T. Silva, "Looking Backwards: How Foundations Formulated Ideology in the Progressive Period," in Philanthropy and Cultural Imperialism: The Foundations at Home and Abroad, ed. Robert Arnove (Boston: G.K. Hall, 1980), pp. 57–62.

9. "Remarks by Mr. Carnegie on Presenting the Trust Deed," _Carnegie Institute of Washington Yearbook_ (_CIWY_) 1 (January 1903): xiv.

10. Trustees and their terms are listed in _CIWY_ 54 (1955): vi.

11. "Proceedings of the Executive Committee," _CIWY_ 1 (January 1903): p. xxxviii.

12. James Leiby, _Carroll D. Wright and the Origins of Labor Statistics_ (Cambridge, Mass.: Harvard University Press, 1960).

13. "Report of the Advisory Committee on Economics," Appendix A--"Reports of Advisory Committees," _CIWY_ 1 (January 1903): 1-2. Both served as foundation managers with Carnegie: Farnam as chairman of the Department of Economics and Sociology after Wright's death and Clark as director of the division of economics and history of the Carnegie Endowment for International Peace, 1911-1923.

14. "Report of the Advisory Committee," p. 19.

15. Lieby, _Carroll D. Wright_.

16. For Seligman as negotiator between CIW and the AEA see "Report of the Secretary," _PAEA_, Part 1, 3d series, 5 (December 1903): 42. The seven AEA council members were Wright, W.F. Willcox, W.Z. Ripley, D.R. Dewey, J.W. Jenks, H.W. Farnam and H.B. Gardner. Many other prominent AEA economists were later assigned subsections of investigation under these section heads: see C.D. Wright, "Report of the Department of Economics and Sociology," _CIWY_ 3 (January 1905): 55-64. On the overall scope of the department, see C.D. Wright, "An Economic History of the United States," _PAEA_, Part 1, 3d series, 4 (May 1905): 390-409.

17. The original concept of the project is clearly restated by H.W. Farnam who took over as chairman in 1909. See H.W. Farnam, "Department of Economics and Sociology," _CIWY_ 8 (February 1910):

81-83. The estimate of overall project cost is from the "Report of the Advisory Committee on Economics," CIWY 1 (January 1903): 1-2. The total figure is cumulated from the annual amounts given in the yearbooks.

18. Robert A. Woodward, "Report of the President of the Institute," CIWY 4 (January 1906): 23.

19. C.D. Wright, "Economics and Sociology: Report of the Director," CIWY 5 (January 1907): 163.

20. H.W. Farnam, "Department of Economics and Sociology," CIWY 8 (February 1910): 81-93.

21. C.D. Wright, "Department of Economics and Sociology," CIWY 7 (February 1909): 74-85.

22. "Report of the President," CIWY 8 (February 1910): 30-31. The department did produce eight volumes of "Indexes of Economic Material in the Documents of the States of the U.S." by 1909. However, the department received a separate allocation for this project, which was not regarded as fulfilling the economic history of the United States for which the collaborators had contracted.

23. "Report of the President of the Institute," CIWY 4 (January 1906): 17, 23, 31.

24. H.W. Farnum, "Department of Economics and Sociology," CIWY 8 (February 1910): 71-83; Robert Woodward, "Report of the President 1910," CIWY 9 (January 1911): 22, and "Report of the President," CIWY 12 (January 1913): 18.

25. David M. Grossman, "Professors and Public Service, 1885-1925: A Chapter in the Professionalization of the Social Sciences," (Ph.D. thesis, Washington University, 1973), pp. 278-290.

26. See H. Farnum's "Department of Economics and Sociology" reports, CIWY 11 (1912): 82, and CIWY 12 (1913): 95-96.

27. In November 1911, when Farnum gained approval for his reorganization scheme, the AEA's leadership contributed 7 of 12 collaborators to the department's board: Commons, Dewey, Farnum, Gardner, Jenks, Meyer and Willcox. See CIWY 10 (1911): 245.

28. Grossman, "Professors and Public Service," p. 289.

29. H. Farnum, "Department of Economics and Sociology," CIWY 11 (1912): 77; CIWY 12 (1913): 90-91; CIWY 15 (1916): 98-102.

30. H. Farnum, "Department of Economics and Sociology," CIWY 15 (1916): 101-102.

31. Ibid.

32. Robert A. Woodward, "Report of the President," CIWY 12 (1913): 18.

33. "Minutes of the Board of Trustees," CIWY 15 (1916): xi-xii.

34. U.S. Congress, Senate, 64th Congress, 1st Session, Sen. Doc. 415, "Industrial Relations: Final Report and Testimony Submitted to Congress by the Commission on Industrial Relations," 16 vols. (Washington, D.C.: USGPO, 1916), 1: 116-126 (hereafter cited as Final Report).

35. "Testimony of John D. Rockefeller, Jr.," Final Report, 8: 7776.

36. On differences in corporate ideology and tactics in the period, see James Weinstein, The Corporate Ideal in the Liberal State, 1900-1918 (Boston: Beacon, 1968); Marguerite Green, The National Civic Foundation and the American Labor Movement, 1900-1925 (Washington, D.C.: Catholic University of America Press, 1956); Albert K. Steigerwalt, The National Association of Manufacturers, 1895-1914 (Ann Arbor, Mich.: University of Michigan Bureau of

Business Research, 1964); and Philip Foner, History of the Labor Movement in the United States, 4 vols. (New York: International, 1963, 1964), vols. 3 and 4.

37. Jerome Greene, Memo RFDR 12, "To Members of the Rockefeller Foundation," October 22, 1913, p. 15, Rockefeller Foundation Archives, North Tarrytown, N.Y.

38. Donald Fisher, "The Ideology of Rockefeller Philanthrophy and the Development of a Policy for the Social Sciences," unpublished MS, Faculty of Education, University of British Columbia, p. 2.

39. Greene, "To Members of the Rockefeller Foundation," p. 16.

40. Ibid., pp. 16-17.

41. Final Report, 9: 8395.

42. Ibid., pp. 8395-8396; Fisher, "The Ideology of Rockefeller Philanthropy," pp. 2-5.

43. George P. West, Report on the Colorado Strike (Washington, D.C.: U.S. Commission on Industrial Relations, 1916) documents the involvement of the eastern Rockefeller office, using IRC subpoenaed correspondence.

44. Fred A. McGregor, The Fall and Rise of Mackenzie King: 1911-1919 (Toronto: Macmillan of Canada, 1961), pp. 121-144; R. MacGregor Dawson, William Lyon Mackenzie King: A Political Biography, 1874-1923 (Toronto: University of Toronto Press, 1958). Henry Ferns and Bernard Ostry, The Age of Mackenzie King (Toronto: Lorimer, 1976), pp. 187ff.; and Paul Craven, An Impartial Umpire: Industrial Relations and the Canadian State (Toronto: University of Toronto Press, 1980), which outlines King's early career and intellectual position that proved so attractive to the Rockefeller managers.

45. Dawson, _King_, pp. 235-255.

46. Graham Adams, Jr., _Age of Industrial Violence, 1910-1915: The Activities and Findings of the U.S. Commission on Industrial Relations_ (New York: Columbia University Press, 1966), pp. 1-80; Weinstein, _The Corporate Ideal_, pp. 172-213.

47. _Survey_ 27, 13 (30 December 1911): 1413-1431; 27, 15 (13 January 1912): 1563; 19, 13 (28 December 1912): 381-382, 385-386; 30, 14 (5 July 1913): 452; _Boston Herald_, 29 December 1912, p. 6; and Adams, _Age of Industrial Violence_, pp. 24-37.

48. Adams, _Age of Industrial Violence_, pp. 1-80, and Jacob Hollander, "Testimony," _Final Report_, pp. 7534-7546.

49. Adams, _Age of Industrial Violence_, pp. 38-46.

50. Adams, _Age of Industrial Violence_, pp. 161-168; Collier and Horowitz, _The Rockefellers_, pp. 119, 123-125.

51. McGregor, _Mackenzie King_, pp. 165-174, quote at pp. 169-170.

52. _Final Report_, vol. 1, section 5, pp. 116-126.

53. William Lyon Mackenzie King, _Industry and Humanity_ (Toronto: University of Toronto Press, 1973).

54. For details on SSRC and ACLS funding, see Joseph C. Kiger, "Foundation Support of Educational Innovation by Learned Societies, Councils, and Institutes," in _Innovation in Education_, ed. Matthew B. Miles (New York: Teachers College Press, 1964), pp. 533-561. For a brief account of the ACLS, consult Whitney J. Oates, "The Humanities and Foundations," in _U.S. Philanthropic Foundations_, ed. Warren Weaver (New York: Harper & Row, 1967), pp. 300-303. On the thrust of Rockefellers' granting, see Fisher, "Ideology of Rockefeller Philanthropy," and the essays in Arnove, _Philanthropy and Cultural Imperialism_.

11
Defense of the Expert Role: Social Science Leaders in The American Association of University Professors

Throughout the Progressive era, social science leaders served as experts in the public and private sectors and used their expertise to build new disciplines. However, service put them in the public eye, and the content of their fields forced them to address issues on which popular passions ran high. As institutionally dependent intellectuals, social scientists were both visible and vulnerable to trustees intent on enforcing orthodoxy in times of social turmoil.

Social scientists were well aware they were in the "danger zone" and sought to protect themselves. To that end, association leaders were able to persuade the fledgling American Association of University Professors (AAUP) to take up the defense of academic freedom and tenure and were also able to shape AAUP policy to incorporate special provisions to protect the expert role. Thus, social scientists had a heavy hand in shaping the twentieth-century American academic role.

But social scientists paid a price for protecting the expert role. To win freedom from arbitrary interference on the part of managers and trustees, they offered to use the AAUP for the conservative management of knowledge. This meant their dissident colleagues were often without safeguards. Professors opposed to the war, professors supportive of radical labor, professors overly critical of the established order were frequently fired. However, the AAUP's definition of academic freedom did allow experts acting as advocates of the existing order to enter the public arena with confidence.

In this chapter, then, we look at ways in which social scientists defended the expert role. We examine the conditions that led social scientist to organize around the issue of academic freedom, inspect their participation in the AAUP as well as their management of Committee A, and analyze their handling of a variety of academic freedom cases. Furthermore, we look at how social scientists and AAUP leaders put their expertise to work during the war and how they participated in refinancing social science research in peace.

The State of Academic Freedom

In 1900 and for a half century to come, faculty had to rest their defense of academic freedom on appeals to professional and public opinion. Neither academic freedom nor tenure was recognized in law. Indeed, the courts had ruled consistently against professors who tried to establish legal right to tenure of office. In laissez-faire interpretations of the right of contract against which AEA leaders had argued on labor's behalf, judges held that governing boards had the power to remove any employee whenever in their judgment the corporate interests of the university required it. "'The professor may leave at his pleasure; the board may terminate his professorship at its pleasure.'"[1] As with workers in the labor market, the fact that institutionally dependent professors were unequal partners in these contracts went unrecognized.

Job security was virtually nonexistent. Many state institutions reviewed all professors annually regardless of rank. As late as 1867 an entire faculty was dismissed at the University of Wisconsin during such an annual review and a similar action was seriously contemplated at Cornell in 1881. Assistant professors as well as men with years on the job most often held their academic place through a series of one-year or short-term renewable appointments ungoverned by rules and precedent. Although some universities, especially those private-sector institutions committed to research, spoke of permanent or indefinite tenure by 1900, this merely meant professors with long service were not subject to a yearly review on which their job turned. They could still be fired at any time without statement of cause or provision for a hearing, let alone a judgment made by peers.[2]

As the graduate school grew and prospered, highly credentialed faculty from a wide array of disciplines began to protest against these conditions, demanding greater professional autonomy. The university self-governance movement, a loose group of professors in the humanities, law and science, argued that professors should have a deciding voice in setting educational and personnel policy.[3] Social scientists, too, urged extending faculty's professional privileges. They were especially interested in establishing the right to address a broad public on subjects where they commanded professional expertise.[4] Regardless of discipline or purpose, all faculty intent on professionalizing were agreed on the institutional mechanism needed to meet their various demands: tenure "as secure as . . . on the Supreme Bench."[5]

Presidents of graduate universities were men in the middle. They were sympathic to faculty efforts to increase professional autonomy, often having risen from faculty ranks themselves. Moreover, they understood that a degree of autonomy was essential to creating working conditions that fostered professors' production of specialized knowledge, which, in turn, enhanced their own autonomy vis-à-vis trustees. But presidents were also sensitive to trustees' well-established prerogatives. And when they tried to balance trustee and professional rights, trustees were rarely asked to concede any of their numerous powers.

In the main, managers tried to head off confrontations between faculty and trustees, counting on their own good intentions to resolve conflict. Harvard's Eliot, for example, viewed tenure as "indispensable" for academic freedom but counseled consideration and respect for the position of trustees and benefactors. Taking a long view, he saw the development of professional autonomy as an ever-diminishing problem, solved by the death of living benefactors and the education of future trustees to an appreciation of the limits of their role. In the short run, he suggested that curricula offensive to resource holders be removed from the catalogue.[6]

Like Eliot, Columbia's Nicholas Murray Butler saw no inherent conflict between trustees and faculty. He contended that professors already played a leading part in making academic policy and thought "most abuses of academic freedom are due simply to bad manners and to lack of ordinary tact and judgment." There was no need, he argued, for an "elaborate code of regulations" that stipulated professors' rights and responsibilities of office.[7]

While professors bent on enhancing professional autonomy were generally restive under presidential paternalism, social scientists had a particular and concrete set of concerns. It was they, as AEA leader Simon N. Patten put it, who by virtue of their subject matter were "on the firing line of civilization," and they who needed the protection of academic freedom.[8] For social scientists, the good intentions of presidents were not enough. Indeed, as AEA and Yale President Arthur T. Hadley noted, presidents as well as professors were vulnerable to pressure so long as men of power believed "that the commercial prosperity of the country is dependent upon certain theories of political economy." According to Hadley, trustees and benefactors had a strong interest in the content of social scientists' work and were able to make their influence felt because they had "the material advantage in holding the base of supplies."[9]

However, after the upheaval caused by the Ross case in 1900, (see Chapter 4) social science leaders were not involved in any sensational academic freedom cases until 1912. The calm prevailing at graduate institutions was the product of several factors. First, AEA leaders had shown they were willing to fight over Ross by vigorously engaging presidents and trustees in the press and on the public platform. Second, the social science leadership, now middle aged and comfortably settled in the political economic center, by and large had abandoned strident criticism for expert service. Third, neither professors nor presidents were forced to take irreconcilable positions on social issues while the promise of Progressive reform momentarily contained social unrest in the wider society.

Although academic freedom cases rarely made headlines, social scientists were not without constraints. Managers grew skilled at removing or reprimanding troublesome, unconventional or overly ambitious men without undue force or fanfare. Thus, the Socialist economist Lindley M. Keasby was cleverly maneuvered from Bryn Mawr by President Carrie Thomas when he tried to up his salary with another job offer.[10] Although never involved in an academic freedom case, Thorstein Veblen had difficulty in finding a stable academic job as much because of his unconventional teaching and life-style as his unorthodox economics.[11] Charles Merriam's interest in testing his political science expertise in the partisan arena on the Republican ticket was discouraged as unseemly by Chicago's presidents Harper and Judson.[12]

Instances such as these as well as memories of the 1880s and 1890s fed the more critical younger economists' sense of insecurity. As a means of ensuring there would be no need "to cater to special interests or fear what consequences might arise from my words or actions," Scott Nearing taught himself to live sparingly and built "a capital reserve to cover a full year of possible unemployment."[13] Aware that the first decade of the twentieth century might be the still eye of the hurricane, AEA leader Alvin S. Johnson, son of a Nebraska homesteader and future head of the New School for Social Research, bought and held in reserve a farm he could work himself "if ever a storm of academic persecution should blow up."[14]

Clouds began gathering in 1912-1913. The ameliorative reforms social scientists had worked on were not enough. Labor legislation, price indexing, the income tax, the Federal Reserve Board, protective tariffs and administrative reform had ended neither labor unrest nor recurring depression. As the poverty of Progressive reform was revealed, polarization between classes increased. Industrial strife was rampant; the years between 1911 and 1916 were "among the most violent in American history, except for the Civil War."[15] The Socialist party grew in strength and was thought a political force to be reckoned with after Debs' showing at the polls in the 1912 presidential election.[16] The International Workers of the World (IWW) made up in increased militance what they lacked in organizational strength and led strikes in the Louisiana timberlands, in Lawrence, in Paterson, and the Wheatland hop fields. Tension was building in the Colorado coalfields and the Mesabi iron range.[17]

As labor and management intensified their struggles, so did faculty and trustees. In 1913 philosopher John Mecklin was driven out of Lafayette College for his evolutionary social views and law professor J.H. Lewis was dismissed from the University of North Dakota after attending a conference of Progressive party leaders. AEA leader Willard Fisher had to leave Wesleyan for political activity and an irreverent attitude toward religion while economists Clyde King and Scott Nearing at the University of Pennsylvania were rumored to have been denied deserved promotions as a result of statistical inquiries touching on local and state enterprises.[18]

Alarmed by these storm warnings, AEA leaders took action. In December 1913 Frank Fetter, who had resigned from Stanford over the Ross case, brought a resolution asking for an investigation of "the present situation in American educational institutions as to liberty of thought, freedom of speech, and security of tenure."[19] The AEA appointed E.R.A. Seligman, also a veteran of the Ross struggle, chair of a committee including Fetter and Richard T. Ely, who had survived a heresy trial at Wisconsin and gone on to participate in the Stanford investigation.[20] AEA overtures to political scientists and sociologists were quickly accepted, and together the AEA, APSA, and ASS formed a Joint Committee on Academic Freedom and Tenure, with three members representing each association.[21]

Issued in December 1914, the Preliminary Report of the Joint Committee found "freedom of speech or liberty of expressing in spoken or written word the results of scientific research" the most problematic aspect of academic freedom. Social scientists, more so than other academics, saw themselves in the "danger zone."[22] Their very subject matter caused them to touch on issues of power and resources in the wider society. Especially in tumultuous times, their work as experts invited public scrutiny and made them vulnerable.

The report raised hard questions for collective consideration. How was the social scientist to distinguish his actions as expert from his conduct as a citizen? Had not the community the right to profit by the opinion of the expert, or might not taking a definite stand on political or economic issues impair his reputation for impartiality? To what extent should concessions to public sentiment be made in utterances outside the university?

While the joint committee was working on a final position paper that would treat the questions raised in the preliminary report, the situation in the wide society went from bad to worse. Two senior professors were fired from the University of Utah, and 17 resigned. Scott Nearing was fired from Pennsylvania, James Brewster from Colorado and Joseph Hart from the University of Washington.[23] But the most serious challenge to social scientists came from Wisconsin, where academics' right to serve the state was questioned. The Board of Public Affairs, an economy and efficiency agency for which Progressives like President Van Hise and reforming political scientist Charles McCarthy had held high hopes, fell into the hands of a conservative governor, who used it to undermine the "Wisconsin Idea." As professors were accused of neglecting their classes while playing at state politics, bills were introduced to the legislature that would have forbidden "the appointment of university professors to government advisory posts."[24] Thus, the final report of the joint committee was written as social scientists saw threats to the role they had tried to carve out for themselves since 1885.

The AAUP Declaration of Principles

As social scientists were writing the preliminary report, academics concerned with self-governance were trying to create an organization broader than the specialist associations, one that would speak to the needs of all professionalizing faculty. The need for protection of outspoken academics was brought home to the group organizing the AAUP when Nicholas Murray Butler tried to force one of their most fiery leaders, James McKeen Cattell, into early retirement.[25] This incident illustrated with great clarity the need for a corporate concept of academic freedom that would serve as a bulwark against external judgments of a professor's fitness for tenure of office. Thus, the AAUP was receptive when E.R.A. Seligman, representing the social scientists, moved that the AAUP establish a committee to be merged with the social scientists Joint Committee on Academic Freedom and Tenure, creating the renowned Committee A.[26]

Seligman remained chair, and eligible members of the entire Joint Committee--professors who had served a decade or more--were incorporated. All in all, seven social science association leaders accounted for 46.6 percent of the reconstituted committee. The other eight members, appointed by the AAUP, were from a variety of disciplines, all different.[27] Thus, social scientists were the principal authors of the American professorate's basic statement on academic freedom.

Committee A's Declaration of Principles was essentially a defense of the expert role and reflected the special concerns of social scientists. The 1915 declaration remains critical to our understanding of academic freedom. It is an exact statement of the reciprocal rights and responsibilities the academic professional and the community-at-large owe each other.[28] Even in the 1980s the AAUP views its work as confirming and elaborating this initial setting out of obligations between the profession and the public.[29]

Analytically, the declaration can be divided into three parts: formulation of claims to academic freedom, an assessment of the political and economic restraints posed by vested interests, and presentation of the concessions the profession was prepared to make in return for limited job security. Before making any claims, however, the proprietary rights held by American university trustees had to be undercut. As suitable in a document written largely by social scientists, the declaration borrowed from theory AEA leaders had developed to contain the worst abuses of private capital. Specialized knowledge was assumed to be a "natural" monopoly and, like public utilities, whether privately or publicly held, subject to regulation in the public interest. Thus, trustees had "no moral right to bind the reason or conscience of any professor." Indeed, the professor was not a "mere employee" because the university was beyond purely private contractual arrangements. The real responsibility of the professor was "primarily to the public itself and the judgment of his own profession."[30]

Using rhetoric developed in the AEA, APSA and ASS, the declaration saw academic freedom as the only way to meet society's need for specialized, objective knowledge. As the drafting of social science professors from "almost every one of our higher institutions of learning . . . into more or less unofficial participation in public service" indicated, the "complexities of economic, social and political life" in a modern democracy were such that it was no longer possible to solve social problems without "technical knowledge." As important as technical skill was the quality of expert advice--"prolonged and specialized technical training," guaranteed knowledge characterized by "disinterestedness and impartiality," a commodity difficult to come by in a society rife with special interests. As expert technicians certified by graduate training as beyond bias of class, party or creed, academics used objective knowledge to resolve and defuse widespread social conflict. The only way objectivity could be protected was through academic freedom; the only way academic freedom could be ensured was through tenure. Moreover, freedom of conscience and security of position were necessary to attract qualified and dedicated men. Despite the importance of their social functions, the "magnitude of economic rewards" was not great, and academic freedom would compensate. This freedom also enabled professors to better perform their other functions--research and teaching.[31]

The declaration's authors revealed an acute awareness of barriers to the free flow of expertise. Social scientists in particular were in the "danger zone." Their subject matter, by definition, always touched "private or class interests." If housed in "privately endowed institutions" where boards of trustees were "naturally made up of men who through their standing and ability are personally interested in great private enterprises, the points of conflict are numberless." Moreover, the student population of such universities was drawn from "the more prosperous and therefore usually . . . more conservative classes." As a result, "pressure from vested interests" could be used to curtail academic freedom. Conversely, in state institutions, strong popular opinion could result "in the repression of opinions deemed ultra-conservative rather than ultra-radical."[32]

Rather than opposing "vested interests" in the name of science or seeking support from popularly based groups, the declaration denied the revolutionary potential of knowledge. The profession voluntarily undertook the conservative management of new knowledge in return for a commitment to limited job security on the part of university managers. Thus, the university was defined as "likely always to exercise a certain form of conservative influence." Indeed the university

is committed to the principle that knowledge should precede action, to the caution (by no means synonymous with intellectual timidity) which is an essential part of the scientific method, to the practice of taking long views into the future, and to a reasonable regard for the teaching of experience.

The declaration also offered to use the emerging rhetoric of the profession to manage "the hasty and unconsidered impulses of popular feeling." As trained experts representing objective science, their verdict on social and technical issues commanded respect. However, as the Industrial Relations Commission investigation into Rockefeller Foundation activities had revealed, this respect was contingent on the public's belief that the university was organized "in such a way as to make impossible the exercise of pressure on professional opinions." If this were the case, then "the public may respect and be influenced by the counsels of prudence and moderation which are given by men of science." Open commitment to academic freedom by university managers would convince the public of the impartiality of science and allow professors to mold moderate popular sentiment on potentially explosive social issues.[33]

These guarantees that scientific discovery would not go too far or too fast and that results would be used to contain extremes of public opinion reaffirmed social scientists' conception of their role as producers of technical knowledge and ideology serving the political-economic center. Although its rhetoric claimed that academics were responsible to the public and their peers, the institutional reality of elite dominance of higher education was explicitly accommodated. The declaration asked university managers and the educated public to endorse the principle of academic freedom by recognizing that professors needed job security to perform functions necessary to society's well-being. In return, they agreed to blunt the cutting edge of knowledge potentially able to slice through class privilege and power, and thus conceded any absolute right to academic freedom.

In effect, faculty tried to gain some occupational autonomy by assuming trustees' responsibilities for monitoring the social content of knowledge. The rights that came with this responsibility were limited: freedom to follow research where it led, to pursue advanced and controversial ideas with graduate students, to speak freely outside the university in areas of professional competence and with the decorum befitting a professor on general social and political issues. These rights were extended only to professors with long years of service, and their enforcement was uncertain. Rather than demanding firm tenure of office, the AAUP asked only that institutions develop and adhere to a uniform written personnel policy that took account of the rights articulated in the declaration.

The AAUP began investigating academic freedom cases even as the declaration was being completed. It used techniques developed by the AEA in the Ross case. The usual procedures involved examination of facts by a committee composed of eminent academics, painstaking documentation, a case law format and well-placed lofty publicity.

Examination of the cases investigated prior to the First World War indicates that the AAUP placed development of university personnel policy above the merits of individual cases, relied on procedure rather than substantive issues to shape its judgment, and looked for managerial compliance with AAUP rules rather than for structural solutions to the problems created by powerful, wealthy and too often conservative lay boards. In the eight cases investigated prior to the war, 30 professors were fired or resigned in protest over what they regarded as arbitrary dismissals. None were reinstated. Only four institutions had their personnel policies publicly called into question. When these institutions developed procedures approximating the AAUP's, they were commended, regardless of their prior actions.[34]

Two examples serve to illustrate the AAUP's emphasis on procedural rather than substantive justice. The first is provided by the case of James Brewster. A senior law professor from the University of Michigan, Brewster took a job at the University of Colorado late in life to save his health. In 1915 he was fired after testifying for labor at the Industrial Relations Commission hearings in the aftermath of the Ludlow Massacre. Because his appointment was technically a temporary position, the AAUP found his termination did not violate academic freedom.[35]

Scott Nearing, too, was fired in 1915. Nearing was an economist who was dismissed from the University of Pennsylvania following an alumni campaign to oust him for his critique of the distribution of wealth and his strong stand against child labor. Although the AAUP acknowledged that Nearing was wrongfully dismissed, it did not demand restitution, and instead praised Pennsylvania for changing its personnel policy after Nearing's departure.[36]

Although the AAUP chose to make its stand on procedural rather than substantive justice, this choice should be placed in the context of its times. Were there available alternatives? Would they have offered academics better protection?

There were at least two alternatives. First, radical labor was fighting for freedom of speech on First Amendment grounds. From 1908 to 1912, the International Workers of the World ("Wobblies") engaged in free speech fights, beginning what was one of the first popular attempts to define the limits of freedom of expression. Nor were the Wobblies alone in their struggle for the First Amendment rights. Reformers such as Gilbert Roe and Theodore Schroeder joined with radicals and intellectuals such as Emma Goldman, Alexander Berkman, Margaret Sanger and Lincoln Steffens to form the Free Speech League in 1913. Some of these people would go on to work with the National Civil Liberties Bureau (later called the American Civil Liberties Union) during the war.[37]

Second, other reformers thought the best way to ensure professors' academic freedom was through structural change. The Industrial Relations Commission advocated making professors independent of conservative trustees and arbitrary presidents through government funding. They recommended that the existing distribution of wealth be restructured through heavy taxation, and the monies so accrued used to fund knowledge in a way that did not lend itself to influence by vested interests.[38]

Apparently the AAUP considered these alternative approaches to protecting academic freedom to be too risky. Using the First Amendment to defend academic freedom might have involved professors with radical labor and certainly would have put their claims before a judiciary that had thus far proved unfriendly. Restructuring wealth through taxation and using such funds to sponsor academic research might have had some appeal. However, social science leaders would have had to move from the political economic center to implement such a plan, and in so doing they might have forfeited their work as experts for the existing order.

On the whole, AAUP policy made it difficult for academics to sustain positions that deviated far from the center. The strain of opposition either drove them to extremes or forced them to conform. Thus, Scott Nearing was prompted by his experience to reevaluate American society and take an increasingly radical stand. His opposition to the war and the use of the Espionage Act against labor organizers lost him the job he had found at the University of Toledo, and he never held another academic position. For Nearing, the lesson was clear:

So long as I continued to oppose the American Oligarchy, . . . I would be cut off from the country's major channels of publicity. No more of my articles would appear in newspapers or magazines nor would my books be reviewed in them. No more books would be published by representative publishers. I would be excluded from the lecture platform. Most important of all to me, the academic field would be closed tight.[39]

Even those professors who found a safe haven after their firing were marked forever by the experience. John Mecklin, a philosopher too liberal for church-related Lafayette College but hardly a radical had fought with President Warfield and trustees for years to preserve a modicum of intellectual freedom. Several decades after his dismissal from Lafayette, he still vividly recalled the emotional turmoil taken by daily opposition:

Long after the struggle was over I was bedeviled by nightmares from which I awoke with the terrible feeling that my job was gone and my life ruined. I learned to sympathize with the worker's haunting sense of insecurity when he knows his job is completely at the mercy of a hard employer. This feeling of insecurity born of many years of friction with President Warfield had registered itself deep in my subconsciousness. From these hidden depths of soul, of which we are rarely aware in our waking hours, come sudden emotional upsurges of fear, when the barriers of reason are broken down in sleep, and we regain consciousness oppressed by a horrible feeling that we are the victims of some terrible disaster.[40]

While the AAUP's version of academic freedom began to routinize personnel policy, it offered little protection to outspoken critics or radicals like Nearing, even if they were housed at reputedly tolerant graduate universities. And almost no sustenance was provided for men and women of courage, who, like Mecklin, merely tried to uphold widely acknowledged standards of scholarship at institutions not fully committed to the limited exploration implicit in the research tradition.

Experts, the AAUP and the War

World War I provided social scientists and AAUP leaders with an opportunity similar to that offered two decades earlier by the Spanish-American War. Their ideological and technical skills were needed; thus, rewarding government posts were created for them. Social scientists' war work stilled popular doubts raised by the Industrial Relations Commission about academic knowledge as a weapon in wealth's arsenal during class struggle. At the same time, social science leaders were able to demonstrate their utility to men of power by aiding the organization of a war economy. For its part, the AAUP was able to make common cause with academic managers, sending representatives to sit with them on committees designed to increase education's contribution to victory. Thus, social science and AAUP leaders emerged from the war in a stronger position than they held at entry.

However, social scientists' participation in the First World War was different from that in the Spanish-American War in several respects. First, a greater number of social scientists were involved. Second, their services, especially those of economists, were rooted more firmly in their specializations. Third, the associations formally and enthusiastically endorsed the war, refusing to tolerate membership opposition. During the Spanish-American War, ASSA leaders had been allowed honorable opposition. In the First World War so intense was social scientists' involvement that academic freedom was among the first casualties.

Although opinion about U.S. entry into the European war was at first divided, many social science leaders entered the preparedness campaign. Under Harvard president and APSA leader A. Lawrence Lowell's guidance and funded by the Carnegie Endowment for International Peace, many social science leaders worked with the League to Enforce Peace to advocate military readiness. Those who were initially uncertain--such as Hadley, Farnam and Hart--were won over before entry. The few who refused to jump on the bandwagon--Simon N. Patten at the University of Pennsylvania and Charles Beard at Columbia--were increasingly isolated.[41]

When the U.S. declared war, the APSA and ASS quickly offered resolutions of support. They apparently did not view U.S. entry as a political question. Only the AEA acknowledged that endorsement of the war broke with its traditions on nonpartisanship and its refusal to "commit . . . members to any position on practical economics." Initially, the AEA also rejected establishment of committees to deal with the economic problems of war. However, it did agree to register economic experts for government service through the Civil Service Commission.[42]

Economists and other social science leaders were quickly absorbed in such government service. Twenty-three social science leaders were called to Washington to serve with the War Department or in federal agencies specially created to direct the war effort (see Table 5). Economists were most in demand, with more than twice as many serving as the others combined. Fielding an army overseas called for reliable information to inform crucial decisions about the amount and quality of supplies, priorities in manufacturing and complicated logistics. Social scientists, experienced in locating and analyzing data, served largely in the statistical, research and planning units of wartime agencies. Some, however, were called upon to monitor labor agreements and grievances, as close cooperation between capital and labor was necessary for full production. In short, the war called for greater government coordination of the political economy than ever before, and social scientists were able to use and improve the technical and ideological skills they had developed in the Progressive era.

However, these full-time administrative positions give little indication of the extent of economists' involvement in the war. The AEA changed its position on using association expertise to solve war problems in late 1917 and created a series of committees that worked closely with government agencies and corporate capitalists. Its committee on price fixing, chaired by leader T.N. Carver, worked closely with the Food and Fuel Administrations and the War Industries and War Trade Boards.[43] The foreign trade committee, chaired by E.M. Friedman of the War Finance Board, brought together AEA leaders like Paul M. Warburg of Kuhn and Loeb, and Frank Taussig, chair of the U.S. Tariff Commission, with corporate leaders like A. Barton Hepburn of the Chase National Bank and Jason A. Neilson of the Mercantile Bank of the Americas.[44] E.R.A. Seligman raised $1,100 from New York businessmen to underwrite the work of the AEA committee he chaired on war finance and

Table 5: Administrative Service of Social Science
Leaders in Federal War Agencies*

	ALL	AEA	APSA	ASS
War Department	5	2	1	2
War Industries Board	3	3	0	0
War Labor Policies Board	4	3	1	0
War Trade Board	3	2	1	0
War Fuel Administration	1	0	1	0
Shipping Board & related	4	4	0	0
Excess Profits Advisory Board	1	1	0	0
U. S. Food Administration	1	1	0	0
Advisory Tax Board	2	2	0	0
Price Fixing Commission	1	1	0	0
Sugar Equalization Board	1	1	0	0
War Savings, Treasury Department	1	1	0	0
Advisory Commission on the Peace	3	3	0	0
Delegates to Interallied Conferences	4	1	2	1
Sum of Participations	34	25	6	3
Number of Participants	23	16	5	2
Average Participations	1.5	1.6	1.2	1.5

*Data compiled from Allen Johnson, Dumas Malone, Harris E. Starr, Robert
L. Schulyer, Edward T. James and John A. Carrity, eds., Dictionary of
American Biography, 25 vols., (New York: Charles Scribner's Sons, 1928-
1977); National Cyclopedia of American Biography, 91 vols. (Clifton,
New York: James T. White, 1892-1978); Who Was Who in America, 7 vols.
(Chicago: Marquis, 1963-1976).

on which sat leaders such as H.C. Adams, C.J. Bullock, J.H. Hollander and C.C. Plehn.[45]

Economic expertise was not the only social science skill required by war. Leaders from all associations used their ideological and technical skills in a wide variety of semi-official organizations dedicated to enhancing patriotism. Association leaders were especially active in the division of civic and educational publications of the committee on public information, better known as the Creel Committee. This propaganda organization tapped their ideological expertise and fanned the flames of American patriotism at home and abroad, drawing on the skills of leaders like Charles Beard, John R. Commons, William E. Dodd, Albert Bushnell Hart, Monroe Smith and Charles Merriam.

Some social science leaders even went as far as to suppress scholarship and abandon friends. John Bates Clark, at the Carnegie Endowment for International Peace, aided by Alvin S. Johnson, stored in basement vaults studies questioning American involvement that had been commissioned before U.S. entry into the war.[46] At Wisconsin, Commons and Ely were part of a group that turned against their Progressive supporter, LaFollette, interpreting his anti-militarism as pro-Germanism.[47]

The AAUP's commitment to war was as intense as that of the disciplinary associations. The association as a whole vigorously supported the war effort, relinquishing for the duration any commitment to freedom of inquiry and expression. It issued the "Report of the Committee on Academic Freedom in Wartime," which not unexpectedly denied professors the privilege of academic freedom if they disobeyed any statute or executive order relating to the war. However, the AAUP demanded more than the law. Institutions were encouraged to dismiss professors engaged in any propaganda that might cause others to resist the war or who tried to dissuade others from rendering voluntary service to the government. And a special requirement was extracted from professors of German or Austro-Hungarian birth or parentage to refrain from public discussion of the war and avoid any hostile comment toward the U.S. in their private intercourse with neighbors, colleagues and students.[48] In short, professors opposing the war on grounds of science or conscience had no claim to academic freedom.

As AEA leaders had a committee to channel experts to public service, so the AAUP had Committee P, on patriotic service, that pointed members to war work. As the AEA looked to the war to make the U.S. the world center of finance, so the AAUP hoped it would lead to American dominance in the world of scholarship. To accomplish this, the AAUP's Committee V on the apparatus of productive scholarship focused on building American capacity for the infra-structure of scholarship--bibliographies, centralized clearinghouses for abstracts, systemic and regularly updated treatises on the states of various fields and more specialized journals.[49] As F.J. Teggert, chair of Committee V, put it, there was no longer any need to think of the tools "of scholarship . . . as 'made in Germany.'" Indeed, there was no reason "why American scholarship should not get to the front in the same way as the American army."[50]

The AAUP also joined with the Associations of State Universities, American Colleges, Agricultural Colleges and Experiment Stations, Urban Universities, and other managerial groups in the Emergency Council on Education. This organization, which would survive the war as the American Council of Education, saw educators' contribution to the war as providing moral and spiritual values to the nation in the absence of a state religion. It saw this function as important enough to merit department status and cabinet representation for education. Although the emergency council did not win formal presidential recognition, it continued its war work vigorously. Perhaps its greatest contribution was participating in planning the Student Army Training Corps in an effort to prevent disintegration of academic institutions as a result of mobilization.[51]

Thus, the associations and the AAUP were formally and fully committed to the war. Social science leaders acted as adjuncts to policy makers and were able to assemble data sets in agencies geared to national planning that they had only dreamed of before the war. The AAUP was able to advance the claims of American scholarship in an international arena and work with university managers who had refused to give them much official attention in the Progressive era.

But not all academics enlisted for the duration and those who opposed the war paid a heavy price. Almost any behavior construed as un-American resulted in termination. Pacifism, often supported by professors already holding questionable economic and social views, was prima facie evidence of disloyalty. When James McKeen Cattell wrote a confidential letter to his congressman in October 1917 supporting a bill for a volunteer rather than a conscripted army, President Butler seized the chance to be rid of a man who had long been a torment. Although a draft act had not yet been passed, Butler fired him under the guise of patriotism.[52] When Butler suspected Henry R. Dana of lack of enthusiasm for the war, he too was forced to leave. These dismissals prompted APSA leader Charles Beard to resign from Columbia and the AAUP, abandoning academia altogether.[53] AEA leader Simon Patten, whose economic views had always verged on the unorthodox, was retired early from the University of Pennsylvania after renting a hall in which a pacifist speaker appeared.[54] Political scientist William Schaper of University of Minnesota was a member of the Nonpartisan League, vocal in his opposition to the state's corporate interests and opposed to the war; he was dismissed even though he stopped his anti-war activity on U.S. entry. There were at least 18 other known war-related terminations and perhaps many more at institutions where accurate chronicles were not kept.[55] In the main, those dismissed were ideological deviants, regarded as overly critical of American institutions. Thus, the war provided an opportunity for managers to rid themselves of professors who created problems, and neither the social science nor AAUP leadership attempted to stop it.

Again, it is necessary to place the social science associations and the AAUP in the context of their times, and ask if there were widely understood alternatives. At least one organization with a small staff of professionals did resist efforts to silence those who spoke out against the war and social injustice. The National Civil Liberties Bureau, later the American Civil Liberties Union (ACLU), grew out of the militant wing of the pacifist movement. Although attorneys, reformers, publicists and a few businessmen worked with the bureau during the war years, the only social science or AAUP leaders who supported it were the AAUP's John Dewey and ASSA and AEA leader John Graham Brooks. A handful of academics worked with the bureau, but they were not association leaders.[56]

Although the ACLU provided an alternative to the academic community's position on the war, it was not viable for social science and AAUP leaders. Defending opposition to the war on civil libertarian grounds was perceived as radical by Wilson and the Washington bureaucracy, and social scientists had eschewed extremes. In the years since the Spanish-American War, they had deepened and made public their commitment to the center and to a conservative definition of social knowledge, making impossible organizational support of positions firmly defined as deviant by Americans in positions of power.

Experts, the AAUP and Victory

Throughout the war, social science leaders made plans for peace. In the main, these plans stressed the need to keep in place or expand the information and planning capacities developed during the war. For example, social science leaders in the National Civil Service Reform League wanted the war-swollen federal bureaucracy kept intact in peace to deal better with planned reconstruction. Academic experts in the National Municipal League thought government should retain the special powers acquired during war, using its agencies to monitor for "national efficiency." The AEA sought to preserve and make available for study records of the agencies with which its members had worked, arguing strongly for the development of organizations to continue gathering "exact quantitative data" for grounding peacetime policy.[57] Social science leaders, of course, were expected to play a major part in shaping what amounted to a national information-gathering and policy making apparatus.

While the organization of knowledge after the war did not meet the extravagant expectations of social science leaders, victory did bring about a series of organizations that put the production of social knowledge on a firm footing. Among the institutions and organizations established in the wake of the war were general associations such as the American Council of Learned Societies, the National Research Council and the Social Science Research Council, as well as more specialized organizations, such as the Institute for Public Administration, the Council of Foreign Relations, the Institute for Politics, and the Georgetown School of Foreign Service for political scientists, as well as the Industrial Conference Board and the National Bureau of Economic Research for economists. The disciplinary associations were often formally represented on these bodies, as was the case with the AEA and the National Bureau of Economic Research, and the AEA, APSA and ASS with the Social Science Research Council and the American Council of Learned Societies. Individual leaders, such as Charles Merriam, who directed the Social Science Research Council, also often played significant roles. The bulk of the funding for all these organizations continued to come from the great foundations--Carnegie, Rockefeller, Sage, Commonwealth, Falk, Rosenwald--and the research produced remained firmly in the political-economic center.[58]

This refinancing of social science research reflected lessons social scientists and their supporters had learned during the Progressive era and the war. Umbrella organizations--such as the Social Science Research Council--acted as academic holding companies that allowed the great foundations and corporate sponsors to funnel money to more specialized social science organizations without direct involvement. This organizational scheme averted questions like those raised by the Industrial Relations Commission about the control that sponsors exercised over the outcome of research. The confidence both social science and business leaders had in this arrangement was firm, strengthened by their shared experience of national planning in wartime.

As association leaders found seats on research boards after the war, so the AAUP was accepted in management forums. When the Emergency Council on Education became the American Council of Education (ACE) after the war, AAUP leaders were represented in the most comprehensive association of higher educational managers in the U.S. Their work with university managers on a host of academic problems caused them to change their adversary posture to one of collaboration, and in 1925 under ACE auspices the AAUP was able to negotiate limited managerial endorsement of the Declaration of Principles.[59]

The war placed social scientists and AAUP leaders, located primarily at prestigious research universities in an advantageous position, but the majority of the professorate did not fare so well. While the AAUP agitated for general salary increases and fought for years with the Carnegie Foundation's representatives to win fair pensions for all professors, it began to back slowly away from a firm commitment to the rank and file located at minor four-year institutions.[60] In his 1921 AAUP presidential address, E.R.A. Seligman suggested that full academic freedom and inviolable tenure would be more easily protected if extended only to senior professors at research institutions.[61]

Although the AAUP did not want to use its slender resources to fight the battles of colleges left behind in what Seligman called "the uneven development of higher education," it was hostile to the American Federation of Teachers (AFT), the organization most likely to aid professors at non-elite schools. While the American Federation of Labor had not solicited academics and was not quite certain of what to do with them, college locals burgeoned after the war when inflation made fixed salaries intolerable; by 1921 fourteen colleges had signed on.[62] The AAUP strongly opposed this development of academic unionization. Three points were frequently cited: first, union organization would divide and weaken the professorate; second, it was not fitting to pursue primarily economic goals when working at non-profit institutions; third, all faculty, but especially social scientists, "ought to avoid entangling permanent alliances with any groups . . . now struggling with one another to retain or increase their share of the social dividend."[63] Social scientists' own tendency to work in public- and private-sector groups indirectly supported by powerful capitalists went unremarked, especially as funds began to be channeled through the new research institutes.

However, the AAUP did not have long to contend with the possibility of academic unionism. The AFT college locals, formed for the most part at small and isolated four-year schools, disappeared when Palmer raids and the post-war repression made ties with labor a cause for suspicion. The AAUP was then free to label "the distinctive function" of university professors "in the economy of modern society" as furnishing "to other men the results of the experts in the several provinces of thought and knowledge."[64] This crystallized the expert role as the definitive role of research-oriented academics.

In sum, social science leaders were able to confirm the expert role through the AAUP. They directed Committee A toward protecting specialists from reprisals by managers, trustees and legislators who took issue with their learned advice. While the AAUP had only the slight leverage of personnel policy and procedure to stay the very real legal and economic power held by institutional managers, academics were nonetheless able to gain some authentic autonomy. But that autonomy depended upon the expert's acceptance of the conservative nature of social knowledge. When social science expertise supported radical policy that threatened the established order--as was the case with those who opposed the War--academic freedom did not apply. However, most social scientists were so firmly situated in the economic and ideological center that they saw the punishment meted out to their dissident colleagues as aberrant. In the main, they did not turn deliberately or maliciously from colleagues with alternative visions of social reality. Rather, they felt they had the academic freedom necessary to foster their pragmatic goals of influencing national policy and could not understand how this might not be sufficient. For the majority of social science leaders, then, the war was a demonstration of the success of what they had come to see as an objective and value-free social science, and the refinancing of social science research after victory was its just reward.

NOTES

1. As quoted in Walter P. Metzger, "Academic Tenure in American: A Historical Essay," in Faculty Tenure, ed. Commission on Academic Tenure in Higher Education (San Francisco: Jossey-Bass, 1973), p. 134.

2. Ibid., pp. 98-159.

3. "The Case of Professor Ross," Science 13 (March 8, 1901): 361-370, especially pages 364-370 where the AEA report is reprinted.

4. See for example James P. Munro, "Closer Relations Between Faculties and Trustees," Science 12 (1905): 848-855; George M. Stratton, "Externalism in American Universities," Atlantic Monthly 100 (1907): 512-519; Joseph Jastrow, "Academic Aspects of Administration," Popular Science Monthly 73 (October 1908): 326-369.

5. William C. Lawton, "The Decay of Academic Courage," Educational Review 32 (November 1906): 402.

6. Charles W. Eliot, Academic Freedom (Ithaca, N.Y.: Cornell, 1907); pp. 5-24.

7. Nicholas Murray Butler, "Academic Freedom," Educational Review 47 (March 1914): 291-294.

8. Simon N. Patten, "The Making of Economic Literature," American Economic Association Quarterly, 3d series, 10 (April 1909): 8.

9. Arthur T. Hadley, "Academic Freedom in Theory and in Practice," Atlantic Monthly 91 (February 1903): 152-160.

10. Alvin S. Johnson, Pioneers Progress: An Autobiography (New York: Viking, 1952; reprint ed., Lincoln, Neb.: Bison Books, University of Nebraska Press, 1960); pp. 147-150.

11. Joseph Dorfman, _Thorstein Veblen and His America_ (New York: Viking, 1961).

12. Barry D. Karl, _Charles E. Merriam and the Study of Politics_ (Chicago: University of Chicago Press, 1974), p. 46.

13. Scott Nearing, _The Making of a Radical: A Political Autobiography_ (New York: Harper & Row, Torchbook edition, 1972), pp. 44-45.

14. Johnson, _Pioneers Progress_, p. 201.

15. Philip Taft and Philip Ross, "American Labor Violence: Its Causes, Character and Outcome," in _The History of Violence in America: A Report to the National Commission on the Causes and Prevention of Violence_, edited by Hugh Davis Graham and Ted Robert Gurr (New York: Bantam, 1969), p. 320.

16. James Weinstein, _The Decline of Socialism in America, 1912-1925_ (New York: Vintage, 1969), pp. 93-103.

17. Taft and Ross, "American Labor Violence," pp. 320-332.

18. Howard Crosby Warren, "Academic Freedom," _Atlantic Monthly_ 114 (November 1914): 689-699.

19. "Minutes of the Business Meeting at Minneapolis," _American Economic Review_ 4 (Supplement, March 1914): 196-197.

20. For an account of the Ely trial, see Chapter 4.

21. The APSA members were F.N. Judson, chair, James Q. Dealy and Herbert Croly. The ASS members were U.G. Weatherly, chair, and James Lichtenberger and Roscoe Pound. Croly, Pound and Judson were public members appointed to indicate that the investigation was not being made by a special interest group. Judson was also an APSA leader, and Lichtenberger was not an ASS leader.

22. "Preliminary Report of the Joint Committee on Academic Freedom and Tenure," American Economic Review (AER) (Supplement, March 1915): 318.

23. See "Report of the Committee of Inquiry Concerning Charges of Violation of Academic Freedom at the University of Colorado," American Association of University Professors Bulletin (BAAUP) 2 (April 1916): 3-72, for Brewster; "Report of the Committee of Inquiry on the Case of Professor Scott Nearing of the University of Pennsylvania," BAAUP 2 (May 1916): 7-57, for Nearing; and Sheila Slaughter, "The Danger Zone: Academic Freedom and Civil Liberties," Annals of the American Academy of Political and Social Science 448 (March 1980): 52.

24. Merle Curti and Vernon Carstensen, The University of Wisconsin, 2 vols. (Madison, Wisc.: University of Wisconsin Press, 1949), 2: 267-294, quote from p. 289.

25. William Grabner, "The Origins of Retirement in Higher Education: the Carnegie Pension System," Academe 65 (March 1979): 97-103. See also "Columbia University vs. Professor Cattell," BAAUP (November 1922): 20-41.

26. "Meeting for the Organization of the Association, New York, January, 1915," BAAUP 2 (March 1916): 16-17.

27. "General Report of the Committee on Academic Freedom and Tenure; Prefatory Note," BAAUP 1 (December 1915): 17-18.

28. "General Report of the Committee on Academic Freedom and Academic Tenure: General Declaration of Principles and Practical Proposals," BAAUP 1 (December 1915): 20-43.

29. Ralph S. Brown, Jr., and Matthew W. Finkin, "The Usefulness of AAUP Policy Statements," Academe 64 (March 1978): 5-11.

30. "General Report of the Committee on Academic Freedom and Tenure," AAUP (December 1915): 20-43.

31. Ibid. All quotes in this paragraph taken from pp. 11-16.

32. Ibid., p. 19. Although the AAUP may have anticipated state universities suppressing professors who were political conservatives, there is only one well-known instance in the period, that of Kansas State University, where Populists gained control, fired conservatives and introduced radicals. Within several years this policy was reversed. See Mary O. Furner, Advocacy and Objectivity (Lexington, Ky.: The University Press of Kentucky, 1975), pp. 214-215.

33. "Report of the Committee on Academic Freedom and Tenure," all quotes in this paragraph from pp. 17-19.

34. Compiled from cases reported in BAAUP, 1916-1917.

35. "Report of Committees Concerning Charges of Violations of Academic Freedom at the University of Colorado and at Wesleyan University," BAAUP 2 (April 1916): 3. See also "Report at the University of Colorado," BAAUP 2 (April 1916): 3-35.

36. "Report of the Committee of Inquiry on the Case of Professor Scott Nearing of the University of Pennsylvania," BAAUP 2 (May 1916): 7-52; and Commission on Industrial Relations, Final Report and Testimony, 16 vols. (Washington, D.C.: U.S. Government Printing Office, 1916), 1: 82-86.

37. See, for example, Paul F. Brissenden, The I.W.W.: A Study of American Syndicalism (New York: Columbia University, 1920), p. 265; Theodore Schroeder, Free Speech for Radicals (New York: Free Speech League, 1916), pp. 116-190; Paul Murphy, The Meaning of Freedom of Speech (Westport, Conn.: Greenwood Press, 1972).

38. Commission on Industrial Relations, Final Report and Testimony, 16 vols., 415 (Washington, D.C.: U.S. Government Printing Office, 1916); 1: 84.

39. Nearing, The Making of a Radical, pp. 120-121.

40. John M. Mecklin, My Quest for Freedom (New York: Charles Scribner's Sons, 1945), p. 187.

41. Carol Singer Gruber, Mars and Minerva: World War I and the Uses of the Higher Learning in America (Baton Rouge, La.: Louisiana State University Press, 1975), pp. 81-117; C. Roland Marchand, The American Peace Movement and Social Reform, 1898-1918 (Princeton, N.J.: Princeton University Press, 1972), pp. 145-175.

42. A.A. Young, "Report of the Secretary for the Year Ending December 18, 1917," AER 8 (Supplement, March 1918): 300.

43. "Report of the Secretary for the Year Ending December 18, 1918," AER 9 (Supplement, March 1919): 354-358.

44. "Report of the Committee on Foreign Trade," AER 10 (Supplement, March 1920): 241-247.

45. For Seligman's part, see "Report of the Secretary . . . 1918," p. 355. For the work of the committee, see "Report of the Committee on War Finance of the American Economic Association," AER 9 (Supplement 2, March 1919): 1-142.

46. Johnson, Pioneers Progress, p. 229.

47. Curtis and Carstensen, The University of Wisconsin, 2: 15.

48. "Report of the Committee on Academic Freedom in Wartime," BAAUP 4 (February/March 1918): 29-47.

49. "General Announcements: Annual Meeting," BAAUP 4 (January 1918): 6-8.

50. F.J. Teggert, "Preliminary Report of Committee V on the Apparatus for Productive Scholarship," BAAUP 5 (March 1919): 35, 39.

51. "General Announcements," BAAUP 4 (May 1918): 1-2; "Emergency Council on Education," BAAUP 4 (February/March 1918): 5-9.

52. "Columbia University vs. Professor Cattell," BAAUP 8 (November 1922): 21-41. The AAUP supported Cattell in its last stand before initiating its wartime policy.

53. William Summerscales, Affirmation and Dissent: Columbia's Response to the Crisis of World War I (New York: Teachers College Press, Columbia University, 1970), pp. 94-95.

54. Daniel M. Fox, The Discovery of Abundance: Simon N. Patten and the Transformation of Social Theory (Ithaca, N.Y.: Cornell University Press, 1967), pp. 126-177.

55. Gruber, Mars and Minerva, pp. 176-177.

56. For Dewey's participation, see Donald Johnson, The Challenge to American Freedoms: World War I and the Rise of the American Civil Liberties Union (Lexington, Ky.: University of Kentucky Press, 1963), p. 88. For Brooks's participation, see Peggy Lamson, Roger Baldwin: A Portrait (Boston: Houghton Mifflin, 1976), p. 80.

57. See, for example, "News and Notes," APSR 12 (1918): pp. 137-138; J.P. Chamberlain, "The International Union of Academies and the American Council of Learned Societies Devoted to Humanistic Studies," APSR 14 (August 1920): 499-503; "The National Bureau of Economic Research," AER 11 (Supplement, March 1921): 180-181.

58. For account of the formation of these institutes, see Barry D. Karl, Charles E. Merriam and the Study of Politics (Chicago:

University of Chicago Press, 1974), especially chapter 7, "An Organization for Social Research;" and Herbert Heaton, A Scholar in Action: Edwin F. Gay (Cambridge, Mass.: Harvard University Press, 1952; reprint ed., New York: Greenwood Press, 1968), especially 196-206; as well as David W. Eakins, "The Development of Corporate Liberal Policy Research in the United States, 1885-1965" (Ph.D. dissertation, University of Wisconsin, 1966).

59. For a good description of the ACE, see "General Announcements," BAAUP 6 (March 1920): 4-7. See "Committee A, Academic Freedom and Tenure," BAAUP 8 (February 1922): 57, for authorization of these negotiations.

60. For agitation for salary increases, see Arthur O. Lovejoy, "Annual Message of the President," BAAUP 5 (November/December 1919): 10-40. For an account of the AAUP's work on pensions, see "Committee P, Pensions and Insurance," BAAUP 8 (February 1922): 73-86.

61. Edwin R.A. Seligman, "Our Association--Its Aims and Accomplishments," BAAUP 8 (February 1922): 8-26.

62. Jeannette Lester, "The American Federation of Teachers in Higher Education: A History of Union Organization of Faculty Members in Colleges and Universities," (Ph.D. dissertation, University of Toledo, 1968.)

63. Arthur O. Lovejoy, "Annual Message," BAAUP 5 (November-December 1919): 27.

64. A.O. Lovejoy, untitled remarks, reprinted from Weekly Review in BAAUP 6 (October 1920): 11.

Epilogue
Prometheus Bound in the
Age of Monopoly Capitalism

Members of the academic community tend to see academic freedom as a well-established and liberating tangible right, the privilege of professors that distinguishes them from other cultural workers. This view errs in several ways. First, minimal academic freedom--the right to pursue ideas to systematic intellectual conclusions protected by organizational due process and tenured job security--far from being well established was not widespread until 1940. And since then--as before--it has been under constant and vigorous attack by educational managers and resource suppliers. Far from being well established and routinely available, academic freedom is a fragile and weakly institutionalized expectation more desired by university-based cultural workers than acknowledged by educational managers.[1] Second, an adequate academic freedom--one permitting systematically developed ideas to be tested pragmatically and corrected in everyday life--does not exist. And if the evidence of the last decade is a sound guide, it will not[2] exist in the present climate of rationalization and retrenchment. Third, and most importantly, academics fail to comprehend the historical causes and consequences of the exchanges that shaped their highly prized but essentially illusionary academic freedom. For academic freedom, as presently constituted, far from being the liberating right to test the limits of thought and deed, is in fact the very chain that immobilizes university-based intellectuals, always separating their thoughts from deeds and keeping their ideas from reaching systematic limits.

It is understandable, though not admirable, that natural and physical scientists, mathematicians and humanists hold such flawed notions of their academic situations. That academic social scientists share these errors is a severe indictment of their collective wisdom resting as it does on historical amnesia, a suggestion of the larger invalidity of university-based social thought, and a sure affirmation that their expertise is bound, Prometheus-like, in the service of institutionalized power. Indeed, social scientists helped forge the chains of academic freedom. As we have seen, the American Association of Universities (AAU) was formed in 1900 to provide a forum for university managers at the leading research institutions. Here higher education's managers discussed and elaborated their expectations about their rights and obligations to resource suppliers, professors, students and the community-at-large. In 1915 academics at these managers' institutions began their own forum group, the American Association of University Professors (AAUP), to discuss and elaborate similar expectations. Then, ever sensitive to their positions' vulnerabilities, the social scientists' joint committee became a majority of the AAUP's Committee A, with its over-riding concern with academic freedom. And, in Metzger's felicitous phrase, Committee A became the AAUP.[3]

The essential exchanges involved in the discipline-leader-dominated joint committee becoming Committee A are clear-cut. The AAUP acknowledged the expertise of the social scientists in the qualities of mind and rhetoric necessary to comprehend the social world. Here were precisely the fourth faculty specialists, certified fit and qualified to articulate and argue an academic freedom adequate for intellectual activities at America's emerging research universities. For their part, the social scientists, by agreeing to staff Committee A, greatly broadened their bargaining base. Now they could seek a socially necessary intellectual freedom for the entire research professorate and claim their own disciplinarian rights from those granted to all academics. But gaining the leverage of a broader social base required trimming their own expectations to those shared by all academics. Here the social scientists let go of their claims to extraordinary rights as the fourth faculty's most specialized guides through the social chaos of America's rapid industrialization. These claims to extraordinary academic freedoms were never advanced by Committee A speaking for the entire profession, and their accomplishment remains unattempted by the disciplinarian associations.

The exchanges occurring with Committee A becoming the AAUP are similarly straightforward. The AAUP gradually shut down an entire alphabet of committees focused on every conceivable aspect of university and college life. It thus gave up the research professorate's comprehensive claims to create and implement academic policy writ large. In essence, the AAUP narrowed its negotiable interests to personnel policies guaranteeing job security. To say that Committee A became the AAUP is to note that the AAUP became something of a company union, accepting management initiatives and authority in most areas of university life. And as academic management consolidated its increasingly uncontested control over American universities and colleges, present and future, it granted the professorate a limited and inadequate academic freedom, but one consistent with higher education's enormous resource requirements. Thus was Prometheus bound in the higher learning, as we see in the documents marking the AAUP's negotiations with academic management from the 1920s to the present. In this half century, the AAUP consistently continued to uphold its 1915 agreement to manage knowledge conservatively in the fourth faculty's house of intellect,[4] going even as far as trading the professorate's constitutional civil liberties for a foreshortened version of academic freedom.

The 1925 Conference Statement

After World War I, the AAUP was not the only educational organization concerned with academic freedom. Associations of managers--like the Association of American Colleges--were equally interested in definitions of academic freedom, especially as they impinged on personnel policy. Their interest was obvious; they had to develop procedures that took the profession's demand for academic freedom into account while still preserving managerial prerogatives and safeguarding the resource base of their institutions from being jeopardized by professors who took positions openly at odds with trustees. For its part, Committee A noted in 1924 that "by ourselves we can only investigate cases and point out wherein principles which we believe to be fundamental have been violated. . . . This is not nearly as effective as would be an enunciation of principles made not only by professors but by professors and bodies authorized to speak for the institutions themselves."[5]

The 1925 conference statement made by the AAUP and the American Association of Colleges under the sponsorship of the American Council of Education was essentially an accommodation between professors and university management. It was more or less a manual of operating procedures augmenting the 1915 declaration by making the code of conduct governing freedom of expression more explicit. The university teacher in the classroom was enjoined to confine himself to his field of expertise, to present all sides of controversial questions, and to show special restraint when instructing immature students. When speaking outside the university in his area of specialization, he had full "freedom of exposition in his own subject," as well as the same political rights as any other citizen.

Although some universities had instituted tenure, the association did not yet insist that it be uniformly incorporated into personnel policy. However, if academics observed the rules of classroom conduct, the only grounds for termination of a permanent or long-term appointment were "gross immorality or treason, when the facts are admitted." The statement, then, recognized tenure where it existed and offered some protection to senior faculty, the most likely to hold long-term appointments at institutions without tenure.

The AAUP, one other professional organization, and seven major associations of higher education managers endorsed the statement.[6] Although endorsement did not guarantee the good conduct of member institutions, the AAUP's cautious definition of academic freedom and the corresponding need to show cause for terminating a long-standing or permanent appointment began to be recognized as a condition of academic employment with which managers would have to deal.

The 1925 conference statement was formulated under conditions of "normalcy" and did not withstand the onslaught of the depression. Systemic economic crisis produced intense ideological conflict. In many instances, political and economic elites responsible for the governance of universities refused to tolerate their faculties' outspoken participation in activities overly critical of capitalism. The number of academic freedom cases on the AAUP docket piled up rapidly. The point at which professors most often alleged violation of academic freedom was in exercise of their civil liberties. The association had approved almost without reservation academics' right to engage in political activity and was now asked to offer protection.

However, the AAUP was sometimes unwilling and often unable to intervene effectively. When radical groups demanded protection of professors' right to dissent and engaged in litigation as well as active protest to win reinstatement for ousted colleagues, they acted on the revolutionary potential of social knowledge and went farther and faster than stipulated in the gentlemen's agreement established by the 1915 declaration. And the AAUP was reluctant to move beyond its narrow definition of academic freedom.

Thus, when both the AAUP and the American Federation of Teachers (AFT) investigated the celebrated Jerome Davis case, they came to different conclusions. Davis, an associate professor employed for many years by the Yale Divinity School, was long on radical activity and short on publications. When he wrote an open letter to President Roosevelt in 1936 criticizing reform capitalism, he was dismissed. The AFT found Yale guilty of violating academic freedom, and demanded that Davis be reinstated while the AAUP found him professionally inadequate but tempered this judgment with a recommendation of a year's severance pay.[7]

Bound by its 1915 commitment to conservative management of knowledge and the molding of a moderate public opinion, the AAUP side-stepped the radical thrust of the 1930s. The 1925 accommodation with management further limited its scope for vigorous, independent action. While managers might support freedom of inquiry within the university, they could not condone radical political activism without endangering material and political support for their institutions in a time of great economic uncertainty.

Throughout the 1930s the AAUP more often than not interpreted alleged violations of academic freedom as administrative quarrels or personality clashes, even though 21 states had legislated loyalty oaths aimed at eliminating radical educators and professors from public educational systems by 1935.[8] As a result of the AAUP's reluctance to take a militant stand, many professors turned to more aggressive organizations, such as the AFT or the American Civil Liberties Union (ACLU). These organizations were not concerned with personnel policy as a safeguard for academic freedom, but with substantive protection of civil liberties. The AFT, for example, mounted crusades to attract attention to the plights of Professor W.G. Bergman, dismissed from Detroit Teachers College on charges of sedition based on his opposition to military training; Professor J.C. Granbury, Texas Tech, dismissed for enonomic liberalism and pacifism; Leo Gallagher, Los Angeles law professor dismissed for defending political minorities; G. McLean, an economics professor in Memphis who lost his job for serving as an advisory member of the Unemployed Citizens League; and Hugh De Lacy, a Washington English professor and AFT delegate to the Seattle Central Labor Union who was dismissed when he ran for political office.[9]

The AAUP had recognized the inadequacy of the 1925 conference statement in the early 1930s, and started working with managerial groups on a more comprehensive agreement. The need for a new document became more urgent as the 1930s drew to a close and firings increased. Moreover, AAUP membership held steady while other organizations were growing rapidly.[10] If the AAUP were to continue to speak for the profession as a whole without abandoning its commitment to defense of academic freedom through uniform personnel policy, it would have to offer professors something tangible in the way of job security.

The 1940 Statement of Principles

The 1940 statement drawn up conjointly with the Association of American Colleges is of critical importance, since it still stands, subject to 1970 interpretations, as the AAUP's basic formulation of academic freedom and tenure. The 1940 statement in essence exchanges professors' civil liberties for tenure. And the profession, faced with organized repression in the form of the Ives Laws and the MacNaboe, Dies and Rapp-Courdet Investigating Committees, accepted the bargain.

With regard to "extra-mural utterances" made in the course of exercising the political rights of a citizen, the professor no longer has the same latitude as other men and women. "His special position in the community imposes special obligations." While the professor should be "free from institutional censorship or discipline," he should nonetheless always keep in mind "that the public may judge his profession and his institution by his utterances. Hence he should at all times be accurate, should exercise appropriate restraint, should show respect for the opinions of others, and should make every effort to indicate that he is not an institutional spokesman."

In return, precise definition is given for the first time to the tenure process. After a probationary period of a maximum of seven years, professors, after review, should have permanent or continuous tenure of office that can be terminated only by "adequate cause." What adequate cause might be is not addressed, but the interpretation appended to the 1940 document specifically states that the exercise of professor's political rights as a citizen might legitimately be considered sufficient.[11]

Exactly how a professor may fail to meet his "special obligations" is not treated; indeed, it still remains subject to a variety of interpretations both inside and outside the association. However, in 1940, the AAUP was no longer obligated to insist that professors be accorded the same rights as all citizens in a time of widespread social unrest. As a president of the AAUP, William Van Alstyne, has pointed out:

the trade-off that the AAUP appeared to have accepted with the Association of American Colleges in 1940 (namely, to cultivate public confidence in the profession by laying down a professionally taxing standard of institutional accountability for all utterances of a public character made by a member of the profession) is substantially more inhibiting of a faculty member's civil freedom of speech than any standard that government is constitutionally privileged to impose in respect to the personal political or social utterances of other kinds of public employees.[12]

Essentially, political activity was left to the discretion of individual professors. However, the AAUP no longer had an obligation to defend professors engaged in such activity. The association was relieved of antagonizing university managers, trustees and other representatives of vested interest controlling higher education's funding. For example, when the Rapp-Courdet Committee began hearings in New York City in 1941 to investigate Communism in the schools, the AAUP was not forced to take a definitive position even though 69 faculty members in the City College system were called before the tribunal.[13]

The AAUP, then, traded civil liberties for tenure. Academic freedom was permitted in the classroom, within the confines of the scholarly community, and in seemly extra-mural utterance in one's field of expertise but did not extend to intercourse with the general public in the political arena. The commitment to manage knowledge conservatively was honored by protecting the silent majority of professors, those displaying conventional behavior and acceptable ideologies, while placing political deviants and activists in jeopardy.

Academic Freedom and the Quest for National Security: The 1956 Report

During World War II, the AAUP made a deliberate effort not to let history repeat itself and was justly proud of the fact no emergency measures were taken. Indeed, only two cases involving conscientious objectors were brought to the formal attention of Committee A during the war years.[14] Communists and fellow travelers did not present the problems they had in the 1930s, so long as the U.S.S.R. remained an ally. The AAUP's confrontation with the conflicting claims of academic freedom and national security was delayed until after the war. Then the very success of science in the dramatic end to hostilities in the Pacific theater turned governmental and public attention to the university.

As World War II gave way to the Cold War, instances like the Lattimore and Oppenheimer cases made the university, as the home of scientists and intellectuals, a target for national security. The Un-American Activities Committee (HUAC) was made a permanent committee of the House of Representatives in 1945; Truman instituted the Federal Loyalty Program by executive order in 1947; the National Security Act was passed in 1950; numerous states began to conduct their own investigations into professors' pasts. Education became one of the major battlefields in the post-war struggle for control of domestic policy.[15] Professors who throughout World War II had planned for a new peace in a more democratic social order were among the first to fall in this ideological struggle that stifled even liberal critiques of capitalism. The AAUP, having traded civil liberties for tenure, had nothing left to give and was unable to protect the profession from persecution on grounds of political activity. In fact, the AAUP affirmed its giveaway of civil liberties by undermining the validity of the faculty's claim to Fifth Amendment rights.

According to the AAUP's own calculations, there were at least 77 dismissals between 1949 and 1955. Tenure offered little security, since its protection did not extend to the professor in his role as citizen outside the university. And almost all firings were the result of professors' alleged participation in politics. Thus, in 1949 three tenured professors at the University of Washington were dismissed without severence pay, two for membership in the Communist party, one for refusal to testify; in 1950, at the University of California, 32 faculty members, more than half of them tenured, were dismissed for their refusal to take a regent-imposed disclaimer oath in regard to past or present party membership; in the New York City Municipal Colleges, 14 were dismissed in 1953 after refusing to testify at congressional hearings, four more in 1954 and 1955 under the Feinberg Law. Another 24 individuals were dismissed from an additional 20 institutions, in most cases for refusal to testify[16] before a university, state or federal investigating committee.

These dismissals are only a rough index of the degree to which academic freedom was curtailed. When professors were falsely accused, as was the case with Melvin Rader at the University of Washington, or mistakenly identified and forced to spend thousands of dollars in legal fees as well as endless hours in proving perjury on the part of a witness or correcting a bureaucratic mistake, all professors felt themselves vulnerable.[17] As Paul Lazarsfeld and Wagner Thielens, Jr., have pointed out, the climate of repression significantly affected academics' willingness to treat controversial issues even in their own fields of expertise.[18]

In 1956 prodded by membership pressure and encouraged by recent judicial decisions, the association issued a position paper. Presented as a reappraisal of the question of national security, this statement is a massive equivocation. Basically, the document argues that a professor cannot be dismissed for past or present Communist party membership, as long as it is demonstrated that these do not affect fitness to teach. Nor can he be compelled to testify. However, participation in educational subversion is evidence of unfitness, refusal to testify may be a strong indication of such subversive activity and, if questioned by institutional authorities,the professor has a duty to disclose, even though this means loss of Fifth Amendment protection in inquiries outside the university.[19] Confined by the 1940 statement, the AAUP had little scope for argument; what was needed was full protection of civil liberties, and this the association could not give without abrogating its earlier document.

The courts moved faster than the AAUP. When they upheld the legality of the Fifth Amendment, Committee A had to issue a supplement to its 1956 document. The association, however, was not as liberal as the courts. Its 1958 supplement still insisted that the institution had a right to information touching on a faculty member's fitness. As a strategy it was suggested that professors under institutional investigation offer off-the-record testimony to officials. If this candid gesture compromising one's constitutional liberty was rejected, then the professor had fulfilled his obligation to this employer, and the institution was open to possible censure by the AAUP.[20]

In summary, the association continued to put its faith in personnel policy that accommodated university managers and trustees while professors were forced publicly to recant ideological sins committed a decade or more before. However, uniform promotion and tenure policy protected those faculty members who stayed away from politics, and this was the lesson that the profession learned. The vast majority of the professorate kept their jobs and held their tongues.

1970 Interpretative Comments

The safeguards offered by the courts in the mid-1950s may have been a turning point in terms of the AAUP's role in defining and protecting academic freedom and tenure. The AAUP's failure to redefine academic freedom to include civil liberties marks the time when professors consistently began to use litigation to protect their employment while exercising their constitutional right to free speech.

The 1970 interpretative comments did little to revitalize the association's claim to speak for the profession as a whole. Although the comments were formulated during the campus upheavals of the 1960s and substantive revision of the 1940 statement was expected, little was changed. Professors still have a "particular obligation" as representatives of the academy outside the university.[21] Even in the 1970s professors' claims to civil liberties are not firm.

However, the AAUP still wields considerable force when it comes to defining tenure. The courts recognize the association as the custodian of "professional custom" and often turn to its precedents when ruling. Many colleges and universities have adopted the 1940 statement as their personnel policy; thus the document becomes part of the formal contract between professors and university, governing litigation as well as day-to-day procedures. Unions, too, are informed by the AAUP definition of tenure and offer no greater substantive protection of academic freedom than the association.

The problem with all these definitions remains the same as in 1915. Tenure does not necessarily insure academic freedom, let alone the exercise of civil liberties. Although tenure does offer job security to senior faculty, even this is limited. Tenured professors can still be fired for incompetence, financial exigency or failing to act in a manner that fulfills their "particular obligation" as faculty members. While the courts offer some protection, they have not established binding definitions of academic freedom. Since the concept has no constitutional status, professors must defend their civil liberties under the First Amendment and tenure as property right under the Fourteenth. Clearly an adequate academic freedom is not a condition of employment in higher education.

And What Now?

Although we tell ourselves that the day is past when wholesale attacks on academic freedom are possible, evidence argues the contrary. In the years 1965-1975 professors were fired on overtly political grounds at a rate unmatched since the height of the McCarthy era. As always, professors in the danger zone were political activists, often using their academic expertise to challenge dominant ideologists.

Among the more well-known cases were George Murray, English instructor at San Francisco State and Black Panther "Minister of Education," suspended for allegedly advocating that minority students arm themselves for self-protection; Staughton Lynd, historian who traveled to North Vietman in defiance of state department orders in 1966, denied employment by the Board of Governors of the State Colleges and Universities in Illinois because his journey went "beyond mere dissent"; Angela Davis, U.C.L.A. philosopher fired for her Communist party membership; Michael Parenti, anti-war political science professor at the University of Vermont, denied renewal despite unanimous recommendations by department, dean and university administration on grounds of unbecoming "professional conduct" detrimental to the image of the university; Peter Bohmer, radical economics professor at San Francisco State, fired on charges of discriminating in his grading practices against conservative students even after being cleared of the charges in three separate investigations; Morris Starsky, activist philosophy professor at Arizona State, fired in connection with his anti-war stance despite[22] support from two faculty committees and the university president.

When professors combine intellectual work with outspoken political activism, they are vulnerable. At that point trustees exercise their legal authority, often reversing the decisions of the faculty and university administrators by asserting their own definition of ideological orthodoxy and the limits of professors' civil liberties.

Dismissals on political grounds are, of course, the exception; they occur only in the relatively few instances when professors regularly and vehemently challenge the established order in a public arena. However, such dismissals are an index of managerial concern about the beliefs, values, and ideologies of resource holders. These concerns are widely shared by senior faculty and by university administrators, who often use what power they have to screen out potentially troublesome colleagues through devices such as the tenure review process and budget cuts.

Indeed, the tenure review process, governed by senior faculty who have already proved to be responsible, respectful, and conscious of their particular obligations, is probably the major mechanism for insuring the continued conservative management of knowledge. Ideologically suspect and politically active young faculty are often denied permanent positions on grounds of professional inadequacy. In the late 1960s and early 1970s, the campus climate was such that these charges could not be lightly made. Junior faculty who thought their tenure decisions turned on their politics often asked for and received public hearings.[23] But as tenure slots become scarce and students apathetic, activist and junior faculty are more easily let go, often internalizing   their   senior   colleagues'   verdict of professional inadequacy without serious question.

Current economic conditions also allow administrators wider scope in removing ideological deviants, activists and "difficult" faculty. The dissolution of the radical activist School of Criminal Justice at Berkeley on grounds of financial exigency is a case in point. At a time when economic uncertainty is increasing and administrators are routinely asked to turn in retrenchment plans, the importance of holding jobs makes faculty less likely to speak out and identify themselves as targets for budget cuts. These internal controls on academic freedom--tenure review and the budget--are pervasive, subtle and not easily fought.

While tenure may not protect academic freedom or even guarantee job security, given the vulnerability of men and women prepared to voice or act on ideas at odds with the dominant culture, it may be necessary, if only to make dismissals more difficult. However, it is perhaps time to raise the question of how the profession can better protect academic freedom that guarantees civil liberties. Our inability to safeguard the rights we claim is painfully apparent. When economic instability is compounded by ideological conflict--as was the case in the Progressive era, the 1930s, and the period following World War II--academic freedom has no real meaning. With both academia and the economy in an unsteady condition, we should remember our collective past and use our insight to repossess the future. We might begin by confronting the chains that bind us to a corporate capitalism committed to a world system of production planned for profit, institutionalized inequality, political corruption and dictatorship. Surely, the central problematic requiring academic attention is how to untie social sciences from an epoch of bondage to monopoly capital. And perhaps the first item on our question list should be to identify and consolidate an alternative resource base, one capable of sustaining the unbinding of Prometheus and the widest use of social science for the greatest good.

For example, given the widely reported, left-of-center tendencies among sociologists,[24] one would suppose a large proportion of the ASA's university-based membership to sense the resource potential inherent in the many millions of their fellow citizens living in relative poverty and powerlessness. Such ASAers might open a dialogue and practice on the knowledge needed by their fellows, using the established academic forums: the cycle of regional and national association meetings and departmental colloquia everywhere. Furthermore, academics might offer their well-honed skills at ideological construction and technical amelioration in exchange for popular resource support and legitimation. Professors might present themselves at the forums frequented by the wider working class: union meetings, labor schools, cooperative conferences, even service club luncheons, church groups, and parent-teacher associations.

At the ideological level, university-based social scientists could offer systematic oppositional analysis of current events as well as enduring inequalities. Here the point would be to strengthen the de-legitimation routinely presented by everyday experience in advanced corporate capitalist society. Here the task is to deepen such de-legitimation by uncloaking the corporate center's authority as raw power serving its own narrow interests. But simply revealing raw power immobilizes those who might oppose it, or worse, transforms decent concern into cynical opportunism. What is needed is more than mere de-legitimation. Indeed, as many decent citizens have long held the theory of "the just war" against intransigent immorality, so sociologists must create an ideology to guide and give meaning to oppositional practice. We need a new and energizing theory of "the just revolution," one specifying the social conditions morally condemning North American capitalism to the trash heap of out-moded social structures while compelling its replacement by a clearly more just and equitable society. Here is a task worthy of the profession's very considerable ideological talents.[25]

Beyond ideological combat and renewal are the imperatives of technical amelioration and two similar tasks. First, better social service delivery systems should be designed, building on the ideological critiques offered in working-class forums. Given the structural insensitivity of the present system to the culturally defined needs of its participants, the possibilities are virtually limitless. Occupational health and safety touches most blue- and white-collar workers, as does decent and affordable housing, care for old and young, and polluted air, food and water. Here again, redesign isn't enough, for by itself it endlessly absorbs the energies of its architects. Even more important is drafting plans for the future, plans that combine traditional cultural aspirations with the material abundance available in North America. For example, what would auto workers do on the job in a decent society? What would a healthy and safe auto plant look like? What kind of autos would be congruent with a society that maximized human safety and technical efficiency on the highway as well? What sort of transportation mix would express the population's enduring commitment to egalitarianism[26] and the still undepleted resources of our society? The need is for a liberating "futurology," one opening up popular, democratic alternatives to the continuing crisis of centralist corporate capitalism at home and abroad.

As simply put as possible, having come of age in academia during the waning years of North American monopoly capitalism, we the professionals that staff the universities can realistically begin to discuss and design a more useful and humane social system. Indeed, given that the alternative to thoughtful revolution is centralist repression,[27] we have little choice if we are to remain true to our own traditions of knowledge in the service of humanity.

NOTES

1. Sheila Slaughter, "The Danger Zone: Academic Freedom and Civil Liberties," Annals of the American Academy of Political and Social Science, 448 (March 1980): 46-61.

2. Sheila Slaughter, "Political Action, Occupational Autonomy and Retrenchment: A Decade of Academic Freedom, 1970-80," in Higher Education in American Society, ed. Philip Altbach and Robert Berhdahl (Buffalo, N.Y.: Prometheus Press, 1981), pp. 73-100.

3. Walter P. Metzger, "Origins of the Association: An Anniversary Address," American Association of University Professors Bulletin, (BAAUP) 51 (June 1965): 236.

4. For the details of this 1915 agreement, see Chapter 11.

5. "Committee Reports Report of Committee A," BAAUP 10 (February 1915): 12.

6. "American Council On Education: Conference on Academic Freedom and Tenure," BAAUP 11 (February 1925): 99-102.

7. Robert Iverson, The Communists and the Schools (New York: Harcourt Brace, 1959), pp. 166-169.

8. See Lionel Lewis, Scaling the Ivory Tower (Baltimore: Johns Hopkins University Press, 1975) Chapter 6, The Bearing of Merit on Academic Freedom.

   For another view of the nature of academic dismissals, see "Restrictions on Professors," in The Gag on Teaching (American Civil Liberties Union Pamphlet, April 1936), pp. 34-37.

9. Compiled from the American Teacher, 1930-1940.

10. Jeanette A. Lester, "The American Federation of Teachers in Higher Education: A History of Union Organization of Faculty Members in Colleges and Universities" (Ph.D. dissertation, University of Toledo, 1968), Figure 1, Membership in AFT College Locals and the AAUP, p. 25.

11. "The 1940 Statement of Principles on Academic Freedom and Tenure," in Academic Freedom and Tenure: A Handbook of the AAUP, ed. Louis Joughlin (Madison, Wisc.: University of Wisconsin Press, 1967), pp. 33-39.

12. William Van Alstyne, "The Specific Theory of Academic Freedom and the General Issue of Civil Liberty," in The Concept of Academic Freedom, ed. Edmund L. Pincoffs (Austin, Tex.: University of Texas Press, 1975), pp. 81-82.

13. Iverson, The Communists and the Schools, pp. 215-216.

14. Edward C. Kirkland, "Academic Freedom and Tenure: Report of Committee A for 1945," BAAUP 32 (Spring 1946): 6.

15. Richard M. Freeland, The Truman Doctrine and the Origins of McCarthyism: Foreign Policy, Domestic Politics and Internal Security, 1946-1948 (New York: Schocken Books, 1974).

16. Compiled from "Academic Freedom and Tenure in the Quest for National Security: Report of a Special Committee of the AAUP," in The American Concept of Academic Freedom in Formation, ed. W.P. Metzger (New York: Arno, 1977), irregular pagination, pp. 61-107.

17. Melvin Rader gives his account and others in False Witness (Seattle, Wash.: University of Washington Press, 1979 edition).

18. See Paul L. Lazarsfeld and Wagner Thielens, Jr., The Academic Mind: Social Scientists in Times of Crisis (Glencoe, Ill.: The Free Press, 1958).

19. "Academic Freedom and Tenure in the Quest for National Security: [1956] Report of a Special Committee," in Academic Freedom and Tenure: A Handbook, pp. 47-56.

20. "A [1958] Statement of the Committee on Academic Freedom and Tenure Supplementary to the 1956 Report," in Academic Freedom and Tenure: A Handbook, pp. 56-63.

21. "Academic Freedom and Tenure: 1940 Statement of Principles and [1970] Interpretative Comments," AAUP Policy Documents and Reports (Washington, D.C.: AAUP, 1977 edition), pp. 1-4.

22. Robert Justin Goldstein, Political Repression in Modern America, 1870 to the Present (Cambridge, Mass.: Schenkman, 1978), pp. 522-523.

23. For a sense of the departmental dynamics involved at the University of Wisconsin, see the essays in "Part Two: The Faculty," in Academic Super Markets: A Critical Case Study of a University, ed. Philip G. Altbach, Robert S. Laufer and Sheila Slaughter McVey (San Francisco: Jossey-Bass, 1971), pp. 155-269.

24. See for example, Everett Ladd and S.M. Lipset, The Divided Academy: Professors and Politics (New York: McGraw-Hill, 1975).

25. For a beginning of the theory of the just revolution based on recent North American experience, see Peter L. Berger and Richard J. Neuhaus, Movement and Revolution (New York: Anchor, 1970), especially pp. 143 ff.

26. Richard F. Hamilton, Class and Politics in the United States (New York: John Wiley & Sons, 1972).

27. See Ralph Miliband, The State in Capitalist Society (New York: Basic Books, 1969), pp. 265-277, as well as the pages of current newspapers.

Appendix A
Social Characteristics of Association Leaders

Table 1: Primary Data Sources

	ASSA 1865–1886	AEA 1885–1903	AEA 1904–1920	APSA 1903–1920	ASS 1905–1920
Dictionary of Amer. Biography	81.4%	70.6%	55.3%	62.8%	47.1%
National Cyclopedia	7.0	17.6	29.8	16.3	29.4
Who Was Who and Others	4.7	8.8	12.8	20.9	17.6
No Data	7.0	2.9	2.1	0.0	5.9
TOTALS	100.1% N=43	99.9% N=34	100.0% N=47	100.0% N=43	100.0% N=17

Table 2: Family Settlement

	ASSA 1865–1886	AEA 1885–1903	AEA 1904–1920	APSA 1903–1920	ASS 1905–1920
Before 1700	67.5%	48.5%	28.3%	32.6%	31.3%
1701 and After	10.0	21.2	39.1	18.6	31.3
Never Settled	15.0	3.0	4.3	11.6	0.0
No Data	7.5	27.3	28.3	37.2	37.5
TOTALS	100.0% N=40	100.0% N=33	100.0% N=46	100.0% N=43	100.2% N=16

Table 3: Region^1 of Birth

	ASSA 1865–1886	AEA 1885–1903	AEA 1904–1920	APSA 1903–1920	ASS 1905–1920
New England	72.5%	33.3%	17.4%	16.3%	18.8%
Mid-Atlantic	15.0	21.2	32.6	16.3	25.0
South	0.0	0.0	6.5	14.0	0.0
Midwest	5.0	39.4	34.8	41.7	43.8
Farwest	0.0	0.0	2.2	0.0	0.0
Foreign	7.5	6.1	6.5	11.6	12.5
TOTALS	100.0%	100.0%	100.0%	99.9%	100.1%

Table 4: Region of Adult Residence³

New England	72.5%	21.2%	23.9%	25.6%	12.5%
Mid-Atlantic	12.5	45.5	34.8	32.6	31.3
South	2.5	0.0	4.3	4.7	0.0
Midwest	12.5	33.3	28.3	27.9	56.3
Far West	0.0	0.0	8.7	4.7	0.0
Foreign	0.0	0.0	0.0	4.7	0.0
TOTALS²	100.0%	100.0%	100.0%	100.2%	100.1%

Table 5: Region Graduated College

New England	60.0%	42.4%	19.6%	27.9%	31.3%
Mid-Atlantic	2.5	24.2	21.7	14.0	18.8
South	2.5	0.0	4.3	7.0	0.0
Midwest	2.5	18.2	30.4	32.6	31.3
Far West	0.0	0.0	6.5	2.3	6.3
Foreign	5.0	3.0	4.3	11.6	6.3
Attend, does not Graduate	7.5	12.1	8.7	4.7	6.3
Does Not Attend	20.0	0.0	4.3	0.0	0.0
TOTALS²	100.0%	99.9%	99.8%	100.1%	100.3%

Table 6: Region of Graduate Education

New England	35.0%	9.1%	17.3%	20.9%	6.3%
Mid-Atlantic	5.0	24.2	34.7	32.6	37.5
South	0.0	0.0	0.0	0.0	0.0
Midwest	0.0	9.0	15.2	14.0	37.5
Far West	0.0	0.0	0.0	0.0	0.0
Foreign	15.0	45.5	8.7	20.9	12.5
Does Not Attend	45.0	12.1	23.9	11.6	6.3
TOTALS²	100.0%	99.9%	99.8%	100.0%	100.0%

Table 7: Graduate Education: Highest Attained

Attends/Graduates Law School	17.5%	3.0%	8.7%	18.6%	0.0%
Attends/Graduates Medical School	5.0	0.0	0.0	0.0	0.0
Attends/Graduates Theology School	10.0	0.0	0.0	0.0	6.3
Attends/Graduates School, no Ph.D.	12.5	18.1	13.0	9.3	12.5
Earns Ph.D.	10.0	66.7	54.3	58.1	75.0
Does Not Attend	45.0	12.1	23.9	14.0	6.3
TOTALS^2	100.0%	99.9%	99.9%	100.0%	100.1%

Table 8: Father's Principal Occupation^4

Farmer	20.0%	6.1%	8.7%	7.0%	12.5%
Business, Manufacture, Commerce	32.5	36.4	23.9	23.3	6.3
Professional (total)	(35.0)	(30.3)	(37.0)	(32.6)	(31.3)
Clergy	5.0	21.2	10.9	7.0	18.8
Legal	15.0	0.0	13.0	7.0	6.3
Medical	5.0	0.0	8.7	11.6	0.0
Other	10.0	9.1	4.3	7.0	6.3
Public Official	5.0	0.0	0.0	4.7	0.0
Skilled Worker	2.5	3.0	6.5	0.0	12.5
Unskilled Worker	0.0	0.0	0.0	0.0	0.0
No Data	5.0	24.0	23.9	32.6	37.5
TOTALS^2	100.0	100.0	100.0	100.2	100.1

324   Appendix A

Table 9: Leader's Principal Occupation[4]

Higher Education Careerist (total)	(35.0)%	(84.8)%	(56.5)%	(62.8)%	(81.3)%
Professor	20.0	66.7	50.0	48.8	75.0
Prof./Pres.	15.0	18.2	6.5	14.0	6.3
Other Professional (total)	(37.5)	(3.0)	(17.3)	(16.3)	(6.3)
Clergy	2.5	0.0	0.0	0.0	0.0
Law	12.5	0.0	13.0	7.0	0.0
Medical	5.0	0.0	0.0	0.0	0.0
Cultural	17.5	3.0	4.3	9.3	6.3
Business, Manufacture, Commerce	17.5	9.1	23.9	9.3	6.3
Public Officials	5.0	3.0	2.2	11.6	6.3
Farmers and Workers	0.0	0.0	0.0	0.0	0.0
Outside the Labor Force	5.0	0.0	0.0	0.0	0.0
TOTALS[2]	100.0	99.9	99.9	100.0	100.2

Table 10: Leaders Political Service, 1865-1921: Persons (and Posts) by Level[5]

Holding Expert-Appointive Office (and Their Posts)

Local	7.5(7.1)	6.1(3.3)	13.0(7.2)	18.6(11.4)	0.0(0.0)
State	25.0(25.0)	30.3(16.7)	28.3(20.6)	32.6(19.0)	25.0(30.0)
Federal, domestic	27.5(41.1)	36.4(51.7)	52.2(59.8)	30.2(21.9)	25.0(61.5)
Federal, foreign	22.5(25.0)	21.2(23.3)	13.0(11.3)	25.6(40.0)	6.3(7.7)
International	2.5(1.7)	6.1(5.0)	2.1(1.0)	11.6(7.6)	0.0(0.0)
TOTALS: % persons (% posts) =	60.0(99.9)	60.6(100.0)	69.7(99.9)	67.4(99.9)	50.0(100.0)
N2 =	40 (56)	33 (60)	46 (97)	43 (105)	16 (13)

Holding Expert-Elective Office (and Their Posts)

Local	12.5(17.0)	0.0(0.0)	13.0(58.8)	7.0(29.3)	6.3(40.0)
State	32.5(70.2)	6.1(67.7)	2.2(5.9)	9.3(41.2)	6.3(40.0)
Federal	10.0(12.7)	3.0(33.3)	6.5(35.3)	9.3(29.3)	6.3(20.0)
TOTALS: % persons (% posts) N^2 =	42.5(99.9) 40 (47)	6.1(100.0) 33 (3)	17.4(100.0) 46 (17)	18.6(99.8) 43 (17)	6.3(100.0) 16 (5)
Ratio of Appointive to Elective Service	1.4(1.2)	10.0(20.0)	5.8(5.7)	5.4(6.2)	8.0(2.6)

NOTES TO APPENDIX

1. Regions are defined as follows. New England=Maine, Vermont, New Hampshire, Massachusetts, Connecticut and Rhode Island. Mid-Atlantic= New York, New Jersey, Pennsylvania, Maryland, the District of Columbia, Delaware and West Virginia. South=Virginia, North and South Carolina, Georgia, Alabama, Missouri, Mississippi, Arkansas, Louisiana, Texas and Florida. Midwest=Ohio, Michigan, Illinois, Indiana, Wisconsin, Minnesota, Iowa, Nebraska, Kansas, South and North Dakota, Oklahoma, Tennessee, and Kentucky. Far West= Washington, Oregon, California, Idaho, Colorado, Utah, Wyoming, New Mexico, Arizona, Montana and Nevada.

2. The data base for the total is shown in Table 2 and includes only leaders for which some biographical material was found.

3. Adult residence is defined as the place lived for one-half or more of one's life after school leaving.

4. Principal occupation is defined as the type of job held for at least one-half the time of gainful employment between school leaving and retirement.

5. Cell entries show both the percentages for persons (and posts). Since some experts hold several posts at various govermental levels, the number of posts sometimes exceeds the number of leaders at each level and in the totals.

Appendix B
Association Leadership Samples

ASSA Leaders

Adams, Charles Francis	b. 1835
Adams, Henry Carter	b. 1851
Barnard, James M	
Blatchford, J.D.	
Boutwell, George Sewall	b. 1818
Bradford, Gamaliel	b. 1831
Channing, Walter	b. 1786
Curtis, George William	b. 1824
Eaton, John	b. 1829
Eliot, Charles William	b. 1834
Eliot, Samuel	b. 1821
Farnam, Henry Walcott	b. 1853
Gilman, Daniel Coit	b. 1831
Hammond, William Gardiner	b. 1829
Harris, William Torrey	b. 1835
Hill, Hamilton Andrews	b. 1827
Hill, Thomas	b. 1818
Howe, Samuel Gridley	b. 1801
James, Edmund Janes	b. 1855
Jarvis, Edward	b. 1803
Kingsbury, Frederick John	b. 1823
Leiber, Francis	b. 1800
May, Abigail Williams	b. 1829
Nichols, George Ward	b. 1831
Peirce, Benajmin	b. 1809
Rice, Alexander Hamilton	b. 1818
Rogers, William Barton	b. 1804
Sanborn, Franklin Benajmin	b. 1831
Stokes, Anson Phelps	b. 1838
Sumner, William Graham	b. 1840
Talbot, Emily Fairbanks	b. 1834
Thayer, James Bradley	b. 1831
Townsend, William Kneeland	b. 1849
Villard, Henry	b. 1835
Washburn, Emory	b. 1800
Wayland, Francis	b. 1826
Wells, David Ames	b. 1828
Wells, John	b. 1819
White, Andrew Dickson	b. 1832
Whitman, Mrs. Henry	
Woolsey, Theodore Dwight	b. 1801
Woolsey, Theodore Salisbury	b. 1852
Wright, Carroll Davidson	b. 1840

AEA Leaders, 1885-1903

Adams, Henry Carter	b. 1851
Canfield, James Hulme	b. 1847
Clark, John Bates	b. 1847
Dunbar, Charles Franklin	b. 1830
Daniels, Winthrop More	b. 1867
Ely, Richard Theodore	b. 1854
Falkner, Roland Post	b. 1866
Farnam, Henry Walcott	b. 1853
Fetter, Frank Albert	b. 1863
Folwell, William Watts	b. 1833
Gardner, Henry Brayton	b. 1863
Giddings, Franklin Henry	b. 1855
Gould, Elgin Raltson Lovell	b. 1860
Gray, John Henry	b. 1859
Hadley, Arthur Twining	b. 1856
Hawley, Frederick B.	
Hull, Charles Henry	b. 1864
James, Edmund Janes	b. 1855
Jenks, Jeremiah Whipple	b. 1856
Kinley, David	b. 1861
Knight, Geroge Wells	b. 1858
Marburg, Theodore	b. 1862
Mayo-Smith, Richmond	b. 1854
Moore, Frederick Wightman	b. 1863
Patten, Simon Nelson	b. 1852
Ripley, William Zebina	b. 1867
Ross, Edward Alsworth	b. 1866
Seligman, Edwin Robert Anderson	b. 1861
Schwab, John Christopher	b. 1865
Taylor, Fred Manville	b. 1855
Walker, Francis Amasa	b. 1840
Ward, Lester Frank	b. 1841
Willcox, Walter Francis	b. 1861
Wood, Stuart	b. 1853

APSA Leaders 1903-1921

Baldwin, Simeon Eben	b. 1840
Barrows, David Prescott	b. 1873
Beard, Charles Austin	b. 1874
Bryce, James W.	
Childs, Richard Spencer	b. 1882
Cleveland, Frederick Albert	b. 1865
Corwin, Edward Samuel	b. 1978
Dealey, James Quayle	b. 1861
Dodd, Walter Fairleigh	b. 1880
Ford, Henry Jones	b. 1851
Freund, Ernst	b. 1864
Garfield, Harry Augustus	b. 1863
Garner, James Wilford	b. 1871
Goodnow, Frank Johnson	b. 1859
Hart, Albert Bushnell	b. 1854
Hatton, Augustus (Raymond) Rutan	b. 1873
James, Edmund Janes	b. 1855
Jenks, Jeremiah Whipple	b. 1856
Jones, Chester L.	b. 1881
Judson, Frederick Newton	b. 1845
Loeb, Isidor	b. 1868
Lowell, Abbott Lawrence	b. 1856
McLain, Emlin	b. 1851
Macy, Jessie	b. 1842
Merriam, Charles Edward, Jr.	b. 1874
Moore, John Bassett	b. 1860
Moses, Bernard	b. 1846
Munro, William Bennett	b. 1875
Ogg, Frederic Austin	b. 1978
Porritt, Edward	b. 1860
Powell, Thomas Reed	b. 1880
Reinsch, Paul Samuel	b. 1869
Rowe, Leo Stanton	b. 1871
Shambaugh, Benjamin Franklin	b. 1871
Shaw, Albert	b. 1857
Shortt, Adam	b. 1859
Smith, Munroe	b. 1854
Swayze, Francis Joseph	b. 1861
Willoughby, Westel Woodbury	b. 1867
Willoughby, William Franklin	b. 1867
Wilson, George Grafton	b. 1863
Wilson, Woodrow	b. 1856
Woolsey, Theodore S.	b. 1852

330   Appendix B

AEA Leaders 1904-1921

Abbott, Edith	b. 1876
Adams, Thomas Sewall	b. 1873
Burton, Theodore Elijah	b. 1851
Bogart, Ernest Ludlow	b. 1870
Brooks, John Graham	b. 1846
Brookings, Robert Somers	b. 1850
Carver, Thomas Nixon	b. 1865
Commons, John Rogers	b. 1862
Cooke, Thorton	b. 1873
Crane, Charles Richard	b. 1858
Davenport, Herbert Joseph	b. 1861
Dewey, Davis Rich	b. 1858
Dill, James Brooks	b. 1854
Durand, E. Dana	
Fairchild, Charles Stebbins	b. 1842
Field, James Alfred	b. 1880
Fillebrown, Charles Bowdoin	b. 1842
Fisher, Irving	b. 1867
Fisher, Willard Clark	b. 1865
Franklin, Fabian	b. 1853
Glenn, John Mark	b. 1858
Hammond, Matthew Brown	b. 1868
Hatfield, Henry Rand	b. 1866
Hollander, Jacob Harry	b. 1871
Hotchkiss, Willard Eugene	b. 1874
Houston, David Franklin	b. 1866
Johnson, Alvin Saunders	b. 1974
Johnson, Joseph French	b. 1853
Judson, Frederick Newton	b. 1845
Kingsburg, Susan Myra	b. 1870
Knapp, Martin Augustine	b. 1843
LeRossignol, James Edward	b. 1866
MacFarlane, Charles William	b. 1850
McVey, Frank Lerond	b. 1869
Meyer, Balthasar Henry	b. 1866
Neill, Charles Patrick	b. 1865
North, Simon Newton Dexter	b. 1848
Plehn, Carl Copping	b. 1867
Roberts, George Evan	b. 1857
Taussig, Frank William	b. 1859
Vanderlip, Frank Arthur	b. 1864
Warburg, Paul Moritz	b. 1868
Westerfield, Ray Bert	b. 1884
Wicker, Geroge Ray	b. 1870
Wildman, Murray Shipley	b. 1868
White, Horace	b. 1834
Young, Allyn Abbot	b. 1876

ASS Leaders 1905-1921

Bedford, Scott Elias William	b. 1902
Blackmar, Frank Wilson	b. 1854
Burgess, Ernest Watson	b. 1886
Cooley, Charles Horton	b. 1864
Dealey, James Quayle	b. 1861
Hayes, Edward Cary	b. 1868
Howard, George Elliott	b. 1849
Lichtenberger, James Pendleton	b. 1870
Ross, Edward Alsworth	b. 1866
Small, Albion Woodubry	b. 1854
Sumner, William Graham	b. 1840
Tenney, Alvan A.	
Veditz, Charles William Augustus	b. 1872
Vincent, George Edgar	b. 1864
Ward, Lester Frank	b. 1841
Weatherly, Ulysses Grant	b. 1865

Bibliographic Essay

We are deeply indebted to scholars of American social science for their work on the founding of the disciplinary associations. Among the works that inform our understanding of the origins of the association are A.W. Coates, "The First Two Decades of the American Economic Association," _American Economic Review_ 50 (September 1960): 555-574; Joseph Dorfman, _The Economic Mind in American Civilization_, vol. 3 (New York: Viking, 1949); Albert Somit and Joseph Tanenhaus, _The Development of American Political Science: From Burgess to Behavioralism_ (Boston: Allyn and Bacon, 1967); Roscoe C. Hinkle, _Founding Theory of American Sociology, 1881-1915_ (London: (Routledge & Kegan Paul, 1980); and Howard Odum, _American Masters of Social Science_ (New York: Holt, 1927).

More recently scholars have labored to clarify the history and theory of social science professionalization. Among those who have advanced an interpretation that sees social scientists during the last quarter of the nineteenth century as abandoning reform for science, technique and institutionalization in the university are Luther Lee Barnard and Jessie Barnard, _Origins of American Sociology: The Social Science Movement in the United States_ (New York: Crowell, 1943); Mary O. Furner, _Advocacy and Objectivity: A Crisis in the Professionalization of American Social Science, 1865-1905_ (Lexington, Ky.: University Press of Kentucky, 1975); Thomas Haskell, _The Emergence of Professional Social Science: the American Social Science Association and Nineteenth Century Crisis of Authority_ (Urbana, Ill.: University of Illinois Press, 1977); Anthony Oberschall, "The Institutionalization of American Sociology," in his _The Establishment of Empirical Sociology_ (New York: Harper & Row, 1972), pp. 187-251; Robert Church, "The Economists Study Society:

Sociology at Harvard, 1871-1902," in Social Science at Harvard: From Inculcation to Open Mind, ed. Paul Buck (Cambridge, Mass.: Harvard University Press, 1965); and Dorothy Ross, "The Development of the Social Sciences," in The Organization of Knowledge in Modern America, ed. Alexandra Oleson and John Voss (Baltimore, Md.: Johns Hopkins University Press, 1979), pp. 107-138.

Work that has contributed to our understanding of social scientists involvement in public service includes David Grossman, "Professors and Public Service 1885-1925: A chapter in the Professionalization of Social Science," Ph.D. thesis, Washington University, 1973; and Stephen J. Diner, A City and Its Universities: Public Policy in Chicago 1892-1919 (Chapel Hill, N.C.: University of North Carolina Press, 1980). While these works provide a sense of the extent of social scientists' involvement in national and municipal affairs, their service is not put in the context of their institutional dependence.

None of these works fully considers the implications of capitalist industrialization upon the formation of the academic expert role. Useful supplements to these works are Herman and Julia Schwendinger, Sociologists of the Chair (New York: Basic Books, 1974); Magali Sarfatti Larson, The Rise of Professionalism: A Sociological Analysis (Berkeley, Calif.: University of California Press, 1977); Goran Therborn, Science, Class and Society (London: New Left Books, 1976); and David W. Noble, America by Design: Science, Technology and the Rise of Corporate Capitalism (New York: Alfred A. Knopf, 1977).

Some sense of the tensions that existed among university managers, academics and resource suppliers during the rise of graduate school are found in Burton J. Bledstein, The Culture of Professionalism (New York: W.W. Norton, 1977), which interprets and details the views of the leading university presidents; Randall Collins, The Credential Society (New York: Academic Press, 1979) which places professionalization and the American university in a historical sociology of education and stratification; and Laurence R. Veysey's still invaluable The Emergence of the American University (Chicago: University of Chicago Press, 1965). Also interesting are the biographies of university managers and academics and the histories of pace-setting graduate schools, such as Hugh Hawkins, Between Harvard and America: The Educational Leadership of Charles W. Eliot (New York: Oxford, 1972); Daniel M. Fox, The

Discovery of Abundance: Simon N. Patten and the Transformation of Social Theory (Ithaca, N.Y.: Cornell University Press, 1967); and Richard Storr, Harper's University: The Beginnings; a History of the University of Chicago (Chicago: University of Chicago Press, 1966). How these tensions were also expressed at the departmental level is an important element in the formation of the academic expert, on which see James T. Carey, Sociology and Public Affairs: The Chicago School (London: Sage, 1975).

The choices made by new social scientists in deploying their expertise initially in the service of empire can best be understood by looking critically at the development of American foreign policy and at the alternatives foregone. Especially helpful are William Appleman Williams, The Roots of Modern American Empire (New York: Random House, 1969); E. Berkeley Tompkins, Anti-Imperialism in the United States: The Great Debate, 1890-1920 (Philadelphia: University of Pennsylvania Press, 1970); and Daniel B. Schirmer, Republic or Empire: American Resistance to the Philippine War (Cambridge, Mass.: Schenkman, 1972).

The conservative nature of social scientists' decision to support the trust, albeit subject to government regulation, can best be appreciated by seeing their service within the context of the framework of the development of the corporate industrial state. For this perspective, see Gabriel Kolko, The Triumph of Conservatism: A Reinterpretation of American History (Chicago: Quadrangle Paperbacks, 1967) and his Railroads and Regulation, 1877-1916 (New York: W.W. Norton, 1970); and William Appleman Williams, Contours of American History (Chicago: Quadrangle Paperbacks, 1966). Academic service in the business-dominated National Civic Federation is interpreted by James Weinstein, The Corporate Ideal in the Liberal State: 1900-1918 (Boston: Beacon Press, 1968). Continued academic service in such form is treated in William Domhoff, The Higher Circles (New York: Random House, 1973); and Laurence Shoup and William Minter, Imperial Brain Trust: The Council on Foreign Relations and United States Foreign Policy (New York: Monthly Review Press, 1977). Paul S. Reinsch gives a richly detailed personal account of his struggle to serve the U.S. overseas in An American Diplomat in China (Garden City, N.Y.: Doubleday Page, 1922), and this is interpreted and augmented by Noel Harvey Pugach, in "Progress, Prosperity and the Open Door: the Ideas and Career of Paul S. Reinsch,"

Ph.D. dissertation, University of Wisconsin, Madison, 1967.

A great many scholars have contributed to our understanding of government reform movements in the Progressive era. Particularly important to our general interpretation of the place of academics in this movement was Martin J. Schiesl, The Politics of Efficiency: Municipal Administration and Reform in America, 1800-1920 (Berkeley, Calif.: University of California Press, 1977), which treats the relationship between patrician reforms, good government groups, corporate leaders and emerging administrative experts. Barry D. Karl also enriched our view of academics, expertise and reformers with his Charles E. Merriam and the Study of Politics (Chicago: University of Chicago Press, 1974), which deals with professors' sensitivity to resources, ambition for their disciplines and sincere desire to right the system's wrongs. Valuable for their chronicling of reform agencies critical to our analysis are Frank Mann Stewart, A Half Century of Municipal Reform: the History of the National Municipal League (Berkeley, Calif.: University of California Press, 1950) and Jane S. Dahlberg, The New York Bureau of Municipal Research: Pioneers in Government Administration (New York: New York University Press, 1966).

In coming to grips with social scientists' contribution to pre-war foreign policy C. Roland Marchand, The American Peace Movement and Social Reform (Princeton, N.J.: Princeton University Press, 1972) is crucial, delineating as it does the role the peace associations played in the years before the U.S. firmly established its foreign service. Jonathan Spence, To Change China: Western Advisors in China 1620-1960 (Boston: Little, Brown, 1969) provides a framework for understanding the problems social science experts faced when giving advice.

For understanding the origins of the AAUP, a knowledge of Walter P. Metzger's work is essential, particularly his Academic Freedom in the Age of the University (New York: Columbia University Press, 1955). Useful studies of the limits set on academic freedom during the war as well as the expert service professors gave government are Carol Singer Gruber, Mars and Minerva: World War I and the Uses of the Higher Learning in America (Baton Rouge, La.: Louisiana State University Press, 1975), and William Summerscales, Affirmation and Dissent: Columbia's Response to the Crisis of World War I (New York: Teachers College Press, Columbia University, 1970). Scholars' autobiographies that give a sense of the university community's absorption in the war and its consequences for the development of academic expertise are Alvin S. Johnson, _Pioneers Progress: An Autobiography_ (New York: Viking, 1952); John M. Mecklin, _My Quest for Freedom_ (New York: Charles Scribner's Sons, 1945); and Scott Nearing, _The Making of a Radical: A Political Autobiography_ (New York: Harper & Row, Torchbook ed., 1972).

Index

About the Authors

EDWARD T. SILVA is Associate Professor of Sociology at the University of Toronto. He has published extensively in journals such as *Theory and Society, Social Problems, Law and Society Review, Social Forces,* and *Journal of Popular Culture.*

SHEILA A. SLAUGHTER is Associate Professor in the College of Education at the State University of New York at Buffalo. She is the co-editor of *Academic Supermarkets* and *Perspectives on Publishing.* She is on the editorial board of *Review of Higher Education* and has contributed articles to *Philanthropy and Cultural Imperialism, Educational Theory, Higher Education in American Society,* and *Journal of Higher Education.*